ISBN 978-0-282-45920-8
PIBN 10850677

For support please visit www.forgottenbooks.com

1 MONTH OF FREE READING

at

www.ForgottenBooks.com

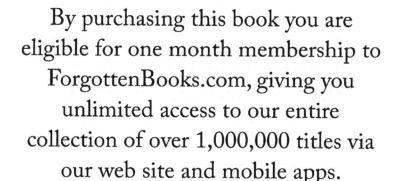

By purchasing this book you are eligible for one month membership to ForgottenBooks.com, giving you unlimited access to our entire collection of over 1,000,000 titles via our web site and mobile apps.

To claim your free month visit:
www.forgottenbooks.com/free850677

BY

STEWART MACPHERSON

Price { Paper Covers 3/- net

Cloth Boards 4/- net

DON: JOSEPH WILLIAMS, LIMITED,
ENFORD STREET, MARYLEBONE, W.1.
J.W., 13,990

RUDIMENTS OF MUSIC

BY

STEWART MACPHERSON

Price { Paper Covers 3/- net
Cloth Boards 4/- net

LONDON: JOSEPH WILLIAMS, LIMITED,
29 ENFORD STREET, MARYLEBONE, W.1.
J.W., 13,990

All prices subject to adjustment.

WORKS SUITABLE FOR BEGINNERS.

	NET
By J. RAYMOND TOBIN	
Fun with Scales (a First-of-all Scale Book on the Musicianship plan) ...	1 6
More Fun with Scales (companion to above) ...	1 6
Fun with Fingering ...	1 6
Fun and Facts (a First-of-all Book of Tunes) ...	2 6
How to Find Key Changes in a Piece ...	1 0
My First Music Book, by F. S. BELLAMY ...	2 6
Very First Piano Tutor, by J. A. JOHNSTONE ...	2 6
My First March Album, by various composers ...	2 6
School Sight-Reading Exercises, by JOHN GREENFIELD. Book I, Primary Grade. Book II, First Grade. Book III, Second Grade ... each	2 6
Music for Sight-Reading, by G. M. BRUXNER (two books) each	2 6
Sight-Reading Made Easy, by DOROTHY BRADLEY and J. RAYMOND TOBIN. A complete graded course (in eight books) ... each	3 6
Scales and Arpeggios, with photographic illustrations (English or foreign fingering), by SYDNEY BLAKISTON ...	4 0
Elementary Sight-Reading Exercises, by LUCY WELCH. 1.—Pitch. 2.—Rhythm. 3.—Phrasing and Form each	2
Six Sight-Reading Studies. JASPER GRAHAM ...	2
Very First Studies. Op. 187. C. GURLITT ...	2
Velocity Studies for Beginners. Op. 186. C. GURLITT...	2 3
Twenty Short Studies for equal training of both hands. Op. 191. B. WOLFF ...	2 0
Studies for Beginners. Op. 225. B. WOLFF ...	2 0
Student's Dictionary of Musical Terms. A. J. GREENISH	3 6
Meadowsweet (six easy pieces), by OLGA MILLS ...	2 0
Four Short Pieces, by LEO LIVENS ...	2 6
Old Tunes for Young People, by MARKHAM LEE ...	2 6
First Tunes at the Piano, by EDITH ROWLAND ...	2 6
In Willow Wood, by GRAHAM CLARKE ...	2 3
*****Music Land**, combining aural training with first piano lessons, by MADELEINE EVANS (in four Books) ... each	3 6
Through the Centuries (1600-1800) by MADELEINE EVANS. Graded classics, with illustrations and biographical notes (in three Books) ... each	
Once upon a time (nine easy pieces), by MADELEINE EVANS	3 8
Sight-Reading Tests (Primary to Higher), by ERNEST NEWTON. Books I, II, III ... each	2 0
A New Approach to Scales and Arpeggios by THOMAS FIELDEN. (Combined with Technical Exercises and notes on Fingering)	1 9

(Descriptive leaflet on application.)

STEWART MACPHERSON'S STANDARD TEXT BOOKS.

	Paper covers. net. s. d.	Cloth covers. net. s. d.
Rudiments of Music (New Edition) ...	3 0	4 0
Questions and Exercises upon the Rudiments of Music ...	2 6	—
Practical Harmony ...	6 6	10 6
Appendix to Practical Harmony ...	5 6	—

RUDIMENTS OF MUSIC

BY

STEWART MACPHERSON

(Fellow, Professor and Lecturer, Royal Academy of Music ; Author of "Form in Music," "Music and its Appreciation," "Melody and Harmony," "Studies in the Art of Counterpoint," etc., etc.)

Price $\left\{\begin{array}{l} \text{Paper Covers 3/- net} \\ \text{Cloth Boards 4/- net} \end{array}\right.$

(New Edition 1939)

LONDON : JOSEPH WILLIAMS, LIMITED
29 Enford Street, Marylebone, W.1

Agents for U.S.A. $\left\{\begin{array}{l} \text{The B. F. Wood Music Co., Boston} \\ \text{Mills Music Inc., New York} \end{array}\right.$

J.W. 13990
(W 3317)

B 30   [Made and printed in Great Britain]

TABLE OF CONTENTS

RUDIMENTS OF MUSIC

INTRODUCTORY.

1.—**Musical sound** is the result of regular and periodic vibrations of air.

2.—The varying height or depth of sound is caused by the difference of the rapidity of these vibrations, and is called the **pitch** of the sound.

3.—The **loudness** or **softness** of a sound depends upon the size, or amplitude, of the vibrations. This is called the **force** of the sound.

4.—The **quality** (or ' timbre ') of a sound depends upon the nature of the vibrating body (i.e., the medium by which vibration is set up, whether string or column of air) ; and also upon the presence, in greater or less degree, of harmonics. (See Appendix A.)

5.—The indication, in writing, of musical sounds requires :—
  (i.) **Notes**—to express *duration.*
  (ii.) **The staff, or stave** ⎱ to express *pitch.*
  (iii.) **Clefs** ⎰

CHAPTER I.

Duration of Sounds.—Notes.

1.—The **relative duration** of musical sounds is made clear to the eye by signs of varying shape called **notes**.

2.—Those now commonly in use are as follows :—*

o ꞌ   Semibreve, or whole-note.

♩ , or ♭   Minim, or half-note.

♩ , or ♭   Crotchet, or quarter-note.

♪ , or ♭   Quaver, or eighth-note.

♪ , or ♭   Semiquaver, or sixteenth-note.

♪ , or ♭   Demi-semiquaver, or thirty-second note.

♪ , or ♭   Semi-demi-semiquaver, or sixty-fourth note.

3.—Each of the above notes in order is, in duration, half the value of the preceding ; in Germany and America it is customary to describe each note according to its numerical value (whole-note, half-note, etc.), a plan that

---

* In old music, other kinds of notes were used, three only of which need be mentioned here, viz., the *Large* ⊒ , the *Long* ⊐ , and the *Breve* (i.e., short) ‖◑‖

This last sign is even now occasionally met with, especially in church music. See also the Fugue in E. No. 33 of Bach's " Das wohltemperirte Clavier " (8th bar).

has much to recommend it ; in England, however, the terms semibreve, minim, etc., are generally used.*

4.—The values of the various notes in relation to one another will be clearly seen by the following example :—†

---

* In France, the notes are called respectively Ronde, Blanche, Noire, Croche, Double Croche, Triple Croche, &c.

† It must be carefully borne in mind that the above notes represent merely the *relative* duration of sounds, the *actual* duration of any particular note depending upon the speed at which the music is to be played or sung. In this way, a semibreve or minim in a quick movement might very well occupy less time than a crotchet or quaver in a slow one, and so on.

5.—It is immaterial whether the stems of minims, crotchets, quavers, etc., be turned up or down ; although this is frequently regulated, for appearance sake, by their position on the *Staff*. (Chap. II, Sec. I.)

6.—When two or more quavers, semiquavers, etc., occur in succession, it is usual for them to be **grouped together** on one tail, thus :—

Such groupings are inseparably connected with the question of *Time*, and will be fully considered later.   (Chap. V.)

7.—The duration of any note may be increased by adding one or more **dots** after it* ; a single dot augmenting its value by *one-half*, e.g.:—

$$\text{♩.} = \text{♩} + \text{♩} = 3 \text{ crotchets.}$$

$$\text{♩.} = \text{♩} + \text{♪} = 3 \text{ quavers, etc.}$$

and two dots, by *three-quarters*, e.g. :—

$$\text{♩..} = \text{♩} + \text{♩} + \text{♪} = 7 \text{ quavers.}$$

$$\text{♩..} = \text{♩} + \text{♪} + \text{♬} = 7 \text{ semiquavers, etc.}$$

Carefully observe that the second dot adds *half the value of the first dot*, i.e., *a quarter* of the original note.   The following rule will be of assistance :—
" **A dot always takes half the value of whatever immediately precedes it, whether note or dot.**"

N.B.—On reflection, it will be seen that, whatever number of dots were to be placed after a note, the sum of such dots could never equal the value of the original note.

8.—Sound frequently ceases during the course of a musical composition, and there is silence for a definite period.   Such silences are indicated by signs called **Rests**, corresponding in duration to the notes whose names they take†, e.g. :—

Semibreve rest.‡   Minim rest.   Crotchet rest.   Quaver rest.

Semiquaver rest.   Demi-semiquaver rest.   Semi-demi-semiquaver rest.

9.—Dots are sometimes placed after rests, and increase their duration in the same manner as in the case of notes, e.g.:—

$$\text{♪·} = \text{♪} + \text{♪}$$

---

* A similar lengthening of a note may be effected by means of a tie, or *bind*. (Chap. X Sec. 10.)
† The employment of rests is further considered in connection with Time. (Chap. V.)
‡ The rest corresponding to the rarely used Breve is written thus :

CHAPTER II.

Pitch of Sounds.—The Staff, and Clefs.

1.—The relative pitch of sounds is expressed by the staff, or stave, a species of ladder consisting of a set of parallel lines and the spaces between them. The higher the position of the notes written upon this ladder, the higher (or acuter) will be their pitch ; and, *vice versa*, the lower their position, the lower (or graver) their pitch.

2.—A staff that will include the combined compass of male and female voices is called the **Great Staff,** and consists of 11 lines and the spaces above and below them :—

The thick line represents " Middle C "—the note nearest the middle of the Pianoforte Keyboard.*

3.—Starting from " **Middle C,**" the sounds in alphabetical succession upwards are :—

1st space above " Middle C "	...		...	...	D.
1st line	,,	,,	...	...	E.
2nd space	,,	,,	...	...	F.
2nd line	,,	,,	...	...	G.
3rd space	,,	,,	...	...	A.
3rd line	,,	,,	...	...	B.
4th space	,,	,,	...	...	C.
4th line	,,	,,	...	...	D.
5th space	,,	,,	...	...	E.
5th line	,,	,,	...	...	F.
6th space	,,	,,	...	...	G.

Similarly, *below* " **Middle C,**" the sounds occur alphabetically as under :—

1st space below " Middle C "	...		...	...	B.
1st line	,,	,,	...	...	A.
2nd space	,,	,,	...	...	G.
2nd line	,,	,,	...	...	F.
3rd space	,,	,,	...	...	E.
3rd line	,,	,,	...	...	D.
4th space	,,	,,	...	...	C.
4th line	,,	,,	...	...	B.
5th space	,,	,,	...	...	A.
5th line	,,	,,	...	...	G.
6th space	,,	,,	...	...	F.

* The first seven letters of the alphabet, A, B, C, **D**, E, F, G, are commonly used in naming sounds ; these letters recurring (as will be seen later) at a higher or lower pitch.

The following example will shew the range of sounds, in alphabetical order, comprised within the limits of the "Great Staff."

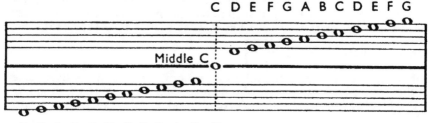

4.—It will be seen, on reference to the above example, that the same letter-name occurs more than once, at a different pitch. Each repetition of a given letter at a higher pitch will produce what is termed the **Octave** above ; and, similarly, each repetition at a lower pitch will produce the **Octave** below ; and it is worthy of note that any two sounds an octave apart have so strong a resemblance to one another (although so distant in actual pitch), that they produce in the mind almost the effect of one sound.

Note.—The number of vibrations in any sound is always *twice* that of the corresponding sound an octave below it.

5.—A staff of eleven lines, such as the above, would not only be found very inconvenient to read from, but the entire compass of any *single* human voice can be comprised within the limits of far fewer lines and spaces. Hence a **selection of a different set** for each separate voice is made, as shewn in the following diagram by the thick lines :—

6.—A **short staff** is thus formed in each instance, consisting of five **lines** and **the spaces** above and below them, and representing one of the above sets,* thus :—

7.—It will now have been seen that the **staff** is used to indicate the *relative* pitch of the various notes placed upon it ; but to represent the

* The five-line staff is now-a-days exclusively used. Formerly, however, staves of four, or even three lines were commonly employed, and, even now, the four-line staff is to be met with in certain music in use in the Church.

efinite height or depth of any sound we need certain signs called clefs (ɼɼ. "clef," a key). These shew which set of five lines is to be used, and so localise the actual position of the sounds ; and, until one of these clefs is placed at the beginning of such a staff, the notes written thereon can bear no names, neither can we know what sounds they represent. For

instance, the note

might represent any one of the following sounds, viz. : C of the Bass voice, G of the Tenor, B of the Alto, D of the Mezzo-Soprano, F of the Soprano, or A of the Treble (right hand in Pianoforte playing), as will be seen on reference to the diagram in Sec. 5.

8.—Clefs are of three kinds, viz. :—

The **G clef**,

The **C clef**, or

The **F clef**, or

The C clef is placed on the staff in such a position as always to indicate "Middle C" ; the F clef is placed upon the F below that note; and the G clef upon the G above it.

Referring again to the example in Sec. 5, the staves and clefs employed for the various voices, &c. there indicated will appear as under :—

The C clef is described in some text-books as a "moveable" clef. The inaccuracy of this statement is shewn at a glance by the above diagram, where it will be seen that the clef in reality remains *always in the same place,* viz., on the line representing "Middle C," the staff in each case being formed by the addition of a greater or less number of lines above or below, as the case may be.

9.—When a staff is formed with the five **highest**, or **five lowest**, lines of the Great Staff, the note "Middle C" is **not included** ; consequently the C clef cannot be used, and the two other clefs, viz. : the F and G, are brought into requisition.

' The "Mezzo-Soprano" clef is omitted, as it is practically obsolete.

† Often called the Violin clef, from the fact that music for the Violin is always written with this clef.

These are the clefs most often seen at the present day, and are the only ones now used in Pianoforte, Harp, or Organ music.

The sounds indicated upon the two staves controlled by the F and G clefs are as follows :—

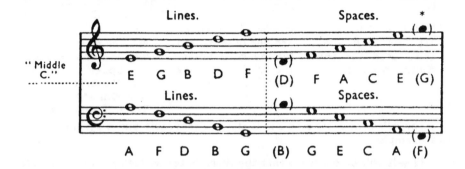

10.—The line for " Middle C " being omitted, this note, when required, is written upon a short line called a **Ledger line** (Fr. *leger*, light), the same distance *below* the Treble staff as it is *above* the Bass, e.g. :—

Other sounds above and below the pitch of those on the staff are indicated by similar ledger lines, and the spaces between them, e.g. :—

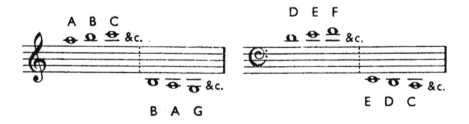

11.—The C clef was formerly more frequently used than at the present time. Now-a-days, its employment is confined to certain orchestral instruments, and occasionally (particularly in foreign scores) to the Soprano,

* The notes and letters enclosed in brackets are, in reality, not actually *upon* the staff, being respectively above and below it ; but it is convenient to indicate them here.

Alto and Tenor voices.* The following table will shew the method of its use :—

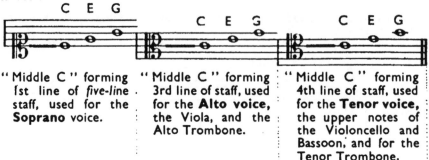

"Middle C" forming 1st line of *five-line* staff, used for the **Soprano** voice.	"Middle C" forming 3rd line of staff, used for the **Alto voice**, the Viola, and the Alto Trombone.	"Middle C" forming 4th line of staff, used for the **Tenor voice**, the upper notes of the Violoncello and Bassoon, and for the Tenor Trombone.

The fallacy of describing the C clef as a moveable one is again shewn in this example.

12.—It will be observed that the three notes written above are in each case **identical in pitch** ; they could be represented in the G and F clefs respectively, thus :—

13.—In music for the Pianoforte, Harp, or Organ, the two staves are usually connected by a sign called a **Brace**, thus :—

and, unless specially indicated otherwise, the notes in the Treble, or G clef, are played with the right hand, and those in the Bass, or F clef, with the left hand.

---

* In England and America, the vocal parts are nearly always written in the F and G clefs ; but a distinct advantage of the use of the C clef is that practically the whole compass of any particular voice is included on the staff, without the use of ledger-lines. When the G clef is used (as it commonly is) for the Tenor voice, the notes are written an octave higher than they sound, a plan tending to obscure their true pitch in the mind of the performer, e.g. :—

written for a Tenor voice would represent

In actual sound.

CHAPTER III.

Pitch of Sounds (continued).—Sharps, Flats, &c.

1.—A chain of sounds such as that given in Chapter II, Sec. 3, although an alphabetical one, is not one in which the distances between the successive notes are in all cases equal, the difference in pitch between the notes B—C and E—F being smaller than that between any other two notes in alphabetical order.

2.—It will be observed that, on the Pianoforte or Organ keyboard, there are in two instances two white keys next to one another, **without a black key between** ; but that, in all other cases, a black key separates two succeeding white ones, thus :—

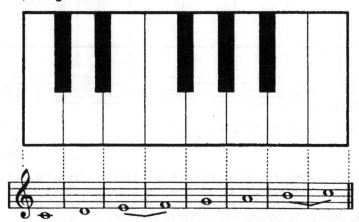

(Sounds represented by the white keys in order, starting from " Middle C.")

3.—In the above diagram, the distance from one white key to another, *when no black key comes between*, is called a **semitone**—being found between E and F, and between B and C, a *whole tone* occurring between any other successive white keys.   The semitone is the **smallest distance** from one note to another on the **Pianoforte or Organ keyboard.***

4.—The black keys represent the sounds lying at the distance of a semitone above or below the adjacent white keys, and are termed **sharps** and **flats**

5.—A sharp, ♯, placed before a note **raises** the pitch of that note one semitone, and a flat, ♭, **lowers** it one semitone.   By the following diagram

---

* Voices, and instruments of the " String " family, such as the Violin, Viola, Violoncello, &c., can produce sounds whose distance from one another is smaller than a semitone ; but, for all practical purposes, the semitone is regarded as the smallest.

it will be seen that, in this way, each black key may represent a sharp or a flat ; a chain of semitones resulting in each case :—*

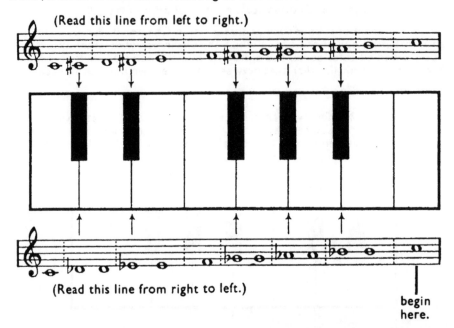

(Read this line from left to right.)

(Read this line from right to left.)

begin here.

6.—When a sharp or a flat is placed **immediately after the clef**, it is intended that all the notes of the same name, occurring during the entire composition (or section of the same) are to be **similarly sharpened or flattened**, unless the contrary is indicated (see Sec. 7) ; e.g.:—

signifies that *all* F's and C's are to be sharp.

signifies that *all* B's, E's and A's are to be flat.

The signs so placed at the beginning of the staff constitute what is known as the **Key-signature.** (Chap. VI, Sec. 8.)

7.—Oftentimes it is necessary **temporarily** to sharpen or flatten a note ; in this case, the sharp or flat is placed immediately **before the note,** and is termed an **Accidental :—**

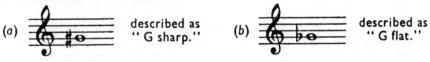

(a)   described as " G sharp."   (b)   described as " G flat."

* When the two notes of a semitone are expressed by the **same letter-name**, as C to C♯, or C to C♭, the semitone is termed chromatic ; when they are expressed by **two different letters**, as C to D♭, or C to B, it is called **diatonic.**

When it is desired to restore such note to its normal pitch a sign called a **Natural,** ♮, is placed before it :—

described as " G natural."

This is called **contradicting** the accidental.*

It will be seen that, after a ♯ has been used, a ♮ *lowers* the pitch of the note a semitone again ; and similarly *raises* it, after a ♭ has been used.

8.—**Double-sharps and double-flats** are frequently met with as accidentals. A double-sharp, X, has the effect of *raising* an already sharpened note a semitone—i.e., a *whole* tone *above*'the " natural " pitch ; and a double-flat, ♭♭, similarly *lowers* an already flattened note a semitone—i.e., a *whole* tone *below* the " natural " pitch, e.g. :—

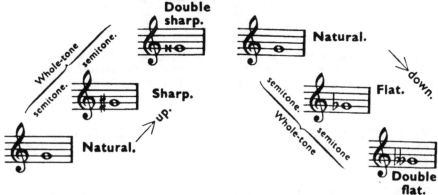

9.—Unfortunately, there are two methods of contradicting double-sharps, or double-flats. In order to **lower a double-sharp** by a' semitone to a single sharp, some composers write—

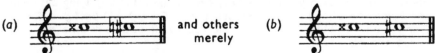

(a) and others merely (b)

and in order to **raise a double-flat,** similarly, to a single flat, both of the following methods are used :—

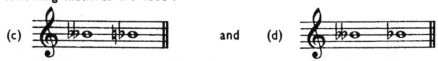

(c) and (d)

The plan adopted at (b) and (d) is to be recommended as being simpler and less cumbersome.

* In cases where the key-signature contains one or more sharps or flats, it is evident that **the natural itself may become an accidental ;** e.g. :—

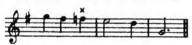

10.—Accidentals, of whatever kind, **affect all notes of the same pitch** throughout an entire *bar*, or *measure* (see Chap. IV, Sec. 3), unless contradicted, but **no further.** If an accidental is to apply to notes of the same letter-name, *but in a different octave*, it should be **indicated again** in that particular position, e.g. :—

11.—When the last note of a *bar*, or *measure*, has been inflected by an accidental, and the next bar begins with a note of the same letter-name, restored to its original pitch, it is safer **specially to indicate** the change, e.g. :—

although, if the rule in Sec. 10 were always acted upon by composers this would not be necessary.

12.—In connection with the subject of sharps and flats, it is worth while to note that each pianoforte key, except the black key lying between G and A, may be called by **three names,** e.g. :—C=B♯ = D♭♭, F♯ = G♭ = E✕, and so on. The black key above referred to can bear only **two names,** viz. : G♯ and A♭.

(See Addenda, page 83.)

CHAPTER IV.

Accent and Time.

1.—To produce a satisfactory musical effect, it is not only necessary that there should be (i) variety of pitch, and (ii) duration of sound, but also (iii) what is termed **Accent.** The grouping of sounds into sets by means of accent produces what is known as **Time.***

2.—In a well-ordered succession of sounds, producing what is commonly called a **Melody,** or Tune, it cannot have escaped the student's notice that

---

* Not to be confused with " Tempo,'' which means the *speed* at which a composition is to be played or sung.

certain of these sounds are **accented more strongly** than others ;* and
that, periodically, there is a recurrence of an accent stronger than the rest,
which, for the sake of convenience, we will call the **Strongest Accent**,
e.g. :—

If this were not the case, music would be chaotic, vague, and lacking in
definite impression.

3.—**To indicate the position** of this constantly recurring Strongest
Accent, it is now-a-days customary to place a perpendicular line—from top
to bottom of the staff—**immediately before** such accent. The above
passage would thus appear as follows :—

Such lines are termed **Bar-lines,** and as much as is contained between any
two successive bar-lines is described as a **Measure** or a **Bar** of music.†

---

* The accenting of certain notes in a melody is analogous to the **scansion** of poetry,
e.g. :—
     (i) **Iambic metre :**

         "As thro' the land at eve we went,

          And pluck'd the ripen'd ears " ;
     (ii) **Trochaic metre :**

         " Who are these like stars appearing ? "
   (iii) **Anapæstic metre :**

         " With a smile on her lips, and a tear in her eye."
   (iv) **Dactylic metre :**

         " God save our gracious King."

† At the conclusion of a composition, or sometimes at the termination of a period, or
musical sentence, two somewhat thicker lines are drawn, called a **Double-bar,** e.g.:—

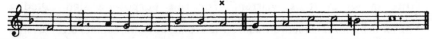 These, however, do not always mark the situation of the accent, neither

do they affect the time (as in the following example) :—

The double-bars here merely indicate the end of a line of words in the nymn to which the
tune is set, and the *time* is not broken at X.

4.—The Strongest Accent in musical passages may recur at a **greater** or less distance **of time,** producing, as a consequence, bars of various lengths—bars in which there are, as the case may be, two, three, or four divisions, *pulses, or **beats** (as they are usually called, from the practice of " beating " time).

5.—The kinds of **Time** produced—depending, be it observed, entirely upon this periodic recurrence of the Strongest Accent—may be classified under three headings, viz. :—

Duple (in which each bar is divisible into **two** beats of equal value), e.g. :—

Triple (in which each bar is divisible into **three** such beats), e.g. :—

Quadruple (in which each bar is divisible into **four** such beats), e.g. :—

NOTE.—Quadruple time being practically an extension of Duple time, an accent will occur on the third beat, but it will be slighter than that on the first beat.

6.—As it is usual for one kind of Time to be maintained for a considerable portion of a composition—often for the whole of it—it is customary to indicate, at the beginning of the piece, the particular **kind of Time** in which it is written. For this purpose a sign called a

---

* Bars with five, or seven such divisions are sometimes met with, but they occur so rarely that it will suffice merely to mention the fact here, particularly as a bar with five divisions generally has the effect of a bar of *three* divisions, followed by one of *two* divisions ; and, a bar of *seven* the effect of one of *four,* followed by one of *three.*

Time-signature is used, which (except in two instances*) consists of two figures, an upper and a lower, thus :—

$$\frac{2}{4}, \qquad \frac{3}{8}, \qquad \frac{4}{16}, \ \&c.$$

the upper figure shewing, the **number of divisions** in a bar, and the lower specifying their **quality,** or **value.**

7.—In order to indicate the **value** of the beats or divisions, whether minims, crotchets, quavers, semiquavers, &c., the lower figure is always an aliquot part of a semibreve (which note is taken as the standard from which the others are reckoned), e.g. :—

$$\overline{2} \qquad \overline{4} \qquad \overline{8} \qquad \overline{16} \ \&c.$$

N.B.—It will be seen, on reference to the table of note-values in Chap. I Sec. 2, that these figures give the fractional part of a semibreve represented by each kind of note in order.

8.—When each beat or a bar is **divisible by two** (i.e., when it can be represented by *two* of the notes next smaller in value), the time is called **Simple.** Thus we have Simple Duple Time, Simple Triple Time, and Simple Quadruple Time, the more usual time-signatures being :—

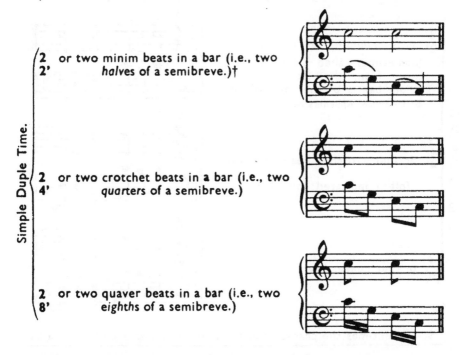

Simple Duple Time.

$\frac{2}{2},$ or two minim beats in a bar (i.e., two *halves* of a semibreve.)†

$\frac{2}{4},$ or two crotchet beats in a bar (i.e., two *quarters* of a semibreve.)

$\frac{2}{8},$ or two quaver beats in a bar (i.e., two *eighths* of a semibreve.)

---

* See under quadruple time in Sec. 8 below ; also Appendix A—" *Alla Breve.*"
† The division of each beat by 2 is shewn on the lower staff in each example.

Simple Triple Time.

$\frac{3}{2}$, or three minim beats in a bar.

$\frac{3}{4}$, or three crotchet beats in a bar.

$\frac{3}{8}$, or three quaver beats in a bar.

Simple Quadruple Time.

$\frac{4}{2}$, or four minim beats in a bar.

(Sometimes called "Alla Breve" time, from the fact that the whole bar is of the value of one Breve)—See Appendix A.

$\frac{4}{4}$, or four crotchet beats in a bar,

(often indicated thus, C).

$\frac{4}{8}$, or four quaver beats in a bar.

9.—Oftentimes the character of the music requires each beat of a bar

* It is very rarely that we find times in which the beats are of the value of semibreves or notes shorter than quavers. There are, however, two rather well-known instances of $\frac{3}{1}$ (three semibreves in a bar) in Clementi's "Gradus ad Parnassum."

to be **divisible by three** (i.e., represented by a *triple* (See Appendix A)) of the notes next smaller in value, e.g. :—

To save the necessity of marking the triplets throughout an entire composition of this kind, a new time-signature is employed, in which the lower figure indicates the **quality of each note of the triplet**—as an aliquot part of a semibreve. Thus, the above passage would appear as follows :—

Here the signature means that six *eighths* of a semibreve (viz., six quavers) are to be taken in each bar, divided into **groups of three,** each group constituting one beat, and being consequently of the value of a dotted crotchet. Hence the above time would be described as having two dotted crotchet-beats in a bar.*

10.—When the beats of a bar are dotted, the time is termed **compound,** and thus we have Compound Duple time, Compound Triple time, and Compound Quadruple time, the more usual time-signatures then being—

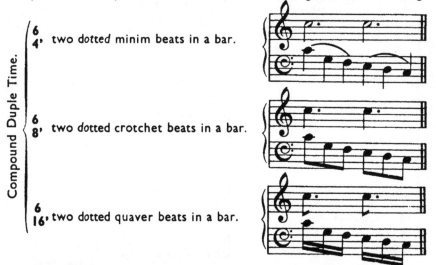

Compound Duple Time.

$\frac{6}{4}$, two *dotted* minim beats in a bar.

$\frac{6}{8}$, two *dotted* crotchet beats in a bar.

$\frac{6}{16}$, two dotted quaver beats in a bar.

*Observe that the **dotted beats** in the second of the above examples are of exactly the **same duration** as the undotted beats in the first.

Compound Triple Time.

9
4'   three dotted minim beats
        in a bar.

9
8'   three dotted crotchet beats
        in a bar.

9
16' three dotted quaver beats
        in a bar.

Compound Quadruple Time.

12
4'   four dotted minim beats
        in a bar.*

12
8'   four dotted crotchet
        beats in a bar.

12
16' four dotted quaver beats
        in a bar.

* Rather rare.

11.—It will be readily understood from the examples in Secs. 8 and 10, that the divisions or beats of a bar may always be expressed by their **equivalent value in notes of shorter or longer duration,** or by an equivalent number of notes and rests, e.g. :—

CHAPTER V.

Accent and Time—(*continued*).

The Grouping of Notes.

1.—When the divisions of a bar are represented by their equivalent value in quavers, semiquavers, &c., it is the custom for these notes to be **grouped together.*** Such groupings should always indicate, as far as possible, the divisions, or beats, in order to make their position clear to the eye. Thus, it may be taken as a safe rule that **only as many notes should be grouped together as would form one beat,** but that the notes belonging to each beat *should* be so grouped, e.g. :—

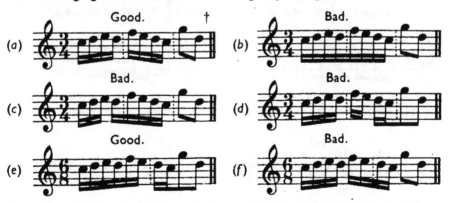

Examples of this rule could easily be multiplied, but the above instances, both of its observance and of its non-observance, will be sufficient to shew

---

* In **vocal music**, only as many notes may be grouped together as are sung to one syllable.

† The dotted lines mark the divisions of the bars.

the necessity of correct groupings, in order to make clear the equal divisions of the bar.

NOTE.—It should be borne in mind, in connection with the question of the sub-division of the beats of a bar, that the first note of any such sub-division is always stronger than the remaining ones, and that it thus forms a **subordinate accent**, e.g.:—

Here the **main accent** of course occurs at the beginning of the **first beat** ; but the F and G (the first note of the second and third beats respectively) are more strongly emphasised than the other notes of their *own groups.*
    This rule applies in a similar way to every further sub-division into groups of shorter notes.

2.—Exceptions to the rule given in Sec. I, occur as under :—

(i.) In the case of $\frac{4}{4}$ time, when it is customary to **group quavers in fours,** where a clear half-bar is indicated *by each four,* e.g.:—

(ii.) In the case of $\frac{3}{4}$ or $\frac{3}{8}$ time, when it is usual to arrange the six quavers of $\frac{3}{4}$, or the six semiquavers of $\frac{3}{8}$, in **one group,** e.g. :—

3.—In the matter of the employment of **rests,** no rest of greater value than one beat should be used (except in two instances mentioned in Sec. 4), e.g.:—

4.—There are two exceptions to this rule, viz. :—

   (i.) In the case of a **whole bar's rest,** when a semibreve rest is used in *all* times, save the true " Alla Breve " $\left(\text{or } \frac{4}{2}\right)$ time, when a breve rest is used, appropriately :—

   (ii.) In the case of a **clear half-bar at either end** of a bar of quadruple time, when a rest of the value of that half-bar should be used :—

5.—With regard to notes, a greater freedom is permissible, and a sound lasting during more than one beat is often represented by a **single note,** e.g. :—

Observe, however, that in *compound* times, this can only occur when the sound **lasts for two or more whole beats :**—

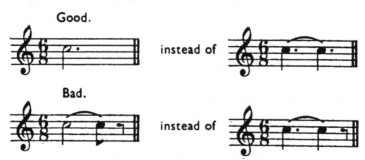

Good.

instead of

Bad.

instead of

6.—When a bar has to be **completed with rests,** care must be taken that each beat (or sub-division of the same) must be finished **before the next is begun.** The following example will illustrate this :—

Good.

(a)

Here, in $\frac{3}{4}$ time, each beat consists of a crotchet. The note at the beginning of the bar has taken a *quarter* of the first beat ; therefore, a semiquaver rest must succeed, to fill up the first *half* ; a quaver rest following, by which the entire beat is completed. The second beat of the bar is intact, consequently a crotchet rest is used. In the case of the third beat the semiquaver note at the end of the bar represents the *last* quarter of that beat, which will be completed in the same manner as in the case of the first part of the bar—**only in the reverse order.**†

Bad.

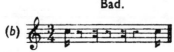

(b)

This example, although it contains the same rests as the bar at (a), is totally incorrect, as their order gives no idea of the position of the various divisions, or sub-divisions.

7.—If $\frac{6}{8}$ (compound duple) were to be substituted for $\frac{3}{4}$ in Ex. (a), the order of rests would be as follows :—

Here **each beat** is of the value of a **dotted note,** as shewn by the small notes above the example, and it should be remembered that in the case

---

* Here the minim totally obliterates the idea of the division of a bar of $\frac{6}{8}$ into two dotted crochet beats, and suggests a bar of $\frac{3}{4}$.

† N.B.—When any division of a bar begins or ends with a short note, the *next* rest in that division will always be of identical value.

of compound times, the value of each of such notes—*without* its dot—should always be completed with rests first, **a separate rest being used for the dot.** Hence, in the above example, the first crotchet having been broken into, is completed by the addition of, first, a semiquaver rest, and then a quaver rest (*vide* Sec. 6)—a second quaver rest then succeeding, as the equivalent of the dot.

In the second half-bar, the case is different. The semiquaver note at the end of the bar has taken the latter half of the *dot*, and consequently needs a semiquaver rest before it, to fill up the value of that dot. A crotchet rest (*not two quaver rests*) then precedes, to represent the unbroken crotchet at the beginning of the second beat.

8.—**Syncopation** is an effect in music caused by throwing additional emphasis upon what is usually a weaker part of a bar. The most common instances of this are found when a note is begun

> (i.) On a comparatively unaccented part of a bar, and prolonged into the next accent, as at (*a*) ; or
>
> (ii.) In the midst of one beat, and prolonged into the next, as at (*b*).

The effect of syncopation is, moreover, produced whenever the *natural* accent is **disturbed by any means**—by ties, rests, &c., e.g. :—

A strong instance of syncopation in triple time is to be found in the *scherzo* of Beethoven's " Eroica " symphony, where the following passage occurs :—

CHAPTER VI.

Scales.

The Major Scale.

1.—A **scale** (L. *scala*, a ladder) is an alphabetical succession of sounds, having reference to one particular sound as its starting-point, or **key-note**.

2.—As was stated in Chap. II, Sec. 2 (foot-note), the first seven letters of the alphabet are employed to express the different sounds in use. The re-appearance of the same letter at a different pitch produces what is known as the **octave** of the sound originally indicated by that letter, thus :—

A continuation, alphabetically, of this series, higher or lower, would be merely a reproduction of these sounds at a higher or lower pitch—in other words, in a higher or lower *octave*.

3.—If the student will play the succession of notes in Sec. 2 on the Pianoforte (represented by the white keys), he will find that the distances between the notes are not in all cases equal. (Chap. III, Sec. 1.)

For instance, the first four notes contain two steps of a *tone* each, and one of a semitone, thus :—

tone.   tone.   semitone.

Proceeding further, it will be seen that the remaining four sounds of the octave are on exactly the same pattern :—

semitone.

tone.   tone.

Each of these groups of four notes alphabetically arranged is called a **tetrachord** (Gr. τέτρα, four ; χορδή, a string), and together form what is termed the **Major Diatonic scale** (Gr. διά, through ; τόνος, a tone, i.e., through the tones, or sounds).

(Scale of C major.)

4.—This **Major Scale**—i.e., a scale having a semitone between its 3rd and 4th degrees, and also between its 7th and 8th degrees—may not only begin upon C as its **key-note**, or starting point, but may be reproduced at a different pitch, any one of the seven letters* above-mentioned being taken as the key-note.

Clearly, however, the white keys of the Pianoforte, or natural notes, would not suffice for the purpose, as were they only to be used, the above order of tones and semitones would not be preserved, e.g. :—

Hence, we must employ the black keys, representing certain sharps and flats, e.g. :—

(Scale of G major, with one sharp, F.)

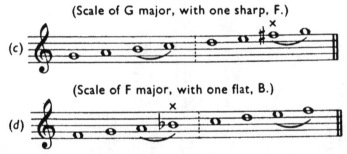

(Scale of F major, with one flat, B.)

by which the tones and semitones are brought into their right positions.

5.—It will be seen, by Ex. (c) above, that the **first** tetrachord of the scale of G major corresponds to the **second** tetrachord of C major, and that the scale of G is completed by adding a **new tetrachord**, containing a sharpened note (*the* **seventh** *of the entire scale*).

Similarly, if we take the **second** tetrachord of this scale (G) as the **first** tetrachord of a new scale, and then add another tetrachord, we shall find it necessary again to **sharpen the note before the last**, in order to preserve the order of tones and semitones :—

(Scale of D major, with two sharps, F and C.)

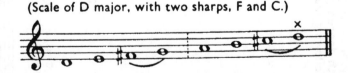

* Or these letters inflected by sharps or flats.

6.—It will thus be found that a series of major scales can be formed, each succeeding scale beginning on the 5th note of the preceding, and having one sharp more, the extra sharp being always the **7th degree** (or Leading-note—see Sec. 9) of the entire scale. The following diagram will show this at a glance :—

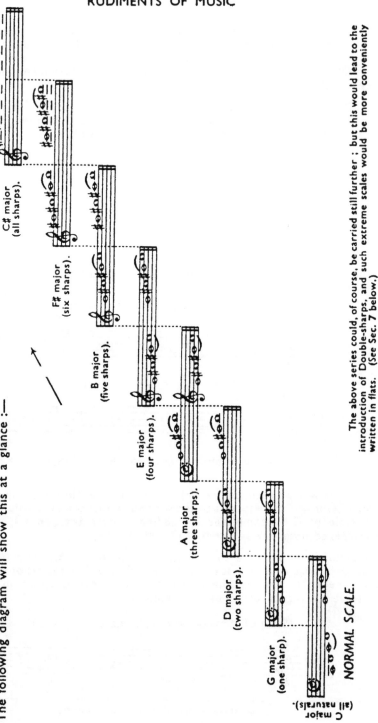

C♯ major (all sharps).

F♯ major (six sharps).

B major (five sharps).

E major (four sharps).

A major (three sharps).

D major (two sharps).

G major (one sharp).

C major (all naturals). *NORMAL SCALE.*

The above series could, of course, be carried still further ; but this would lead to the introduction of Double-sharps, and such extreme scales would be more conveniently written in flats. (See Sec. 7 below.)

7.—Similarly, a series of major scales with **flats** can be formed—(each succeeding scale beginning on the 4th degree of the preceding, i.e., five notes *lower*)—the **extra flat** always being the **4th degree** of the new scale thus produced :—

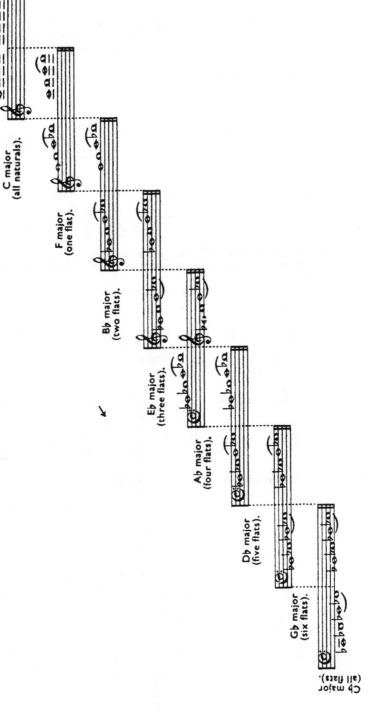

NORMAL SCALE.

C major (all naturals).

F major (one flat).

B♭ major (two flats).

E♭ major (three flats).

A♭ major (four flats).

D♭ major (five flats).

G♭ major (six flats).

C♭ major (all flats).

8.—To save unnecessary complication in writing, the sharps and flats in such scales are placed at the beginning of a musical composition, immediately after the clef. They then form what is known as the **key-signature.** (Chap. III, Sec. 6.)

The key-signatures of the above two series of scales would appear as under :—

(*a*) Scales with sharps.

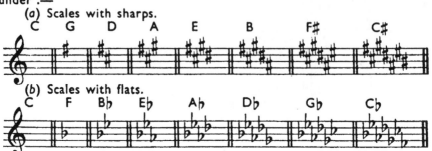

(*b*) Scales with flats.

It should be observed that these sharps and flats must be placed in the signature in regular order, as developed from the *natural* scale according to the plan mentioned in Secs. 6 and 7 above. (*See* Addenda, page 84.)

9.—Every degree of a (major or minor) diatonic scale has a technical name, as follows :—

1st degree	**Tonic,** or Key-note	:	The note from which the whole scale, key, or tonality springs.
2nd ,,	**Super-tonic**	...	The note next *above* the Tonic.
3rd ,,	**Mediant** ...	...	The note *midway* between the Tonic and the Dominant.*
4th ,,	**Sub-dominant**	...	*Under-dominant,* holding same position *under* the Tonic as the Dominant does above it.†
5th ,,	**Dominant...**	...	The note next in importance to the Tonic, having a *dominating* influence over the key.
6th ,,	**Sub-mediant**	...	*Under-mediant,* the note holding the same position *below* the Tonic, midway between it and the Sub-dominant, as the Mediant does *above* the Tonic, midway between it and the Dominant.‡
7th ,,	**Leading-note**	...	The note that leads the ear to expect the Tonic, or Key-note.

* e.g., in scale of C.   † e.g., in scale of C.   ‡ e.g., in the scale of C.

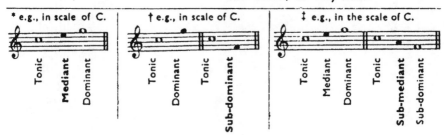

CHAPTER VII.

Scales—(continued).

The Minor Scale.

1.—The **Minor scale** derives its name from the fact that its 3rd degree is a chromatic semitone lower than the corresponding degree of the major scale, consequently producing a smaller (or **minor**) interval from the Tonic to the Mediant, e.g.:—

(In C major.)   (In C minor.)

2.—The Minor scale exists in more than one form ; in each of which, however, the **first tetrachord** is the same, e.g. :—

(C minor.)

the semitone occurring between the 2nd and 3rd degrees, instead of between the 3rd and 4th, as in the Major scale.

3.—The **second tetrachord** may be found in either of the following forms :—

(i.)   (ii.)   (iii.)

It will be seen that No. i. has the step of a semitone between the 7th and 8th degrees, No. iii. between the 5th and 6th ; whereas No. ii. has semitones both between the 5th and 6th, and the 7th and 8th degrees.

4.—The most usual (and useful) form now-a-days is that termed the **Harmonic Minor Scale,** in which the second tetrachord is that given as No. ii. above :—

3 semi-
tones.‡

This scale is termed *Harmonic*, as it is the one from which the harmonies of a minor key are most usually formed.

---

*The difference in pitch (i.e., the *interval*) between C and E is termed a major 3rd ; that between C and E♭ a minor 3rd.   (See Chap. IX.)
† Used only in descending.
‡ Interval of augmented 2nd.   (See Chap. IX, Sec. 9.)

5.—The tetrachords given as Nos. i. and iii. in Sec. 3 are rarely found except as the ascending and descending forms, respectively, of the scale known as the **Melodic Minor Scale** :—

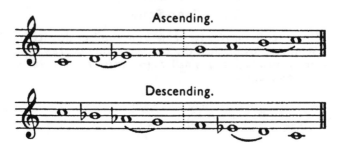

a scale used by composers at times to avoid the somewhat hard effect in *melody* (see App. A), of the step of a tone-and-a-half between the 6th and 7th degrees of the Harmonic Minor Scale.

It should be noticed that, in the Melodic Minor Scale, as shewn above, the Tonic is approached by step of a semitone, ascending ; and the Dominant by a similar step, descending.

6.—The method of writing the **signature** of a Minor scale is a **singularly unfortunate one,** representing neither of the above forms accurately. The plan is to make the signature of a minor scale coincide with that of the major scale that begins on its 3rd degree, e.g.:—

A minor has the same signature as **C** major
E   ,,   ,,   ,,   **G** major
and so on.

These scales, having the same signature, are termed **relative** major and minor scales.

7.—Returning for a moment to the harmonic scale of C minor given in Sec. 4 above, and applying this rule, it will be found that its signature is that of the scale of Eb major (its 3rd degree), thus :—

the Leading-note being written with an accidental to cause the semitone to occur between the 7th and 8th degrees.

Here the **anomalous character of the signature** will be seen, for a B♭ appears therein, only to be contradicted when we arrive at the Leading-note of the scale.

When the Melodic Minor Scale is considered, the matter is no better, as A♮ is required in ascending, and the signature contains A♭.

8.—The **signatures** of the various minor keys are therefore as follows :—

A MINOR, with same signature as *C MAJOR,*

1.—Sharp keys.

E MINOR, with same signature as *G MAJOR,*

B MINOR, *D MAJOR,*

F♯ MINOR, ,, ,, *A MAJOR,*

C♯ MINOR, ,, *E MAJOR,*

G♯ MINOR, ,, *B MAJOR,*

D♯ MINOR, ,, ,, *F♯ MAJOR,*

A♯ MINOR, ,, ,, *C♯ MAJOR,*

A MINOR, with same signature as *C MAJOR,*

2.—Flat keys.

D MINOR, with same signature as *F MAJOR,*

G MINOR, ,, ,, *B♭ MAJOR,*

C MINOR, ,, ,, *E♭ MAJOR,*

F MINOR, ,, *A♭ MAJOR,*

B♭ MINOR, ,, ,, *D♭ MAJOR,*

E♭ MINOR, ,, ,, *G♭ MAJOR,*

A♭ MINOR, ,, ,, *C♭ MAJOR.*

9.—A major and a minor scale starting from the same tonic, or key-note, are termed respectively the **Tonic Major,** or **Tonic Minor,** of each other :—

  (i.) C major : Tonic minor = C minor.
  (ii.) C minor : Tonic major = C major.

It will be seen from the diagram in Sec. 8 that there is always a difference of three signs between the signatures of a major scale and its Tonic minor.

CHAPTER VIII.

Scales—(continued).

The Chromatic Scale.

1.—A **Chromatic Scale** (Gr. Χρῶμα, colour), is a scale proceeding entirely by semitones, the **number of sounds** between any note and its octave being **twelve,** e.g. :—

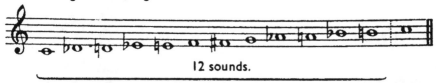

12 sounds.

2.—The student will observe that all the Pianoforte keys, black as well as white, are needed to form this scale.

3.—The **Chromatic scale** is found written in more ways than one, that given in Sec. i. being termed the **Harmonic Chromatic Scale,** from the fact that the chromatic harmonies (*see* App. A, *Chromatic* and *Chromatic Chord*) of any key need this particular notation for their proper formation.

4.—The Harmonic Chromatic Scale is constructed as follows, and **each key has its own chromatic scale,** formed upon exactly the same plan :—

  (*a*) Take the notes of the **Major** diatonic scale of the particular key in question—e.g. (in key of C) :—

  (*b*) Add the notes that differ from these in both forms of the **Minor** diatonic scale :—

In Harmonic Minor.

In Melodic Minor (descending form).

We now have the following :—

with gaps as yet between the Tonic and Supertonic, and between the Sub-dominant and Dominant. To complete the Chromatic Scale, we must finally add the **diatonic semitone** (Chap. III, Sec. 5, foot-note) **above the key-note** (i), and the **chromatic semitone above the sub-dominant** (ii). The following examples will make this clear :—

In key of C.

In key of B♭.

In key of E.

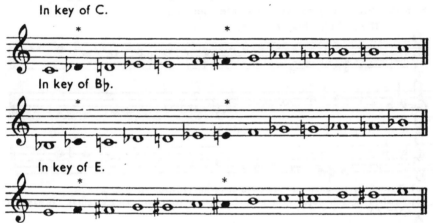

5.—The above is the chromatic scale, formed upon a harmonic basis, but it is often found **modified in notation,** for the purpose of lessening the number of accidentals, and so simplifying matters for the reader of music. These alterations are purely for convenience, however, and vary from time to time, according to the circumstances in which they are needed, the most usual form of **Arbitrary** (or *Melodic*) **Chromatic Scale**— as it is generally termed—being the following :—

(or B♭)

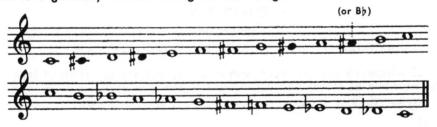

6.—It will be seen, by comparing this form of scale with that given in Sec. 4, that, in ascending, the number of accidentals is much reduced, the scales remaining, however, identical in notation in the descending form.

(i.) The minor 2nd above the key-note. }
(ii.) The Augmented 4th   „   „   } (Chap. IX, Secs. 7 and 9.)

7.—From this we may form the **rules** that are generally **observed in writing** the Arbitrary Chromatic Scale, viz. :—

    (i.) That the notes that are *diatonic* in the particular key are always kept unaltered ;

    (ii.) That *the raised Sub-dominant** is always used, ascending or descending, in preference to the *lowered Dominant,*† as being more closely related to the key ;

    (iii.) That the remaining notes are formed by raising existing ones a *chromatic* semitone in ascending, and by lowering them a semitone in descending.

N.B.—The same letter-name must never occur more than twice in succession.

The following examples will illustrate these rules :—

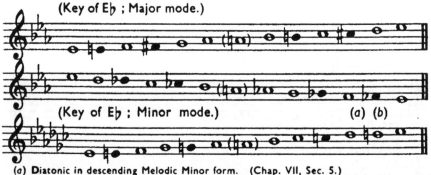

(Key of E♭ ; Major mode.)

(Key of E♭ ; Minor mode.)   (a) (b)

(a) Diatonic in descending Melodic Minor form.   (Chap. VII, Sec. 5.)

(b) Really a diatonic note in the key, although written with an accidental.   (Chap. VII, Sec. 7.)

N.B.—The notes corresponding to Rule (i.) are printed as open notes.
    The note corresponding to Rule (ii.) is printed as an open note enclosed in brackets.
    The notes corresponding to Rule (iii.) are printed as black-headed notes.

CHAPTER IX.

Intervals.

1.—An **Interval** is the *difference in pitch between two sounds.*

2.—Intervals are described **numerically,** and are so reckoned from the **number of letter-names** included in their formation, e.g. :—

1st or unison.‡   2nd.   3rd.   4th.   5th.

---

* Augmented 4th from key-note.   } (Chap. IX.)
† Diminished 5th   ,,   ,,
‡ The 1st, or unison, is, strictly speaking, not an interval at all, there being no *difference in pitch* between the two sounds ; but it is convenient to classify it as such.

6th.　　　　7th.　　　　8th or Octave.

Here it will be seen that the 1st, or unison, contains only one letter-name ; a 2nd, two ;
a 3rd, three, and so on.

3.—The **inflection** of either note of an interval—or of both—by an accidental **does not alter** its numerical description ; but, as will be seen later, it causes its **quality** to be varied.

Thus, each of the following comes under the description of a 3rd, as between C and E there is only one letter-name, D :—

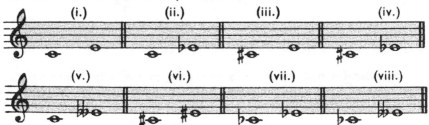

(i.)　　　(ii.)　　　(iii.)　　　(iv.)

(v.)　　　(vi.)　　　(vii.)　　　(viii.)

4.—The **quality** of an interval depends upon the **number of semitones** contained therein. For instance, Exs. (i.), (vi.), and (vii.) contain *four* semitones each ; Exs. (ii.), (iii.), and (viii.), *three* ; and Exs. (iv.) and (v.), *two* ; and, according to the number of semitones they contain, would be described as major, minor, and diminished 3rds, respectively.

5.—The various kinds of interval produced in this way bear the following names :—

(i.) **Perfect** ... (applied only to 1sts, 4ths, 5ths, and 8ths).

Imperfect. {
(ii.) **Major** ...
(iii.) **Minor** ...
} (,, ,, 2nds, 3rds, 6ths, and 7ths).
(iv.) **Diminished** (,, ,, 3rds, 4ths, 5ths, and 7ths).
(v.) **Augmented** (,, ,, 2nds, 4ths, 5ths, and 6ths).

6.—The intervals **counted from the Tonic** to any of the notes of a major scale are either **major** or **perfect**, e.g. :—

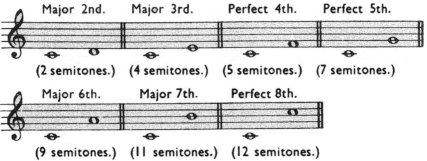

Major 2nd.　Major 3rd.　Perfect 4th.　Perfect 5th.

(2 semitones.)　(4 semitones.)　(5 semitones.)　(7 semitones.)

Major 6th.　Major 7th.　Perfect 8th.

(9 semitones.)　(11 semitones.)　(12 semitones.)

7.—A **minor** interval is formed by **lowering the upper note** of a major interval (*or by raising its lower* note) a chromatic semitone,* e.g. :—

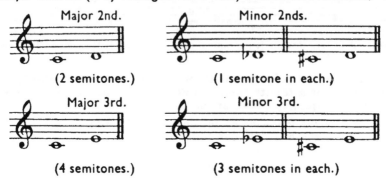

—and similarly with the intervals of 6th and 7th.

8.—A **diminished interval** is produced by similarly **lowering the upper note** of a *minor*, or a perfect interval (or by *raising its lower* note) a chromatic semitone, e.g. :—

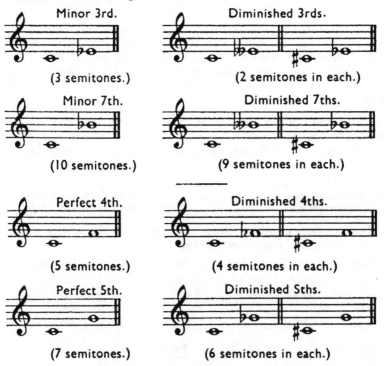

9.—An **augmented interval** is produced, conversely, by **raising the**

---

* Thus retaining letter-names.

upper note of a major, *or a* perfect interval (*or by lowering its under note*) a chromatic semitone, e.g. :—

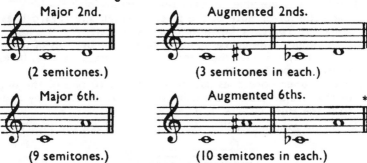

N.B.—The intervals of Diminished 6th and Augmented 3rd are not employed in chord-formation, therefore are not included here, being practically useless.

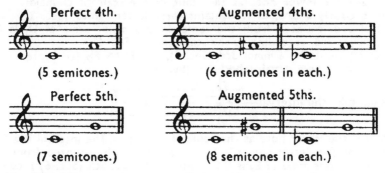

10.—The following diagrams will shew the scheme of varying qualities in intervals at a glance :—

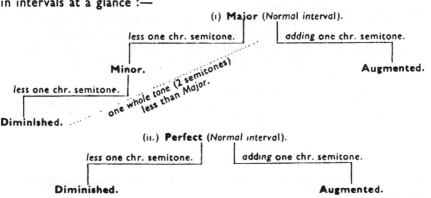

* The 1st and 8ve are sometimes augmented by a similar process ; but they are very rarely found in this form. The augmented 1st is better described as a Chromatic semitone, e.g. :—

11.—In order to **find the interval** between two sounds, it will be of service to remember the rule in Sec. 6. From this, and the statements in Secs. 7, 8 and 9, it is possible to form the following plan :—

    (i.) Take the lower note of the given interval, and regard it as if it were the Tonic, or key-note of a major scale.

    (ii.) If the upper note corresponds to one of the degrees of the major scale of that Tonic, the interval will, as stated above, be either **major** or **perfect.**

    (iii.) If the upper note does *not* so correspond to one of the degrees of that major scale, its quality may easily be found by applying to it the rules in Secs. 7, 8 and 9 above.

The following examples will make this clear. Take the interval :—

Here regard the lower note as the tonic of the scale of D major. The interval is clearly a 3rd, as it contains *three* letter-names (Sec. 2). The interval of 3rd, counted from the tonic, in the major scale of D, is F♯. This is a *major* 3rd, according to the statement in Sec. 6.

D to F♮ would be a *minor* 3rd (Sec. 7), and **D to F♭** (the interval in question) would be a **diminished** 3rd (Sec. 8).

Again, take the interval—

Here regard the lower note as the tonic of E major. The interval is a 5th, as it contains *five* letter-names. The interval of 5th, counted from the tonic, in the major scale of E, is B♮. This is a *perfect* 5th (Sec. 6) ; consequently **E to B♯** is an **augmented** 5th (Sec. 9).

12.—An interval is termed—

    Consonant, or *Concordant,* when it is satisfactory *in itself,* and requires no other to follow it to complete its effect ; and

    Dissonant, or *Discordant,* when, on the contrary, it *does* require another to follow it, to render its effect satisfactory.

In the first class are :

    (i.) Major and Minor 3rds and 6ths.

    (ii.) All Perfect intervals (except, occasionally, the perfect 4th). (See Chap. XIII, Sec. 13, foot-note).

In the second are included :

    (i.) All 2nds, 7ths, and 9ths.

    (ii.) All Diminished and Augmented intervals.

13.—Intervals beyond the limits of an Octave are called **Compound Intervals,** e.g. :—

Major 9th.   Minor 9th.

The intervals of 10th, 11th, 12th, &c., are more often spoken of, however, as 3rds, 4ths, 5ths, &c.

14.—The terms **Diatonic** and **Chromatic** are also applied to intervals. The former are those which can be found in any diatonic scale ; the latter those which occur only in the chromatic scale, viz. :—

(i.) The Chromatic semitone (or augmented 1st).

(ii.) The Diminished 3rd.

(iii.) The Augmented 6th.

(iv.) The Diminished 8th.

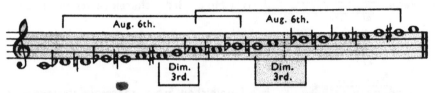

Chromatic semitones and Diminished 8ths clearly occur between any two notes with the same letter-name, one of which is, however, of a different quality, e.g. :—

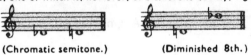

(Chromatic semitone.)   (Diminished 8th.)

15.—By **inverting** an interval is meant the changing of the relative position of the two notes, effected by placing the lower note an 8ve higher, or the higher note an 8ve lower, e.g.:—

Original interval.   Inverted interval.

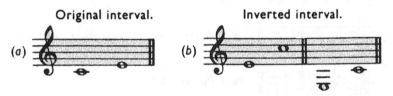

16.—The number of the original interval added to the number of the inverted interval produces **nine** :—

A 2nd inverted becomes a	7th	$2 + 7 = 9.$
A 3rd ,, ,,	6th	$3 + 6 = 9.$
A 4th ,, ,,	5th	$4 + 5 = 9.$
A 5th ,, ,,	4th	$5 + 4 = 9.$
A 6th ,, ,,	3rd	$6 + 3 = 9.$
A 7th ,, ,,	2nd	$7 + 2 = 9.$
An 8th ,, ,,	1st	$8 + 1 = 9.$

17.—Further, it should be observed that, when inverted—

    { (i.) *Major* intervals become *Minor.* }
    { (ii.) *Minor* intervals become *Major.* }

    { (iii.) *Diminished* intervals become *Augmented.* }
    { (iv.) *Augmented* intervals become *Diminished.* }

but that— (v.) *Perfect* intervals **remain** *Perfect.**

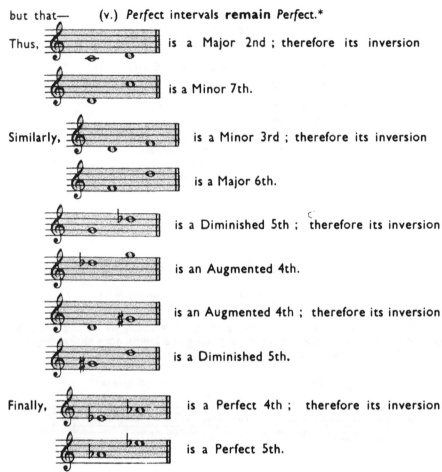

Thus, is a Major 2nd ; therefore its inversion

is a Minor 7th.

Similarly, is a Minor 3rd ; therefore its inversion

is a Major 6th.

is a Diminished 5th ; therefore its inversion

is an Augmented 4th.

is an Augmented 4th ; therefore its inversion

is a Diminished 5th.

Finally, is a Perfect 4th ; therefore its inversion

is a Perfect 5th.

 Instances might be multipled, but the above will be quite sufficient to shew the working of the rules of inversion, as applied to intervals.

 18.—The number of **semitones** contained in any interval added to those contained in its inversion will necessarily produce the number of semitones contained in an 8ve, viz. :—**12**, e.g.:—

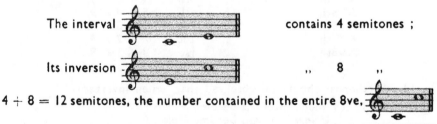

The interval   contains 4 semitones ;

Its inversion   ,,   8   ,,

4 + 8 = 12 semitones, the number contained in the entire 8ve,

---

 * It is worth while to observe that the two notes of a perfect interval are always of the same quality, i.e., both sharp, both natural, &c.—with the exception of the perfect 5th between any B and F, and its inversion, the perfect 4th between any F and B.

CHAPTER X.

Signs of Abbreviation, Embellishment, &c.

1.—When it is desired that a section of a composition shall be **repeated,** such repeat is usually indicated by that particular section being marked off, at beginning and end, by double bars, the first of which has two or four **dots** placed *after* it, and the second, similar dots placed *before* it, thus :—

2.—If the repeat is to be made from the *beginning* of a piece of music, the first double-bar is unnecessary.

3.—When, on the repetition, an **alteration of the termination** of the passage is needed, this is indicated as under :—

Here, when the repeat is made, the bars marked 2*nd time* are to be substituted for those marked 1st *time.*

4.—Sometimes a repeat from the commencement of a piece is indicated by the words **Da Capo** (i.e., from the beginning), or merely the initials **D.C.,** placed at that point from which the return is to be made.

The term **Dal Segno** (i.e., from the sign), or merely the initials **D.S.,** similarly direct that such return shall be made to a point marked by this sign 𝄋. In both these cases the repetition is continued until the word **Fine** (end) occurs.†

5.—The word **bis** over a bar, or similar short passage, signifies that such bar or passage is to be performed twice. This sign is rarely met with now-a-days, except in MS. music.

6.—The sign ⌢, a **Pause,** over or under a note or rest has the effect of prolonging its length, the precise amount of such lengthening being left to the discretion of the performer. (See, however, foot-note to Sec. 4.) The words **Lunga pausa** (a long pause) shew that the pause is to be of considerable duration.

The initials **G.P.** (*Grosse, or General, Pause*) are sometimes met with in orchestral music, and indicate a pause for the whole band.

---

* Sometimes expressed in Italian, 1ma volta, (i.e., prima volta), and 2da volta (i.e., seconda volta) ; and sometimes by merely the figures 1 and 2 respectively.

† Sometimes a Pause ⌢, over a double bar is substituted for *Fine.*

7.—To avoid the use of an inconvenient number of ledger lines, the extreme high notes above the staff are frequently written thus :—

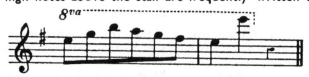

the sign **8va** (or merely 8.........), being an abbreviation of the word **ottava,** and indicating that the sounds over which it and the dots following it are placed are to be played an octave higher. The resumption of the ordinary pitch is indicated by the cessation of the dots, or sometimes by the term **loco** (*in place*).

8va bassa (Ottava bassa), or **8va sotto** (Ottava sotto), under the bass staff indicates similarly that such notes are to be played an octave *lower*.

Con 8 (or **8**) under a bass-note means that such bass-note is to be accompanied by its

Octave below, thus :—

8.—The signs and placed before a chord (see App. A), indicate that the notes of that chord are not to be played together, but in **arpeggio** (Ital. *arpa*, a harp), i.e., in rapid succession, beginning with the lowest :—

the whole chord being held when all the notes have been sounded.

9.—The term **legato** (i.e., bound) implies that two or more consecutive notes (or chords) are to be performed in a smooth, connected manner ; and, in an extended passage, this word is sometimes written to express this effect. Much more frequently, however, a curved line, ⌢ or ⌣ (called a **slur**) is used, and it is understood that all notes included within such curve are to be played *legato*,* e.g. :—

---

* The use of the **slur** is inseparably bound up with the art of **phrasing**, into which it is impossible to enter fully here. Suffice it to say that, in **Pianoforte-playing**, when two successive notes, or chords are connected by a slur, the first of such notes or chords is to be played with additional stress, and the second not only made slighter than usual, but perceptibly shorter, by the hand being raised from the keys, e.g. :—

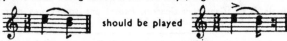

In **music for bowed instruments** the slur usually indicates the number of notes to be taken with one stroke of the bow ; in **vocal music**, the number of notes to be sung to one syllable.

10.—In the first of the above examples, it will be noticed that the two C's at the commencement of the passage are joined by a small curve. When two notes **of the same pitch** are so connected, the curve is not a " slur," but a **tie** (or " bind "), and indicates that only the first of such notes is to be struck, but that this is to be **prolonged** by the value of the second. This same rule would hold good, whatever number of notes were tied together, e.g.:—

In every case the prolonged sound is **equal in duration** to that of all the notes so tied together.

Occasionally, in the works of Beethoven and Chopin, two notes of the same pitch are connected by a curved line, the second of the two having a " staccato " mark over it, thus :—

In such cases they are not intended to be tied. The first note is to be played with the usual amount of tone, and connected closely with the second, which is played with a much diminished tone—producing somewhat of the effect of an echo. This was originally a " grace " connected with the old clavichord, and it is not possible to reproduce it accurately on the modern Pianoforte, although the above-named writers have sought to imitate it in this way. It was entitled the " Bebung."

11.—When, in contradistinction to *legato*, notes are to be **detached** from one another, and played or sung in a short, crisp, manner, the effect so produced is called **staccato.**

There are **three kinds** of *staccato* in general use, indicated by one of the following signs placed over (or under) the notes desired to be so performed :—

(i.) By a dash :—

sounding approximately thus :—

(ii.) By a dot :—

sounding approximately thus :—

(iii.) By a dot combined with a curve, or slur (generally termed **mezzo-staccato** or **portamento**) :—

sounding approximately thus :—

12.—Two or three abbreviations, more frequently found in music for orchestral instruments than in that written for the pianoforte or organ, remain to be noticed.

(i) **The signs for reiterated notes, e.g.:—**

representing

One stroke through the stem of a note signifying *quaver* repetitions ; *two* strokes, semiquaver repetitions ; *three* strokes, demi-semiquaver repetitions ; and so on. In the case of notes having already one or more hooks, or tails, each hook or tail counts for one stroke (See (*a*) above, sounding as at (*b*)). In the case of a semibreve, the strokes are placed above or below, e.g.:—

 representing

When very rapid, this effect is called *tremolo*.

(ii.) **The signs for rapid alternations of notes**, e.g. (sometimes called " legato tremolo ") :—

(c) (d)

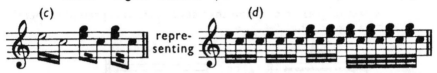 repre-senting

NOTE.—When two minims (or two semibreves) are joined by quaver, semiquaver, or demi-semiquaver, &c., tails, as at (c), the number of alternations is to be equal to the value of *one* of the written notes. (See (d).)

(iii.) **The sign for repeated groups**, e.g.:—

 representing

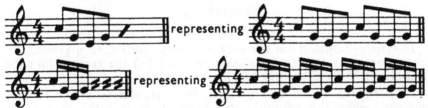 representing

one oblique stroke being used as often as it is desired to repeat a group of quavers ; *two* such strokes being similarly used in the case of semiquavers ; *three* in the case of demi-semiquavers, and so on.

If an **entire bar** is to be repeated, it is often indicated thus :—

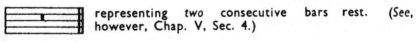

Here, in bars 2 and 3, the figure given in bar 1, is to be played twice more. Sometimes the following sign is used for the same purpose, ⅍.

(iv.) **The signs for rests of more than one bar**, e.g.:—

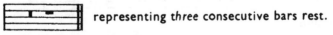 representing *two* consecutive bars rest. (See, however, Chap. V, Sec. 4.)

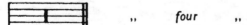 representing *three* consecutive bars rest.

„ *four* „

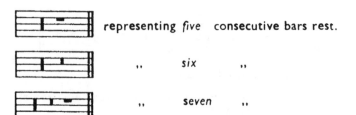

representing *five* consecutive bars rest.

„   *six*   „

„   *seven*   „

A rest of greater duration than seven bars is represented merely by a figure, thus :—

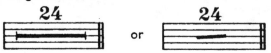

or

This plan is much to be recommended also for the smaller numbers, instead of the cumbersome method described above, for which there would appear to be little reason, and still less practical use.

CHAPTER XI.
Ornaments.

1.—The principal, if not the only, ornaments or graces in general use at the present day are (i.) the **shake**, or *trill* ; (ii.) the **turn** ; (iii.) the **acciaccatura** ; (iv.) the **mordent**.

2.—Formerly, in the days prior to the introduction of the modern Pianoforte—when the expressionless Harpsichord was the only keyed instrument, other than the organ, in general use—composers were obliged to add to the interest of their music by the employment of various other embellishments, in order to give some semblance of accent to their passages, and to compensate, in some small degree, for the lack of variety in tone.

3.—Very many of these ornaments are now entirely obsolete, and are of no interest, except to the musical antiquarian ; one or two, however— notably the **appoggiatura**, and the **extended lower mordent**—have still a practical value for the present-day student. Both of these are constantly to be met with in the works of Bach and Handel, while Haydn and Mozart frequently employ the *appoggiatura*.

4.—The **shake**, or *trill*, consists of a rapid and regular alternation of a principal (written) note with the note alphabetically next above it, and is usually expressed by the letters **tr.** (abbreviation of the Italian *trillo*) above that written note, thus :—

5.—It will be seen that, in the above example, **two small notes** are written (the first being the note *below* the principal note), to form a finish to the shake ; this termination is usually required (even if not indicated in writing).

6.—Sometimes, however, if the shake is followed by one or more unaccented notes, it is played without this form of termination, but care must be used that it always ends on its principal note, e.g. :—

(See also Exs. (b), (c) and (d) in Sec. 8.)

7.—In each of these cases (Secs. 4 and 6), a **triplet** is introduced in order that the shake may finish on the principal note ; if there is an " ending " (or " turn," as it is sometimes called), such as is described in Sec. 5, this triplet will **precede** it (see Ex. in Sec. 4). If, on the contrary, there is **no** " ending," the triplet will come **immediately before the next written note.** (See Ex. in Sec. 6.)*

8.—The **number of alternations** of the two notes of a shake largely depends upon the **speed** of the music, and the **length** of the written note ; in quick time, or in the case of a shake upon a short note, it often assumes such forms as the following :—

.* A point upon which there is some little divergence of opinion is as to whether a shake should begin upon the written note, or upon the note above.
  The matter cannot be dealt with in detail here ; but, generally speaking, the student may take it as a safe rule that, in **modern music** (except at times in that of Chopin), the **shake should begin with the written note** (as in the examples in Secs. 4 and 6). In the case of Haydn and Mozart, and more especially **older masters,** such as Bach and Handel, it is usually more appropriate to begin the shake with the **upper note.** This rule is *inflexible* when the shake is **preceded by another note of the same pitch,** as at (a).

Here the correct rendering would be as follows :—

N.B.—The commencement of a shake upon its *upper note* is now-a-days frequently indicated thus :—

Observe that the **triplet** mentioned in Sec. 7 is necessary **only** when the shake begins **on its principal note.**

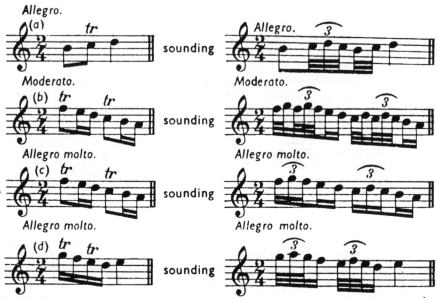

In all these cases, the character of the passage must largely influence the rendering.

9.—A ♮, ♯, ♭, × or ♭♭, over a shake shews that the note above the principal, or written one, should be **inflected** accordingly :—

10.—The **mordent** consists of a **single** rapid alternation of a written note and the note next alphabetically above it, and is indicated thus, ⸙

11.—The **lower mordent,** indicated thus ᷾, implies a similar alternation of a principal note and the note **below** it, e.g. :—

Bach.

&c.

sounding—

&c.

12.—The **turn,** or *grupetto,* ∾ , is an ornament consisting of four notes, played or sung after a principal, written note, as follows :—

  (i.) The note above it.
  (ii.) „ written note.
  (iii.) „ note below it.
  (iv.) „ written note again.

The following example will make this clear :—

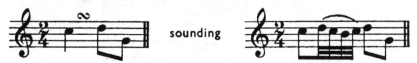

sounding

In performance, the principal note is held for a large part of its value (generally either a *half* in quick "tempo,"† and *three-quarters* in slow "tempo"‡), and the four notes of the turn occupy the remaining half, or quarter, as the case may be,§ e.g. :—

Allegro vivace.   Beethoven.

sounding—

Allegro vivace.

Here the principal note takes one-half of its written value.

---

* The ♯ is here required to conform to the key of B minor, in which the passage is written.
† Or in the case of a comparatively short note.
‡ Or in the case of a comparatively long note.
§ Often, in triple time, or in the case of the *dotted* beats of compound time, the principal note takes **two-thirds,** e.g. :—

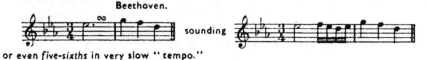

Beethoven.

sounding

or even *five-sixths* in very slow "tempo."

sounding—

Here the principal note takes three-quarters of its written value, to prevent the turn sounding dull and heavy.

13.—When a turn occurs **after a dotted note,** the written note most frequently takes *half* its own value ; the first three notes of the turn take the remaining half, in the form of a triplet ; and its final (fourth) note has *the value of the dot,* e.g.:—

sounding—

N.B.—This rule admits of some relaxation occasionally in slow "tempo," and applies *only* to those cases in which the dot forms the *beginning of a new beat,* or division of a beat.

(Compare this example with that given in foot-note to Sec. 12.)

14.—When a turn is placed **over** a note, the turn generally begins at once with the note above the written one,* e.g.:—

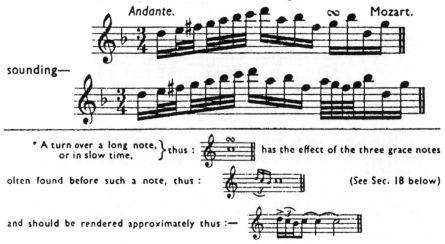

sounding—

---

* A turn over a long note, } thus :   has the effect of the three grace notes
  or in slow time,

often found before such a note, thus :   (See Sec. 18 below)

and should be rendered approximately thus :—

but sometimes the written note is played first, and, together with the four notes of the turn, forms a group of *five* equal notes, e.g.:—

sounding

The character of the passage must largely determine which interpretation the turn is to bear.

15.—An **accidental** written **under** or **over a turn** indicates that the note below or above the written note (as the case may be) is to have a similar accidental, thus—(See also examples in Secs. 13 and 14)

(a) ... sounding

(b) ... sounding

(c) ... sounding

16.—An **inverted turn** (indicated variously by the signs ∾ and Ƨ), is a turn in which the note *below* the principal (written) note comes first, the note *above* appearing later, e.g.:—

sounding

(Compare this with the example given in Sec. 12.
N.B.—This ornament is usually written out in full.

17.—An **acciaccatura** (lit., " crushing-note ") is a quaver of small size, with a stroke through the stem and hook (see (a) in example below) played or sung as quickly as possible, immediately proceeding to the note before which it is placed—and from which it takes no appreciable value :—

(a) Beethoven.

&c.

sounding approximately—

18.—Sometimes **groups of small notes** are found preceding others of full-size. In such a case the group of small notes is performed more or less rapidly, the accent frequently falling on the **principal note**, thus :—

This rule admits, however, of many exceptions, especially in modern music ; the accent often more appropriately falling on the **first of the small notes**, e.g.:—

Chopin.

Such niceties of performance must, of necessity, depend largely upon the character of the passage in question.

___

Ornaments of less frequent occurrence.

19.—As was stated above (Sec. 3), there are two signs of ornament which, though frequent in the works of Bach and Handel, are now practically obsolete, composers preferring to indicate their effect by writing them out in full. These are the **appoggiatura** and the **extended lower mordent.**

The **appoggiatura** (lit., *leaning-note*), is expressed by a small note preceding a principal one, thus :—   differing in

appearance from the *acciaccatura* in the absence of the stroke drawn through the stem.* Moreover, an *appoggiatura* could be of any length, —minim, crotchet, quaver, and so on—the rule being that it should **take its own value from the note that it preceded**—generally *one-half*—as the *appoggiatura* was nearly always written as a small-sized note of half the value of that principal note—the appoggiatura coming *upon* the accent. Thus :—

would sound

___

* It is to be regretted that older composers were often very lax in the writing of these signs, often confusing them, and rendering their performance as '' appoggiaturas '' or '' acciaccaturas '' purely a matter of conjecture based upon the inherent character of the passage.

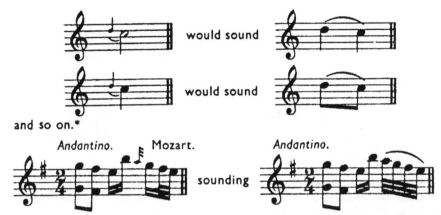

would sound

would sound

and so on.*

Andantino.   Mozart.   *Andantino.*

sounding

20.—An appoggiatura **before a dotted-note** usually takes approximately two-thirds (or sometimes one-third) of the note it precedes, e.g. :—

sounding   or sometimes
                (rarely)

21.—The **prolonged, or extended, lower mordent** is an inverted (or, lower) mordent with *two* alternations instead of one, e.g. :—

Bach.

sounding—

22.—A shake, or trill, is often found indicated **in old music** by one of the following signs, or , a hook sometimes occurring at one end, or at both ends, e.g. :—

Old signs.   *Modern equivalents.*   *Actual renderings.*

(a)

(b)

---

* Modern composers, from Beethoven onwards, write the *appoggiatura* in full-sized notes, **exactly as it sounds.**

23.—In the music of Mozart and Haydn, the **turn** after a **dotted note** is sometimes **inaccurately written** out in four small notes of equal length, as at (*a*) :—

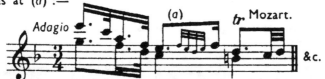

The correct rendering of such a turn would be as follows :—

Fortunately, composers are more particular now-a-days as regards accuracy in expressing the effects they intend, and the meanings of the various signs employed have not to be gauged by the general tenor of the passages in which they occur.

CHAPTER XII.

Italian and other Terms used in Music.

1.—The various degrees of speed and of intensity of sound, as well as directions as to the style in which passages are to be performed are generally indicated by the composer. In former times such indications were often meagre, and much was left to the good sense and taste of the executant ; now-a-days, however, when gradations—especially of tone—are so minute, and so important to the effect of the music, much more care is paid to the marking of the exact manner of performance.

2.—It has always been found advantageous to have these directions written in a language that should be regarded as universal, and Italian has long been used for this purpose, although some German composers, notably Schumann, have preferred to us their own native tongue, the object of which proceeding is not very clear.

3.—The following are the more frequent terms occurring in both vocal and instrumental music :—

Speed :—

Adagio, leisurely ; Molto Adagio, very slow.
Adagissimo, slower than Adagio.
Affrettando, hastening the speed.
Alcuna, some ; e.g., con alcuna licenza, with a certain degree of (i.e., some) license.
Allegro, merry, lively, fast.
Allegretto, not so fast as Allegro.
Andante, going at a moderate pace.
Andantino, not so slow as Andante.
Grave, grave, solemn.
Incalzando, increasing both in tone and speed.
Largamente, } broad, slow.
Largo, }
Larghetto, not so broad as Largo.
Lento, very slow.
Moderato, at a moderate pace.
Presto, quick.
Prestissimo, very quick.
Risvegliato, with animation.
Slargando, } getting slower.
Slentando, }
Sopra, above.
Sotto, below, under.
Tempo comodo, in convenient time.
Tempo ordinario, in ordinary time.
Tempo primo, at the original speed.
Vivace, lively, quickly.

Modifications of Speed :—

Allargando, decreasing the speed, broadening.
A tempo, in time.
Ad libitum or A piacere, at pleasure.
Doppio movimento, at double the pace.
L'istesso tempo, in the same time ; i.e., the beats to have the same duration, however they may be expressed in notation.
Meno allegro, less fast.
Meno mosso, less moved, slower.
Più mosso, more moved, quicker.
Ritardando (ritard.), holding back }
Rallentando (rall.), slackening the pace } getting slower.
Ritenuto (rit.), held back, slower.
Accelerando (accel.), accelerating the pace } getting faster.
Stringendo, pressing onwards }

Intensity of Sound :—

Crescendo (cres.), or < getting louder.
Decrescendo (decres.), } or > getting softer.
Diminuendo (dim.), }
Forte (f), loud.
Fortissimo (ff), very loud.
fff, as loud as possible.

Mezzo-forte (mf), half loud, or moderately loud.
Mezzo-piano (mp), half or moderately soft.
Piano (p), soft.
Pianissimo (pp), very soft.
ppp, as soft as possible.
Dolce, softly, sweetly.

Calando, decreasing.
Mancando, waning in tone.
Morendo, dying away. } Getting slower and softer.
Perdendosi, losing itself.
Smorzando, extinguishing.

Forte piano (fp), loud, then soft.
Sforzando (sf), > or ∧, forcing. } Terms used to indicate
Forzato (fz), forced. } increased accent upon a single
Rinforzando (rf or rinf.), enforcing. } note or chord.

Other terms relating to manner of performance :—

A, at, for, with.
A capella, in the church style.
Affettuoso, affectionately.
Agitato, in an agitated manner.
Amabile, amiably.
Amoroso, lovingly.
Animato, animated.
Appassionato, passionately.
Assai, ▮▮▮▮▮, very.
Attacca, go on at once.
Bene or *Ben*, well.
Ben marcato, well marked.
Brillante, brilliantly.
Brioso, with vigour.
Cantabile or *cantando*, in a singing style.
Col or *Colla*, with the.
Col arco, with the bow (applied to instruments of the violin family).
Colla parte, or *Colla voce*, keeping closely with the solo part or voice.
Come prima, as at first.
Come sopra, as above.
Con, with.
Con amore, with love.
Con anima, with soul.
Con brio, with brightness and vigour.
Con delicatezza, delicately.
Con dolore or *Con duolo*, with grief.
Con espressione, with expression.
Con energia, with energy.
Con forza, with force.
Con fuoco, with fire.
Con grazia, with grace.
Con moto, with movement.
Con sordini, with mutes (applied to instruments of the violin family).
  Also used occasionally (especially by Beethoven) to indicate the
  release of the damper pedal of the Pianoforte.

Con spirito, with spirit.
Con tenerezza, with tenderness.
Da capo, from the beginning.
Dal segno, from the sign.
Deciso, decidedly.
Delicamente or *Delicato*, delicately.
Dolce, sweetly.
Dolente, or *Doloroso*, sadly, with grief.
E or *Ed*, and.
Energico, with energy or force.
Espressivo, with expression.
Forza, force.
Fuoco, fire.
Furioso, impetuously ; with fury.
Giocoso, or *Giocosamente*, gaily, jocosely.
Giojoso, joyously.
Giusto, exact.
Grandioso, grandly.
Grazioso, gracefully.
Il or *La*, the.
Impetuoso, impetuously.
Legato, smoothly ; bound.
Leggiero or *Leggieramente*, lightly.
Lusingando, soothingly.
Ma, but.
Maestoso, majestically.
Maggiore, major.
Main droite (Fr.), or *M.D.*, } with the right hand.
Mano destra (Ital.), or *M.D.*,
Main gauche (Fr.), or *M.G.*, } with the left hand.
Mano sinistra (Ital.), or *M.S.*,
Marcato, marked.
Martellato, with great force ; hammered.
Meno, less.
Mesto, sadly.
Mezzo, half ; *mezza voce*, half voice, ▆▆▆▆▆▆.
Minore, minor.
Molto or *Di molto*, much ; very.
Mosso or *Moto*, movement.
Non, not.
Parlando or *Parlante*, in a speaking manner.
Pastorale, in a pastoral style.
Ped. (abbreviation of *pedale*), indicates the use of the right, or damper, pedal of the Pianoforte.
Pesante, heavily.
Piacevole, pleasantly.
Piangevole, plaintively.
Più, more.
Più tosto, rather more quickly.
Pizzicato (*pizz.*), plucking the string (applied to bowed instruments).
Poco or *Un poco*, a little.
Poco a poco, little by little.

Poi, then.

Pomposo, pompously.   [note to another in singing.

Portamento, implies the extremest smoothness (or carrying) from one

Quasi, almost, as if ; e.g., *Quasi una fantasia* (Beethoven), as if in the style of a fantasia.

Replica, repeat.

Risoluto, resolutely.

Scherzando or *Scherzoso*, in a sprightly, playful manner.

Sciolto, freely, easily.

Sec. (Fr., lit., dry), short, crisp.

Segue, follow on at once.

Semplice, simply.

Sempre, always.

Senza, without ; *senza sordini*, without mutes (applied to instruments of the violin family). Also sometimes used to indicate the depression of the damper pedal of the Pianoforte.

Serioso, seriously.

Simile, in the same manner.

Soave, sweetly, gently.

Sostenuto, sustained.

Sotto voce, in a subdued manner ; lit., under the voice.

Staccato, short and detached.

Strepitoso, in a loud, boisterous manner.

Sul ponticello, near the bridge (applied to bowed-instruments).

Tacet, be silent.

Tanto, so much.

Tempo rubato, robbed time ; the slight alterations of speed which a performer m˜kes for the purpose of expression in particular passages.

Tenuta, Tenute, Tenuto, held on, sustained.

Tranquillo or *Tranquillamente*, tranquilly.   [pedal.

Tre corde (lit., three strings), signifies the release of the left, or soft,

Troppo, too ; too much. *Non troppo*, not too much.

Un or *una*, one.   [the Pianoforte.

Una corda (lit., one string), signifies the use of the left, or soft, pedal of

Veloce, rapidly.

Vigoroso, vigorously.

Vivo or *Con vivacità*, with vivacity.

Volante, in a light, flying manner.

Volti subito or *V.S.*, turn over quickly.

The following German terms are frequently to be met with in Modern Music :—

Aber, but.

Ausdrucksvoll, with expression.

Bestimmt, with decision.

Beweglich, with movement ; the equivalent of *con moto* in Italian.

Bewegt, moved.

Bogen, with the bow, the equivalent of *arco* or *col arco* in Italian.

Breit, broadly.

Doch, but, yet.

Einfach, simply.

Etwas, some, somewhat ; e.g., *etwas bewegt*, somewhat moved.

Gebunden, connected.
Gehalten, sustained.
Gestossen, short, detached ; the equivalent of *Staccato* in Italian.
Geschwind, quickly.
Immer, always.
Kräftig, with energy.
Kurz, short.
Langsam, slowly.
Lebhaft, lively.
Leicht, lightly.
Leise, lightly, softly.
Markirt, marked.
Mässig, moderate ; e.g., *mässig bewegt,* moderately moved, or moderately quickly.
Mit, with.
Munter, lively ; the equivalent of *Allegro* in Italian.
Nicht, not.
Noch, still more ; e.g., *noch schneller,* still quicker.
Rasch, quickly.
Ruhig, calmly.
Schnell, quickly ; *so schnell wie möglich,* as quickly as possible.
Sehr, very.
Stark, strongly.
Und, and.
Wenig, little, e.g., *ein wenig langsamer,* a little slower.
Zart, soft.
Ziemlich, rather moderately.
Zu, too.

_____

CHAPTER XIII.
Harmony.

1.—Broadly, the study of **Harmony** may be said to be concerned with—

    (a) The combination of musical sounds into what are usually spoken of as chords ;

    (b) The classification of such chords ;

    (c) The relation of such chords to one another, particularly as to the various ways in which they may succeed each other.

2.—Closely connected with, and inseparable from, these are—

    (a) **Melody** (or tune).

    (b) **Rhythm** (the intelligent division of music into periods or sentences).

two important factors in modern musical composition, without which Harmony alone would be dead and meaningless.*

---

* Here the author would enter an earnest and emphatic protest against that method of Harmony teaching which neglects—as is so often the case—any consideration of these vital characteristics in the exercises given to the student, exercises in which the only aim seems to be the mechanical classification of chords in his mind, without any attempt being made to cause him to realise that even the simplest chord progressions should be MUSIC !

3.—When two or more musical sounds are sung or played together, a **chord** is produced, and the simplest kind of complete chord is formed by taking a *bass-note* (see App. A), and adding to it its 3rd and 5th; e.g. :—

This is called a **Triad.**

4.—The above example will shew that the quality of 3rd and 5th so added may vary. As a matter of fact, either a major or minor 3rd may be used, and either a perfect, diminished, or augmented 5th.

5.—When a triad has a perfect 5th, it is called a **common chord.** Common chords may have a major or minor 3rd, when they are described as **major or minor common chords** respectively, e.g. :—

6.—Common chords (either major or minor) are **concordant triads,** because they are satisfactory in themselves and need no other chord to follow them. (*See Def. of Concord*—App. A.)

7.—When a triad has a diminished 5th, it always takes with it a minor 3rd, and is called a **diminished triad,** e.g. :—

and when it has an augmented 5th, it always takes with it a major 3rd, and is called an **augmented triad,** e.g. :—

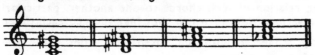

8.—Diminished and augmented triads are termed **discordant,** or **dissonant triads,** as they seem to require some other chord to follow them, to complete their effect. (*See Def. of Discord*—App. A.)

9.—An **inversion of a chord** is produced by placing any other note than its *root* (i.e., the note from which it is derived, and from which it takes its name) in the bass ; e.g. :—

---

* Also described as Major triads.
† Also described as Minor triads.

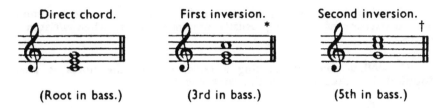

Direct chord. First inversion. Second inversion.

(Root in bass.) (3rd in bass.) (5th in bass.)

10.—Chords are found with their notes placed in various orders, and they may be embellished by the addition of ornamental notes called passing-notes, suspensions, &c.—all of which will be spoken of later.

11.—It must be understood also that, in actual composition, chords are frequently found in a **broken form,** (i.e., with their notes dispersed in " arpeggiated " (*see* App. A, *Arpeggio*) and other figures), e.g. :—

These, and many others that might be given, are all variations upon the chord—

which, in itself, is merely a fuller aspect of the common chord marked (*a*) in Sec. 3 above, caused by writing the bass-note an 8ve lower, and **doubling** it (see Sec. 13) and by placing the 3rd of the chord at the top, and the 5th next to the bass-note.

* The 1st inversion of a triad is often called a " chord of the 6th."
† The 2nd inversion of a triad is often called a " chord of the six-four." (*See* Sec. 26.)

12.—Chords are mostly written in **four parts**—the most complete and satisfactory effect being usually obtainable thus, when written for voices.

13.—When four voices sing a triad, one of the notes is always **doubled**, i.e., used twice in the same chord :—

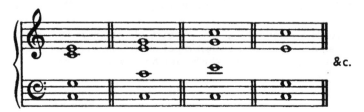

&c.

When a chord is *direct*, this is nearly always the **root**, as in the above example ; in the case of a 1st inversion, either the **3rd or the 6th** *from the bass-note* is doubled, usually, thus :—

while, in a 2nd inversion, the **bass-note** is by far the best note to double, e.g. :—

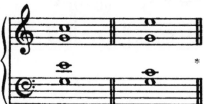

*

14.—Here is a table, shewing the **position of the various triads**, and their inversions, in both major and minor forms of a key.

N.B.—Major Common Chords are written as white notes.
　　　Minor Common Chords are written as black notes.
　　　Diminished and Augmented Triads in small type, in brackets.

＊ The position of the root of the chord as a 4th above the *bass-note* of a 2nd inversion gives somewhat of the effect of a **discord**, requiring some other chord to succeed. This accounts for the fact of a 2nd inversion of a triad being always followed in a definite way. Its **most usual progression** is to a direct common chord upon the same bass-note, e.g. :—

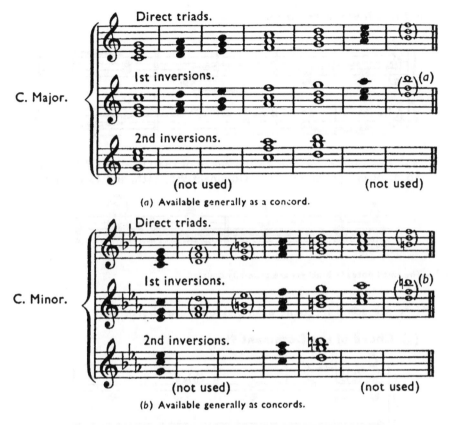

C. Major.

Direct triads.

1st inversions.

2nd inversions.

(not used)   (not used)

(a) Available generally as a concord.

C. Minor.

Direct triads.

1st inversions.

2nd inversions.

(not used)   (not used)

(b) Available generally as concords.

15.—The **Chord of the Dominant 7th** is formed by adding a minor 7th to the common chord on the Dominant of any scale, e.g. :—

(In C major.)   (In C minor.)

It is a discord and consequently requires **resolution**, i.e.. a fixed, definite progression. It most usually resolves upon the common chord of the Tonic, thus :—

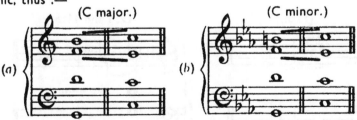

(C major.)   (C minor.)

(a)   (b)

the 3rd of the Dominant 7th chord rising one semitone, and the 7th falling a 2nd (major or minor).

It has **3 inversions,** as follows :—

16.—The addition of 3rds to the chord of the Dominant 7th produces the chords often spoken of as the Dominant 9th, 11th, and 13th, thus :—

N.B.—The small notes in brackets are generally omitted.

Here are some frequent examples of these chords :—

(i.) **Chord of the Dominant 9th.**

N.B.—The 9th may be either a major or a minor 9th in the major form of a key : in the minor form, the 9th is minor.

(ii.) **Chord of the Dominant 11th.**

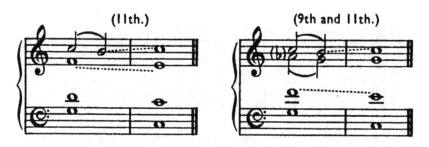

* These examples may occur equally well in the minor mode of the key.

(iii.) Chord of the Dominant 13th.

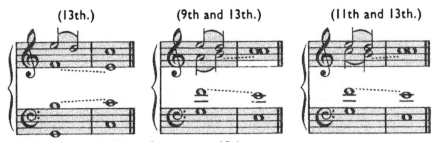

(13th.)   (9th and 13th.)   (11th and 13th.)

N.B.—In the minor form of a key, the 13th is *minor*.

All these chords may be taken in their various inversions, the note upon which the 9th, 11th, or 13th resolves being nearly always omitted from the chord, e.g. :—

Dominant 9th   Dominant 11th   Dominant 13th
(1st inversion).   (2nd inversion).   (3rd inversion).

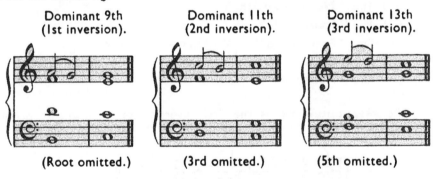

(Root omitted.)   (3rd omitted.)   (5th omitted.)

17.—All these examples can be taken in the minor mode of the key, with the substitution of a *minor* 9th and a *minor* 13th for the major 9th and 13th, respectively.

18.—**Modulation**, or change of key, takes place when a chord *not in the original key* is introduced, and followed by another chord, or chords, defining the new key, e.g. :—

Key C.   Key G.

(See " Practical Harmony," Chap. XI.)

19.—A chromatic chord is a chord that contains **one or more notes** needing *accidentals*, but which does not change the key, e.g. :—

Chromatic chord.

20.—The following specially-named chords are often met with —

(i.) The " **Neapolitan 6th.** "

(ii.) The " **Italian 6th.** "

(iii.) The " **French 6th.** " } Varieties of one chord.

(iv.) The " **German 6th.** "

(v.) The " **Added 6th.** "

The **Neapolitan 6th** is the first inversion of a chromatic major common chord upon the minor 2nd of the scale, e.g. :—

The **Italian, French, and German 6ths** are the three forms of the *chord of the Augmented 6th*, occurring most usually upon the minor 6th of a scale, and resolving generally either upon the common chord of the Tonic or the Dominant, e.g. :—

x German 6th.

The **Added 6th** is the first inversion of a chord of the 7th formed diatonically upon the supertonic of a key—usually called a **secondary 7th**, e.g. :—

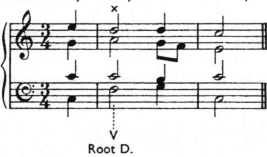

Root D.

21.—**Passing-notes** are notes used to fill the gaps, so to speak, in passing from one note of a chord to another, as at (*a*), or from a note of one chord to a note of another chord, as at (*b*) :—

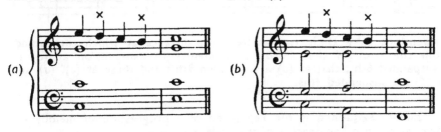

(*a*)   (*b*)

Sometimes a passing-note is **struck with the chord,** when it is called an **Accented Passing-note,** or *Appoggiatura* ; e.g. :—*

N.B.—Passing-notes are foreign to the chords against which they are taken, and are therefore termed **unessential discords.** They are usually approached and quitted by the step of a 2nd.

* Formerly written as a small note. (See Chap. XI, Sec. 19.)

22.—Another class of *unessential discord* is formed by **Suspensions.**
A **Suspension** is the prolonging of a note of one chord while another
chord is being sounded, *of which that note forms no part.* The note so
retained moves by the descent or ascent of a 2nd to a note of the chord
over which it has been held. The following examples will make this clear.
Here is a passage of simple harmony :—

By the delaying of certain of the notes, *suspensions* can be introduced,
thus :—

Suspensions **take their names** from the distance at which they stand
from the **root** of the chord ; consequently the suspension at (*a*) is
a suspended 6th ; that at (*b*) a suspended 9th ; and those at (c), (*d*), (e)
or (*f*) are suspended 4ths.

23.—A **Sequence** is the repetition of a progression of melody or
harmony upon other degrees of the scale, e.g. :—

&c.

24.—A **Pedal,** or **Pedal-note** is a note, usually in the bass, sustained
through a succession of harmonies, of which it may, or may not, form
a part, e.g. :—

The notes almost exclusively used as Pedals are the **Dominant** and the **Tonic** of any key. The above example shews an instance of a Dominant Pedal.

25.—A **Cadence** is the completion of a phrase, or rhythmical period. There are *four* principal cadences, viz. :—

(a) The **Perfect** (or *Authentic*) **Cadence,** when a phrase ends with the Tonic chord, preceded by that of the Dominant ;

(b) The **Imperfect** (or *Half*) **Cadence,** when a phrase ends with the chord of the Dominant ;

(c) The **Interrupted Cadence,** when the course of the music leads one to expect a perfect cadence, but when some other chord is substituted for that of the Tonic : often that of the *Sub-mediant* ;

(d) The **Plagal Cadence,** when a phrase ends with the chord of the Tonic, preceded by that of the Sub-dominant.

26.—When **figures** are found under a bass-note, they Indicate the intervals of the chord counted *from that bass-note*, e.g. :—

where the root of the chord, C, is a 4th above the bass, and the 3rd of the chord, E, is the 6th above the bass. The figuring of the simpler chords (viz., triads and the Dominant 7th) is as follows :—

Triads and their Inversions.

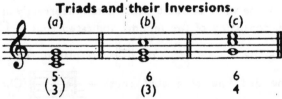

The chord marked (b) is thus often called a **chord of the sixth,** while that at (c) is described as a **chord of the six-four.**

Dominant 7th and its Inversions.

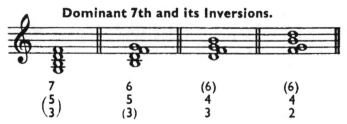

7   6   (6)   (6)

(5)   5   4   4

(3)   (3)   3   2

N.B.—The figures in brackets are usually omitted.

An **accidental** placed **before a figure** indicates that the note represented by that figure is to have a similar accidental, e.g. :—

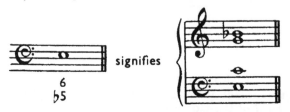

       6
       ♭5   signifies

27.—It is not possible, within the limits of the present primer, to enter more fully into the question of the various chords, &c., described in this Chapter, nor can any attempt be here made to set forth the laws that govern their treatment. The student who desires to prosecute this most important subject can do so by referring to the author's " Practical Harmony,"* where he will find all these matters exhaustively considered.

APPENDIX A.

Table of Definitions.

Accent.—Stress or emphasis. (Chap. IV, Secs. 1 and 2.)

Acciaccatura.—A small note, indicated ♪ , to be played as closely as possible to the full-sized note it precedes. (Chap. XI, Sec. 17.)

Accidental.—A ♮, ♯, ♭, x or 𝄪 occurring incidentally. (Chap. III, Secs. 7-11.)

Agrémens (Fr.).—Ornaments, e.g., the turn, the mordent, etc.

Air.—Melody or tune.

Alla Breve.—A time consisting of *four* minims in a bar ($\frac{4}{2}$), the bar being consequently of the value of one breve. Often incorrectly applied to a bar of *duple* time, consisting of *two* minims, indicated thus :—𝄵.

Alto clef.—The C clef 𝄡, or 𝄢, so placed that " Middle C " occurs as the 3rd line of a staff, thus :—𝄡 (Chap. II, Secs. 8 and 11.)

* Joseph Williams, Ltd., 29 Enford Street, Marylebone, W.1.

Alto voice.—The voice next below the treble in a choir or quartet of voices ; usually called *contralto* when sung by women. Average compass—

Appoggiatura.—A small note, placed before one of full size, and taking its own value from it. Now-a-days always incorporated in the time of the bar. (Chap. XI, Sec. 19 ; Chap. XIII, Sec. 21.)

Arpeggio.—The notes of a chord sounded in succession. (See also Chap. X, Sec. 8.)

B (German).—The note B flat.

Bar.—The music comprised between two successive strongest accents. (Chap. IV, Sec. 3.)

Bar-line.—A vertical line drawn through the staff immediately before the constantly recurring strongest accent. (Chap. IV, Sec. 3.)

Baritone voice.—A voice lighter than a Bass, but fuller than a Tenor, with a compass between the two, approximately—

Bass clef.—The F clef. (Chap. II, Secs. 8 and 9.)

Bass note.—The lowest note in any chord.

Bass voice.—The lowest male voice. Average compass—

Beat.—One of the main divisions of a bar, or measure. (Chap. IV, Sec. 4.)

Bémol (French) ⎫ a flat ; e.g., *Fa bémol* or *Fa bémolle*, signifies F flat.
Bemolle (Italian) ⎭

Bind.—See *Tie*.

Cadence.—The completion of a phrase, or rhythmical period. (Chap. XIII, Sec. 25.)

Chord.—Two or more notes sounded together. (Chap. XIII, Sec. 3.)

Chromatic.—Notes contrary to the key-signature, without causing modulation.

Chromatic chord.—A chord containing one or more such notes. (Chap. XIII, Sec. 19.)

Chromatic interval.—An interval found only in a chromatic scale. (Chap. IX, Sec. 14.)

Chromatic scale.—A scale proceeding entirely by semitones. (Chap. VIII.)

Chromatic semitone.—A semitone, the two notes of which bear the same letter-name, e.g., C to C♯. (Chap. III, Sec. 5, foot-note.)

Clef.—A sign used to fix the absolute pitch of the notes upon a staff. (Chap. II, Secs. 7-12.)

Common Chord.—A chord, consisting of a bass-note, with its major or minor 3rd and perfect 5th. (Chap. XIII, Sec. 5.)

Common Time.—A term sometimes used to denote either Duple or Quadruple time.

Compound interval.—An interval greater than an octave (e.g., a 9th, 10th, &c.). (Chap. IX. Sec. 13.)

Compound times.—Times, in which each beat of a bar is divisible by three, as opposed to *simple times*, in which each beat is divisible by *two*. (Chap. IV, Secs. 9 and 10.)

Concord.—A combination of notes satisfactory *in itself*, needing no other to precede or follow it.

Consonant, or *Concordant intervals.*—The intervals of major and minor 3rd and 6th, and all perfect intervals (except occasionally the perfect 4th). (Chap. IX, Sec. 12 ; Chap. XIII, Sec. 13, foot-note.)

Contralto voice.—See *Alto.*

Counterpoint.—The art of combining separate melodies, or of making vocal or instrumental parts move melodiously one against another.

Couplet.—A group of two notes, to be performed in the time of three of the same quality, indicated by the figure 2 placed over or under the

group, thus :—   (See Addenda, page 84.)

Diapason normal.—The standard of pitch, known as French pitch,

regulated on the principle of  representing a sound of

522 vibrations per second.

Diatonic.—Notes according to the key-signature. N.B.—The major 6th and 7th of a minor scale are, moreover, diatonic, although it is necessary to indicate them by the use of accidentals.

Diatonic chord.—A chord containing only diatonic notes.

Diatonic interval.—An interval that can be found in any major or minor scale. (Chap. IX, Sec. 14.)

Diatonic scale.—A scale proceeding by tones and semitones, in a definite order. (Chaps. VI and VII.)

Diatonic semitone.—A semitone, the two notes of which bear different letter-names, e.g., C to D flat. (Chap. III, Sec. 5, foot-note.)

Dièse (French)
Diesis (Italian) } a sharp ; e.g., *Fa dièse* or *Fa diesis* signifies F sharp.

Discord.—A combination of notes incomplete *in itself* and requiring some other to follow (and sometimes to precede) it.

Dissonant or discordant intervals.—All intervals of 2nd, 7th and 9th, and all diminished and augmented intervals. (Chap. IX, Sec. 12.)

Divisi.—A term used in writing for the bowed-instruments in an orchestra, indicating the *division* of any particular section (e.g., first violins, second violins, &c.) into two or more separate parts.

Do.—The Italian vocal syllable used to denote C.

Dominant.—The name given to the 5th degree of a diatonic scale. (Chap. VI, Sec. 9.)

Double-bar.—Two vertical lines drawn through the staff to indicate the termination of a section of a movement. (Chap. IV, Sec. 3, foot-note.)

Duple.—A term used to describe the species of time containing two beats, or divisions, in each bar. (Chap. IV, Sec. 5.)

Dur.—The German term for a major key, e.g., C *dur* signifies C major.

Enharmonic.—Change of name without change of pitch ; e.g., D♯, E♭ and F♭ are the *enharmonic* of one another.

Es (German).—A syllable affixed to the letter-name of any note, to signify the flattening of that note. (*See* page 83.)

Extended mordent.—A lower mordent with two alternations instead of one. (Chap. XI, Sec. 21.) See *Mordent.*

Extreme parts.—The highest and lowest notes of a chord ; e.g., those sung by the Soprano and Bass voices.

Fa.—The Italian vocal syllable used to denote F.

Full score.—The parts for an orchestra (with or without voices) placed one above another on the same page.

Gamut.—The scale.

Glissando.—Gliding ; applied to the rapid sliding of the fingers over several keys in Pianoforte playing, or over several strings in Harp playing.

Graces.—Musical ornaments. (Chap. XI.)

Great staff.—A staff of eleven lines, including, roughly, the average compass of both male and female voices. (Chap. II, Secs. 2-5.)

H (German).—The note B natural.

Harmonics.—Sounds produced by the fact of a string or column of air vibrating in its fractional parts, as well as in its whole length.

Harmony.—Sounds in combination.

Inflection.—The alteration of the pitch of a note by the addition of an accidental. (Chap. III.)

Interval.—The difference in pitch between two sounds. (Chap. IX.)

Inversion :—
  (i.) *Of an interval* ; the changing of the relative position of the two notes. (Chap. IX, Secs. 15-18.)
  (ii.) *Of a chord* ; the placing of any note of the chord, other than its root, in the bass or lowest part. (Chap. XIII, Sec. 9.)

Is (German).—A syllable affixed to the letter-name of any note, to signify the sharpening of that note. (See page 83.)

Key.—A set of notes (diatonic and chromatic) having a definite relation to a particular starting-point, or key-note (q.v.).

Key-note.—The note forming the starting point of any scale. (Chap. VI, Sec. 1.)

Key-signature.—The sharps or flats necessary to the key of a composition, placed immediately after the clef, in their proper order. (Chap. VI, Sec. 8.)

La.—The Italian vocal syllable used to denote A.

Leading-note.—The 7th degree of a diatonic scale, so called from the fact that it leads the ear to expect the tonic or key-note, from which it stands at the distance of a semitone. (Chap. VI, Sec. 9.)

Ledger lines.—Short lines drawn above or below the staff. (Chap. II, Sec. 10.)

Maggiore (Italian)
Majeur (French) } major.

Major.—(i.) *As applied to intervals* ; a term used to qualify the intervals of 2nd, 3rd, 6th, 7th and 9th. (Chap. IX, Secs. 5 and 6.)
   (ii.) *As applied to chords* ; a common chord having a major (or greater) 3rd. (Chap. XIII, Secs. 5 and 6.)
   (iii.) *As applied to scales* ; a scale having its semitones occurring between the 3rd and 4th, and 7th and 8th degrees. (Chap. VI.)

Measure.—The music comprised between two bar-lines. (See *Bar.*)

Mediant.—The name given to the third degree of a diatonic scale. (Chap. VI, Sec. 9.)

Melody.—Single sounds in succession. Also used as synonymous with tune.

Mezzo-Soprano.—A voice lying between the soprano and contralto

in pitch. Average compass—

Mezzo-Soprano Clef.—The C clef or ▯ , so placed that

" Middle C " occurs as the 2nd line of a staff, thus :—

N.B.—This clef is now obsolete.

Mi.—The Italian vocal syllable used to denote E.

Middle C.—The C nearest to the middle of the Pianoforte keyboard ; a note capable of being sounded by all the various voices, male and female. (Chap. II, Sec. 2, &c.)

Mineur (French)
Minore (Italian) } minor.

Minor.—(i.) *As applied to intervals* ; a term used to qualify the intervals of 2nd, 3rd, 6th, 7th and 9th. (Chap. IX, Sec. 7.) See also *Major.*
   (ii.) *As applied to chords* ; a common chord having a minor (or lesser) third. (Chap. XIII, Secs. 5 and 6.)
   (iii.) *As applied to scales* ; a scale having its semitones occurring between the 2nd and 3rd, 5th and 6th, 7th and 8th degrees. This is called the *Harmonic* minor scale. The *Melodic* minor scale is somewhat differently formed. (Chap. VII.)

Mode.—(i.) A term used to denote a particular aspect of a key, e.g., its *major* mode, or its *minor* mode. Thus C major and C minor are the two opposite *modes* of the key of C.

(ii.) An old Ecclesiastical scale. The chief of such modes, in all of which the semitones occurred between different degrees, were—

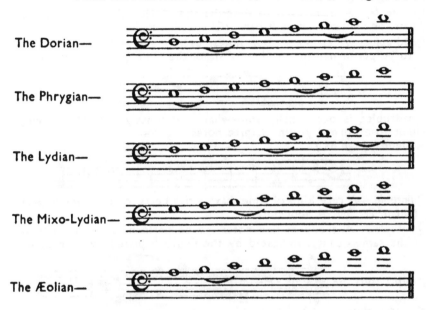

The Dorian—

The Phrygian—

The Lydian—

The Mixo-Lydian—

The Æolian—

(For further information on the Ecclesiastical scales, the student is recommended to the excellent article by the late Mr. W. S. Rockstro, in Grove's '' Dictionary of Music and Musicians.'')

Modulation.—Change of key. (Chap. XIII, Sec. 18.)

Moll.—The German term for a minor key ; e.g., *C moll* signifies C. minor.

Mordent.—A '' grace '' or ornament, consisting of a *single* rapid alternation of a written note and the note next above it, alphabetically. (Chap. XI, Secs. 10 and 11.)

Note.—A sign used to denote relative duration of sound. (Chap. I.)

Octave.—(i.) The interval of an 8th. (Chap. IX, Secs. 2, 5, and 6.)

(ii.) The reproduction of any note at a higher or lower pitch. (Chap. II, Sec. 4.)

(iii.) The sounds contained between any note and such reproduction.

Open Score.—The voice-parts of a chorus, &c., written on separate staves, one above another.

Opus (generally abbreviated thus—*Op.*) ; lit., a work. A term used to denote the *number* of a composition of any particular composer, in order of publication.

Partition (Fr.)
Partitur (Germ.) } A score. (See Score.)

Perfect.—A term used to qualify the intervals of unison, 4th, 5th and 8th. (Chap. IX, Secs. 5 and 6.)

Phrase.—A musical period (often consisting of four bars).

Pitch.—The height or depth of a sound.

Pulse.—The measured " throb " of the music.

Quadruple.—A term used to describe the species of time containing four beats, or divisions, in each bar. (Chap. IV, Sec. 5.)

Quadruplet.—A group of four notes, usually met with in compound times, to be performed in the time of *six* of the same quality, thus :—

The quadruplet is occasionally somewhat inaccurately treated as being equivalent to a normal group of *three* notes, e.g. :—

(See Addenda, page 84.)   Chopin.

Quintuple.—A rare kind of time, having *five* beats, or divisions in each bar. (Chap. IV, Sec. 4, foot-note.)

Quintuplet.—A group of five notes, to be performed in the time of *four* of the same quality, indicated by the figure 5 placed over or under the group ; thus :—

Re.—The Italian vocal syllable used to denote D.

Related keys.—Keys having the greatest number of chords in common.

Relative Major ⎫ A major scale and a minor scale with the same key-
Relative Minor ⎭ signature. (Chap. VII, Sec. 6.)

Resolution.—The fixed progression of a discord

Rest.—A sign used to denote silence for a definite period. (Chap. I, Sec. 8.)

Rhythm.—The vital principle in music by means of which sounds are felt to " progress " to certain points of culmination or of repose, thus forming intelligible *periods* (such as phrases, sentences, &c.).

Root.—The note from which a chord is derived, and from which it takes its name.

Scale.—An alphabetical succession of sounds having reference to some particular starting-point, or *key-note.* (Chaps. VI, VII and VIII.)

Score.—The parts for the various voices or instruments in a composition, placed one above another on the same page.

Semitone.—Half-a-tone. The smallest interval on the Pianoforte or Organ Keyboard. (Chap. III, Sec. 3.)

Sentence.—A musical period (most frequently ending with a perfect cadence) consisting of two or more phrases.

Septolet.—A group of seven notes to be performed in the time of (a) *four,* or (b) *six,* of the same quality, usually indicated by the figure 7 placed over or under the group, thus :—

(a)

(b)

Sextolet.—A group of six notes to be performed in the time of *four* of the same quality, usually indicated by the figure 6 placed over or under

the group, thus :—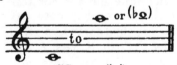

(See Addenda, page 84.)

Shake.—The rapid and regular alternation of a written note with the note next above it alphabetically. (Chap. XI, Secs. 4-9 ; also Sec. 22.)

Short score.—The parts for a chorus, &c., arranged upon two staves, as for the Pianoforte.

Si.—The Italian vocal syllable used to denote B.

Signature.—See Key-signature and Time-signature.

Simple Interval.—Any interval within the octave. (Chap. IX, Sec. 13.)

Simple Times.—Times in which each beat of a bar is divisible by *two*. (Chap. IV, Sec. 8.)

Slur.—A sign used to indicate smoothness of performance. (Chap. X, Sec. 9, and foot-note.)

Sol.—The Italian vocal syllable used to denote G.

Sol-Fa.—The use of the Italian syllables—Do, re, mi, fa, sol, la, si, in singing the notes of the scale.

Soprano.—The highest female voice. Average compass—

Soprano Clef.—The C clef 𝄡, or 𝄡 , so placed that " Middle C " occurs as the 1st line of a staff, thus :— (Chap. II, Secs. 8 and 11.)

Staff (or Stave).—The lines and spaces used to fix the *relative* pitch of sounds. (Chap. II.)

Subdominant.—The name given to the 4th degree of a diatonic scale. (Chap. VI, Sec. 9.)

Submediant.—The name given to the 6th degree of a diatonic scale. (Chap. VI, Sec. 9.)

Supertonic.—The name given to the 2nd degree of a diatonic scale. (Chap. VI, Sec. 9.)

Syncopation.—A disturbance of the normal accent of a bar. (Chap. V, Sec. 8.)

Tempo (Italian).—The speed of a composition.

Tenor.—A high male voice of a comparatively light quality. Average

compass—

Tenor Clef.—The C clef ⟪𝄡⟫ , or ⟪𝄡⟫ , so placed that " Middle C "

occurs as the 4th line of a staff, thus :— 𝄡 (Chap. II, Secs. 8 and 11.)

Tetrachord.—A series of four notes in alphabetical order, most frequently consisting of two tones and a semitone. (Chap. VI, Sec. 3.)

Tie.—A curved line, ⌢ or ⌣, connecting two or more notes of the same letter-name and *quality* (as sharp, flat, natural, &c.), indicating that the first of such notes only is to be struck, and then prolonged by the value of the note or notes with which it is so connected. (Chap. X, Sec. 10.)

Timbre (Fr.).—Quality of tone. (Introduction, Sec. 4.)

Time.—The grouping of sounds into sets by means of accent. (Chap. IV.)

Time-signature.—Figures in fractional form (thus $\frac{2}{4}$, $\frac{3}{8}$, $\frac{12}{16}$, etc.) placed at the commencement of a piece to indicate the position of the accents, i.e., the time in which the piece is written. (Chap. IV, Secs. 6 to 10.)

Tonic.—The name given to the 1st degree, or keynote, of a scale. (Chap. VI, Sec. 9.)

Tonic Major.—⎱ A Major scale and a Minor scale, beginning upon the
Tonic Minor.—⎰   same *tonic*, or key note. (Chap. VII, Sec. 9.)

Treble.—Another name for the soprano voice. (See *Soprano.*)

Treble Clef.—The G clef. (Chap. II, Secs. 8 and 9.)

Triad.—A chord consisting of a bass note, with its major or minor 3rd, and diminished, perfect, or augmented 5th. (Chap. XIII, Sec. 3.)

Trill.—Another name for a shake. (See *Shake.*)

Triple.—A term used to describe the species of time containing three beats, or divisions, in each bar. (Chap. IV, Sec. 5.)

Triplet.—A group of three equal notes performed in the time of *two* of the same quality. The figure 3 is usually placed over such a group,

when it occurs incidentally, thus :—

(Chap. IV, Sec. 9.)   (See also Addenda, page 84.)

Tritone.—(lit., three tones) the step from the 4th to the 7th degree of a diatonic scale. e.g. :—

(In C major.)

forming the interval of augmented 4th.

Turn.—A musical ornament, consisting of four notes, played or sung after a principal, written, note. (Chap. XI, Secs. 12-16.)

Tutti.—All. A term used, principally in orchestral music, to denote that the whole body of performers is to play.

Unison.—The same sound produced by two or more voices or instruments. (Chap. IX, Sec. 2.) *N.B.*—Male and female voices, when they sing in octaves, are described (inaccurately) as singing in *unison*.

Vocal Score.—Vocal parts ranged one above another on the same page.

APPENDIX B.

Rules for finding the number of Keys in which a given Interval may occur.

1.—The interval of **augmented 2nd** occurs *only* in that minor scale of which its *lower* note is the **6th** degree, e.g. :—

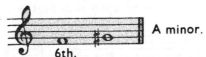

A minor.

6th.

In the case of a **diminished 7th** (the inversion of an augmented 2nd) it will be necessary merely to substitute "upper" for "lower" in the above rule, e.g. :—

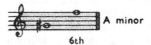

A minor

6th

2.—The interval of **augmented 4th** occurs in that major scale of which its lower note is the 4th degree ; also in the Tonic minor and the Relative minor of that scale, e.g. :—

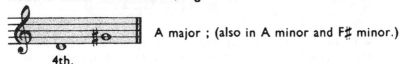

A major ; (also in A minor and F♯ minor.)

4th.

In the case of the inversion of this interval, viz., the **diminished 5th,** again substitute "upper" for "lower."

3.—The interval of **augmented 5th** occurs *only* in that minor scale of which its *lower* note is the 3rd degree, e.g. :—

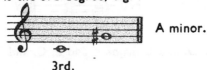

A minor.

3rd.

Here again, in the case of a **diminished 4th** (the inversion of the above interval) substitute "upper" for "lower."

4.—The interval of **augmented 6th** occurs in those *chromatic* scales of which its *lower* note is either the Minor 2nd or Minor 6th degree, e.g. :—

 Chromatic scales of A and D.
(Chap. IX, Sec. 14.)

In the case of the inversion of this interval, viz., the **diminished 3rd,** again substitute " upper " for " *lower.*"

5.—The intervals of **major and minor 2nds and 3rds** (with their inversions, minor and major 7ths and 6ths), and the **perfect 4th** (with its inversion, the perfect 5th), occur in too many keys for rules such as those given above to be of use. The following is the best plan to find the keys in which any one of these intervals occurs :—

Question. In what keys can the interval  (major 3rd) be found ?

If we write a third upon each degree of a major scale, thus :—

we find that major 3rds occur upon the 1st, 4th, and 5th degrees ; therefore, the interval in question could, manifestly, occur on the 1st degree of a major scale, viz., G major ; on the 4th degree of D major ; and on the 5th degree of C major. A similar succession of 3rds built upon a minor scale, thus :—

will shew us that major 3rds occur upon the 3rd, 5th, and 6th degrees ; consequently, the interval in question could occur on the 3rd degree of a minor scale, viz., E minor ; on the 5th degree of C minor ; and the 6th degree of B minor.

Thus, the interval 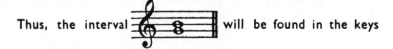 will be found in the keys

of G, D, and C major ; and E, C, and B minor.

NOTE.—It goes without saying, after what has been stated in the preceding sections of this Chapter, that the inversion of this interval (viz., a minor 6th) must of necessity occur in the same six keys.

5.—If the interval given had been a **minor 3rd**, the tables in Sec. 4 would shew (by the black-headed notes) on which degrees minor 3rds are found, and the same process could be gone through as in the case of the major 3rd.

6.—The keys in which **2nds and 4ths** (with their inversions 7ths and 5ths) can appear, can be arrived at in precisely the same way.

ADDENDA

CHAPTER III. **Sharps, Flats, &c.—**

The following table will shew the names given to the various notes of the scale (with their inflections), in English, Italian, French and German.

English.	Italian.	French.	German.
C (natural)	Do	Ut	C
C sharp	Do diesis	Ut dièse	Cis
C flat	Do bemolle	Ut bémol	Ces
D	Re	Re	D
D sharp	Re diesis	Re dièse	Dis
D flat	Re bemolle	Re bémol	Des
E	Mi	Mi	E
E sharp	Mi diesis	Mi dièse	Eis
E flat	Mi bemolle	Mi bémol	Es
F	Fa	Fa	F
F sharp	Fa diesis	Fa dièse	Fis
F flat	Fa bemolle	Fa bémol	Fes
G	Sol	Sol	G
G sharp	Sol diesis	Sol dièse	Gis
G flat	Sol bemolle	Sol bémol	Ges
A	La	La	A
A sharp	La diesis	La dièse	Ais
A flat	La bemolle	La bémol	As
B	Si	Si	H
B sharp	Si diesis	Si dièse	His
B flat	Si bemolle	Si bémol	B

CHAPTER VI.   Scales—Key-signatures—

The following examples will indicate the method of placing sharps and flats on the Staff when the C and F clefs are used :—

Soprano.   Alto.   Tenor.   Bass.

Irregular Groups of Notes—

The true character of the Couplet and the Triplet, and of the Quadruplet and the Sextolet will be gathered from the following diagram :—

It will be seen from the above examples that the Quadruplet results from the sub-division of the Couplet into smaller notes, and that the Sextolet is caused by a similar sub-division of the Triplet.

It will be evident, therefore, that the following group of six notes is not a true Sextolet, but is in reality formed by *two triplets* of semiquavers :—

Lowe and Brydone (Printers) Limited, London

—MUSICIANSHIP PIANO ALBUM SERIES—

	Grade	Net
RAYMOND TOBIN—FUN AND FACTS.—A First-of-all book of tunes and rhythms for developing musicianship ... *—Ideal, for each hand is cultivated alone and within the five finger group.—*	(VE)	2 6
RAYMOND TOBIN—ADVENTURES IN MUSICIANSHIP.—This is a book of "things to do" at the keyboard. In other words a "musical voyage of discovery." Students are *taught to think and do in a most practical and easy manner.*	(ME)	3 0
FREDERICK NICHOLLS and **RAYMOND TOBIN**—ADVENTURES IN IMPROVISATION ... ... This book is designed to assist in the cultivation of improvisation at the keyboard, and is easily assimilated and understood by students and others.	(ME-M)	3 0
FREDERICK NICHOLLS and **RAYMOND TOBIN**—IN ANCIENT EGYPT ... ... *—Six short pieces with Practise and "Study aids."*	(ME)	2 6
RAYMOND TOBIN—MEMORY PLAYING AT THE PIANO.—A "first" book of how to memorise with musical illustrations.	(ME)	2 6
ALEC ROWLEY and **RAYMOND TOBIN—MUSICAL FORM AT THE PIANO** ... ... *—Six simple pieces with explanatory text matter. By this means all essential musical forms are taught in the earliest stages.*	(E)	3 0
ALEC ROWLEY and **RAYMOND TOBIN—TALES OF AN OLD COBBLER** ... ... *—Six easy pieces, with full descriptive notes and a new way of looking at "beginners' music."—*	(E)	2 6
ALEC ROWLEY and **RAYMOND TOBIN—CHILDREN'S ZOO** ... ... *—Six charming "Snapshots in Sound" from Pets' Corner—(with drawings by L. R. Brightwell).*	(E)	2 6
ALEC ROWLEY and **RAYMOND TOBIN—PEOPLE NEAR AND FAR** ... ... *—Easy pieces introducing national rhythms and modes.—*	(E)	2 6
ROBERT McLEOD and **RAYMOND TOBIN—THE JOLLY MILLER** ... ... *—Six short pieces with quick study hints.*	(ME)	2 6
ALEC ROWLEY and **RAYMOND TOBIN—THE ROAD TO ARCADY** ... ... *—Six short pieces with quick study hints.*	(ME)	2 6
ALEC ROWLEY and **RAYMOND TOBIN—ADVENTURES AT SEA** ... ... *—Six descriptive pieces with helpful notes.*	(E)	2 6
DOROTHY BRADLEY and **RAYMOND TOBIN—THE MAGICAL YEAR** ... ... *—Six short pieces with quick study hints.*	(ME)	2 6
THOS. F. DUNHILL and **RAYMOND TOBIN—IN THE COWSLIP MEADOW** ... ... *—Six short pieces with helpful notes.*	(ME)	2 6
LLOYD WEBBER and **RAYMOND TOBIN—RECREATIONS** ... ... *—Six short pieces with helpful notes.*	(ME)	2 6
ALEC ROWLEY and **RAYMOND TOBIN—THE PUPPET SHOW** ... ... *—Six pieces with practice and study aids.*	(ME)	2 6
JOHN C. BRYDSON and **RAYMOND TOBIN**—MINIATURE BALLET FOR A TOY THEATRE ... ... *—Six little pieces with helpful notes.*	(E)	2 6

London: Joseph Williams, Limited, 29 Enford Street, Marylebone, W.I

Date Due

All library items are subject to recall at any time.

APR 0 7 2010		
MAR 3 1 2010		

Cessna 172

AROUND BRITAIN

Dick Flute

IAN ALLAN
Publishing

First published 1994

ISBN 0 7110 2181 4

Published by Ian Allan Ltd,
Shepperton, Surrey; and printed
by Ian Allan Printing Ltd at
their works at Coombelands in
Runnymede, England

To Denise

Contents

Flight Lists:

Flight one: Top Farm (10 miles
west of Cambridge) – Manston –
Lydd (low pass) – Shoreham (west
of Brighton) – Southampton –
Bournemouth – Exeter – Plymouth
– Southampton – Wycombe Air
Park

Flight two: Wycombe Air Park –
Gloucester – Bristol – Cardiff –
Welshpool – Liverpool – Blackpool
– Carlisle – Edinburgh – Perth –
Dundee – Aberdeen – Glasgow –
Prestwick – Newcastle – Tees-side
– Leeds/Bradford – Wycombe Air
Park

Flight three: Wycombe Air Park –
Coventry – Birmingham –
Manchester – Humberside –
Norwich – Wycombe Air Park

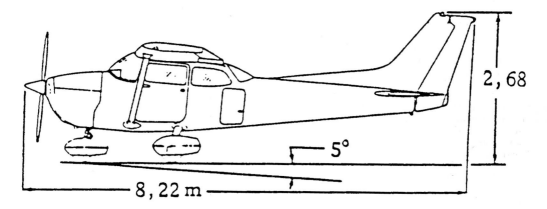

2,68

5°

8,22 m

Specifications and Data

Registration: G-WACL
Type: Reims/Cessna F172N
Vne (Never Exceed Speed): 158kt
Vno (Top manouevring speed with full control deflection): 127kt
Cruise speed (70% power): 105kt
Length: 8.22m
Wing span: 10.97m
Height (tip of tail): 2.68m
Maximum range (still air @ 4,000ft & 70% power): 475nm with 45min reserve
Service ceiling: 14,200ft
Fuel capacity: 163 litres
Typical cruise fuel consumption: 31 litres/hr (6.9 gall/hr)
Engine: Lycoming 0.320 H2AD horizontally-opposed four-cylinder air-cooled developing 160bhp at 2,700rpm
History: Manufactured in Reims, France, and first certified in November 1979. G-WACL had flown 3,800hr by December 1993 and had suffered no damage either by accident or other means. As far as is known G-WACL came straight from France and operated out of Denham aerodrome for the first six years as G-BHGG. In 1986 Charlie Lima was operated by Wycombe Air Centre on a lease-back arrangement before being bought outright in 1988. It was during October 1989 that the registration was changed to the distinctive G-WAC series. Apart from being used as a trainer, 'CL' spends most of its time flying for recreational purposes. Most flights are fairly local. In 1993 the aircraft crossed the Channel to Midden Zeeland in Holland, Calais and Le Torquet in France and Jersey. Two of the longest flights in the UK were to Perranporth in Cornwall and Caernafon in North Wales; the latter trip was flown by the author and Guy Browning.

Introduction

This book tells the story of three flights which set out to visit as many UK airports as possible with quite severe time, weather and financial limitations. The photographs were taken during the flights. They often graphically illustrate the poor weather and visibility which made these flights quite an adventure at times. On top of this, the 'flightdeck' of a Cessna 172 is a small workplace with the glazed areas made of perspex, which does nothing to enhance photography let alone the vision of the pilot! Landings can be very demanding with the actual runway becoming just visible during the final stages. British pilots soon learn to live with poor weather and visibility. Enjoy this account of what it feels like to be there. Visual Flight Rules in the UK allow minima below 3,000ft of visibility 5km, clear of cloud and in sight of ground. Gripping stuff when travelling at over two miles a minute below a continuous 500ft cloudbase in rain.

Dick Flute
London
January 1994

3

1. Ammeter
2. Suction Gauge
3. Oil temperature, oil pressure, and fuel quantity indicators
4. Clock
5. Airspeed indicators
6. Tachometer
7. Gyroscopic turn indicator
8. Gyroscopic directional indicator
9. Artificial horizon
10. Aircraft registration number
11. Secondary altimeter
12. Vertical speed indicator
13. Encoding altimeter
14. ADF bearing indicator
15. Course deviation indicators
16. Transponder
17. Magnetic compass
18. Marker beacon indicator
19. Audio control panel
20. Autopilot control unit
21. Radios
22. Economy mixture indicator
23. Additional instrument space
24. ADF radio
25. Flight hour recorder
26. Map compartment
27. Cabin heat and air control knobs
28. Cigar lighter
29. Wing flap switch and position indicator
30. Mixture control knob
31. Throttle (with friction lock)
32. Static pressure alternate source valve
33. Instrument and radio dial light dimming rheostat
34. Microphone

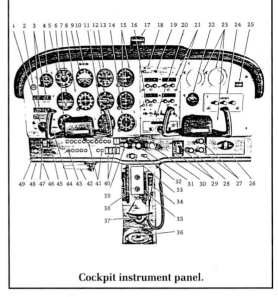

Cockpit instrument panel.

35. Air conditioning controls
36. Fuel selector valve handle
37. Rudder trim control lever
38. Elevator trim control wheel
39. Carburettor heat control knob
40. Electrical switches
41. Circuit breakers
42. Parking break handle
43. Avionics power switch
44. Low-voltage warning light
45. Ignition switch
46. Auxiliary mike jack
47. Master switch
48. Phone jack
49. Primer

Left:
The cockpit of 'Charlie Lima'.

1.
Round Britain VFR

I am sitting at the breakfast table and watching fog thicken. It is 07.30 on a September Monday morning. Half an hour ago it was clear. Ian Allan Publishing have asked the well-know aviation photographer Austin Brown to produce a series of photographs of UK airports. It has become clear that the most practical method of moving from airport to airport is by hiring a light aircraft and this has given rise to another idea. Why not write a book, illustrated with suitable photographs of the trip, to complement Ian Allan's successful series of books on commercial routes 'From the Flightdeck'.

It was a classic case of being in the right place at the right time. I have a Private Pilot's Licence, and have written for various aviation magazines. Aussie and I also happen to be good friends. We have planned to depart from a private farm strip in two hours time. The fog is now down to one hundred metres and the prospect of returning to bed appears the most sensible course of action. The summer weather has been abysmal and the autumn isn't much better. However, we have another more pressing consideration. The days are getting shorter and the light is fading.

It's a quarter past eight and Aussie is knocking at the front door. I have my bags packed and we shall load up the car and drive up to the strip in Cambridgeshire and take it from there. As we drive up the A1 northbound the fog is showing a marked reluctance to lift as forecast. Because of weather delays the Cessna 172 we had originally planned to fly is due for its annual Certificate of Airworthiness inspection. This is the aeronautical equivalent of a very thorough MOT. Consequently we have decided to take a Cessna 150M instead.

When we arrive at the strip the fog is still a problem. The strip is two hundred feet above sea level and looking up we can see clear blue sky. Looking sideways we can see barely one kilometre. The car has been unpacked and the first thing we have to do is weigh the luggage and photographic equipment. The Cessna 150M is a two-seater with limited carrying capacity and it now has to be determined whether the aircraft can carry the load. In order to do this the aircraft manual has to be consulted. In it are tables and graphs which show how specific weights and placements affect the centre of gravity.

Getting these calculations correct is very important. If we get our sums wrong the aircraft may not fly properly. The baggage has been weighed so now we weigh ourselves and then calculate the weight of the full fuel tanks and oil in the engine. The first answers just come within the upper limits but they are close. Being anxious to get the correct answer the exercise is repeated. The answer is the same. Still not 100% satisfied we consult David, the owner, for a second opinion. He checks our figures and thankfully agrees with the findings.

The aircraft has been fully fuelled prior to our arrival so David suggests that as the fog has cleared to nearly three kilometres, we check the aircraft and refresh our flying abilities by doing a few low level circuits.

Aussie has a few business calls to make so I will 'pre-flight' the aircraft. Using my Cessna 152/172 check-list I start inside the cabin. Climbing inside I notice that the control lock has already been removed and stowed in a side pocket. Next the brakes are checked ON, and the throttle full closed. All the switches are OFF so the battery side of the Master (electrical) switch is turned ON. This is the right hand side. The switch is divided into two segments and the left hand segment is the Alternator side. On pressing the right hand side, the gyro for the electrical turn and slip indicator is heard winding up. Almost immediately the little red warning flag in the centre field of the instrument flicks OFF. The fuel gauges are checked for contents and both show FULL. The fuel cut-off valve is checked ON and the flaps are lowered in ten degree stages. On this fairly early example 150/152 the flap position indicator is located towards the top of the left hand 'A' post just in front of the left hand door.

Above:
The author (left) and Austin Brown enjoying the research for this book!

people, flying will always be associated with wet feet. I'm well inured to this by now and squelch around quite contentedly. I am now looking for the landing light and (if fitted) taxi light. Sometimes they are on the wing and sometimes on the nose.

On this aircraft the lights are on the nose. I reach back inside the cabin, switch both landing and taxi ON, take a quick look around the cowling and turn them OFF quickly. The reason I'm doing one part of the electrical equipment at a time is to conserve the battery. I don't know who flew it last or what duties it performed. Therefore it is specially prudent to give the aircraft a very thorough inspection when first taking over. It is quite possible, given the weather over the last few days, that it has hardly flown at all. I will check the aircraft log, of course, but it's three hundred metres away.

With these checks complete the Master switch can be turned OFF. The next stage is to give the

I don't just rely on the indicator gauge. As each ten degrees of flap is lowered I look out of both the left and right cabin windows to see that the flaps are in position. Several fatal accidents have occurred when flaps have operated asymmetrically. Aussie is very aware of this problem and has advised me not to let go of the flap lever when lowering flaps on the approach. If the flaps come down unevenly the aircraft will roll over incredibly quickly and even if you retract the flaps as quickly as possible it may not be possible to recover. Armed with this knowledge I pay particular attention to ascertain that the degree of deflection is the same on both sides.

Next the anti-collision beacon is switched ON. At the same time the Pitot Head heater is switched ON. This is my own particular preference. I then get out of the cabin, check the 'Anti-Coll' beacon which is the flashing red light on top of the tail then reach inside the cabin and turn the 'Anti-Coll' and Pitot heat OFF. Reaching out I feel the front of the Pitot head to make sure it is warm.

I have only just closed the cabin door when I am reminded straight away of one of the unavoidable realities of flying from grass aerodromes. My feet are soaking wet. The problem is that I don't like to fly with heavy-weight shoes let alone wellies. Standing here, beside a small aircraft on the dew laden grass, memories of my first serious flying lessons come flooding back as they also took place in the autumn. For a lot of

Right:
A classic landmark for VFR flight, the Forth Rail Bridge.

cabin interior a good look round. I'm looking for loose items that could get trapped in the control runs and I'm also noting the position of the First Aid Kit and the Fire Extinguisher. Next the security and condition of the straps and harnesses. This 150M is an Aerobat version so it has a hefty four-point harness. It also has the 130hp Continental 0-240 engine. Most Cessna 150/152 variants have the 110hp Lycoming. The extra 20hp goes most of the way to explain why we can carry the extra weight. I have flown this aircraft before but with just two adults and a flight case on board.

Everything looks good so now it is time for the external check. The idea is to start at the left-hand cabin door and work around the extremities of the aircraft in a clockwise direction. First I'll do the fuel check. I have a handy clear plastic cylindrical fuel tester for this purpose. The tester has a prong which pushes up into the self-sealing valve beneath each fuel tank. I draw off half an egg cup full and hold it up to the light. Any water or sediment will be clearly visible. There, clear as a bell.

Now I'll work my way around the undercarriage and along the trailing edge. The flaps are secure as are the ailerons and wing tips. The leading edge and under-surfaces are closely inspected. The hole in the front of the stall-warner and pitot head are clear as is the static-vent on the side of the fuselage. Very important these are. A bug squashed on the front of the pitot head can disrupt or even stop the pitot from giving an accurate reading of the airspeed. There are three pressure instruments on this aircraft and the readings are obtained when the instrument compares one form of moving or dynamic air pressure with a static one.

The three pressure instruments are the airspeed indicator, altimeter and vertical speed indicator. Forward speed is measured by the ASI, (Airspeed Indicator), altitude or height by the Altimeter, and the rate of climb or descent by the VSI, (Vertical Speed Indicator). As an example the air pressure entering the tiny hole in the front of the pitot is compared with static air in a tube of similar length. The faster the aircraft moves the greater the pressure in the pitot. This is also why the pitot is heated. As you know, when you push your hand out of a car window at speed, it soon feels cold. On top of this the atmosphere gets colder as you climb higher. Typically the temperature falls by two degrees Centigrade for every one thousand feet. Combine the two effects and you can easily see that rain can quickly freeze into ice on the pitot. The altimeter on the other hand is very similar

Above:
One of the many memorable moments of the trip was the spectacular approach to Liverpool over the Mersey.

in principle to the barometer seen in many homes.

As you can imagine the intricacies of these instruments are very substantial and it is far wiser to trust the instruments than the seat of your pants. There aren't many quick cross checks but I do know one. I quite often obtain the QNH, (air pressure at sea level), from the control tower and set the subscale in the altimeter accordingly. As the height of the aerodrome above sea level is known the altimeter should correspond. In the UK the typical altimeter subscale range will be 950-1050 millibars.

Anyone wishing really to learn a thing or two about these subjects should refer to the many excellent books readily available. As an ordinary holder of a PPL (Private Pilot's Licence), my opinions should not be relied upon, but let's get back to the pre-flight check. An awful lot of procedure concerning flying is about check and double-check. It is too late to regret a mistake once the aircraft is airborne. So, I am clambering up on the foot-holds to unscrew the fuel tank filler caps and I'll soon see if the tanks are really full. The left tank is and I'll check the right-hand side in a moment.

My next concern is the oil level and fuel-flow. On some aircraft a substantial part of the nose cowling lifts up. On Cessna aircraft there is a hatch into which you peer. The oil level is correct and I pull a plunger which releases a stream of fuel onto the ground near the nosewheel. In this way I can ascertain that a good flow of fuel is being delivered to the carburettor. This is also a good time to see if any major oil leak problems have occurred.

Above:
A tight squeeze; all our baggage and cameras stacked on the apron before loading into Charlie Lima at Wycombe.

Above:
The pitot head provides air speed information and is heated to prevent icing.

Most piston aero-engines leak oil especially if they are used for aerobatics. Consequently some oil is seen splashed around the compartment behind the cylinder and crankcase partition. I can't see any undue residues so I close the hatch and move on. The propeller is obviously very important so this item is closely inspected. There is no sign of damage or cracks and the leading face, the *rear facing* side, is relatively clean. A good tug is given to the 'fan-belt' to the alternator and, bending down, the air-intake filter and nose-wheel assembly are given a thorough scrutiny.

Points to watch are that no oil is leaking from the engine compartment through the nosewheel leg aperture and that the oleo leg is inflated. The oleo is the shock absorber. Grabbing hold of the torque-link which aligns the actual wheel with the airframe and the anti-shimmy damper I can feel that they are both firmly attached. Most modern nose-wheels are prone to shimmy and this can get very unpleasant at high take-off and

Below:
The instrument panel facing the left hand seat and the central radio stack.

landing speeds. Shimmy is the term used for 'wheel wobble' although it isn't usually caused by the wheel being out of balance. Everything looks serviceable and I remember to check for tyre creep. You can probably imagine the forces exerted on a stationary tyre as it contacts the runway on landing especially if the landing is heavy and fast. It is pretty demanding stuff for tyres and they can rotate on the wheel even on small aeroplanes. The simple solution is to paint a line, (usually red), across the rim onto the tyre. If the tyre rotates the split line is easy to notice.

As the aircraft is worked round I realise why my instructors made me do this time and time again. There are dozens of minor points that catch my eye, Screws and fasteners, rivets and pins. After a while you get a feel for it and can work through the checks quite quickly. The point to remember is to be thorough. Don't skimp. I've now spent nearly fifteen minutes and have reached the tail section. I move the elevators through their full travel and inspect the hinges, rods and cables. The tail-plane itself is firmly held to make sure it is securely attached to the fuselage. Squatting down low the under-surfaces are inspected to make sure that damage hasn't been inflicted by objects like stones being thrown up by propeller backwash or the wheels.

We intend taking a lot of photographs of the approaches plus some extras whilst taking-off and taxiing. The windscreen and windows are made of perspex which is very flexible but easily scratched. Grabbing a bottle of REPCON from my flight case I give the glazed areas a good polish. The improvement is clearly visible but a lot of scratches remain. We shall just have to live with this. The prevailing winds in England are from the south-west and the long term forecast tells us that this will be the case for the next few days. Consequently most of our landings will be into sun! Very undesirable from a photographic standpoint and not very comfortable to the Mk1 eyeball.

"How's it going?" Aussie is walking across the grass from his car. "She's fine Aussie. Fully fed and watered and no visible defects", I tell him. We get ready to go flying. The Cessna has been nosed into a corner by the fuel tank. I jump inside and release the park brake. We struggle on the wet grass to push the aircraft back. It weighs barely more than half a tonne. Once clear of the pump I lean across the rear fuselage until the nose-wheel is clear of the ground. Aussie grabs a strut and we heave the aircraft round through 180°. "You've flown this one before, so I'll take the right-hand seat", said

Above:
The ASI (Airspeed Indicator) centre, flanked by the clock and the artificial horizon.

Below:
The author takes Charlie Lima up for a test flight.

Bottom:
Charlie Lima landing after a circuit at Wycombe, the author at the controls and 30 degrees of flap on.

Aussie. Happy with this I clamber into the left-hand seat and re-apply the parking brake. We adjust our seats and strap on our harnesses. There is very little room in a 150 and we're both fair sized people. We end up shoulder to shoulder. The baggage has been left on the ground. Before commencing the pre-start-up checks I'd better take this opportunity to give you an idea of the equipment and layout in our cockpit. I have already referred to the three pressure instruments. These are part of a six instrument bank situated on the left hand side. The layout is pretty much universal these days and this makes moving from one aircraft type to another both easier and safer. When in busy stages of flight you don't want to waste time searching the panel. The primary flight instruments comprise a rectangle with two lines of three. In the upper left hand corner is the Airspeed Indicator (ASI). Centre top is the Artificial Horizon, a beautiful piece of design and workmanship. It is a gyroscopic instrument powered from a vacuum pump driven by the engine. A symbol resembling the rear view of the aircraft is placed in front of a movable display that represents the horizon. Below the centre-line it is coloured tawny brown and above mid-blue. Degrees of bank angle are marked around the upper half with a pointer and degrees of pitch angle are marked in the centre field. Designs do vary but they all give the same information. The top right is the altimeter.

Below:
Charlie Lima moments before flaring to land after a steep glide approach with 40 degrees of flap.

In the bottom left hand is the turn and bank indicator, also gyroscopic but electrically driven. This instrument gives the rate of turn as opposed to bank-angle and also incorporates a 'banana' shaped spirit level in the bottom segment. This is immensely useful if the aircraft is being flown out of balance especially when climbing at full power. The force of the propeller backwash tends to push the tail out together with the torque effect from the engine. The spirit level ball will be seen out of centre if this happens. If it's out to the left you bring it back to the centre by applying left rudder and vice-versa on the right.

The lower centre instrument is the Direction Indicator (DI) which shows a circular compass with a plan view of the aircraft pointing upwards. This is set before beginning a flight by referring to the Magnetic Compass. It is very important to remove all metal objects like headphones from the vicinity as they will produce false readings. The DI has a 'slaving-knob' by which the compass card is aligned to the 'twelve o'clock' position. In other words, if the Magnetic Compass shows a heading of 240° the DI compass is swivelled around until 24 points straight up. The DI is also gyroscopic and is powered by the vacuum pump. The principal benefits are two-fold. The usual Magnetic Compass is harder to read and wobbles about a lot. The DI doesn't wobble but it does suffer from 'Mechanical Drift' which is brought about by tiny amounts of friction etc. The DI is also easier to read because it doesn't suffer from acceleration error and turning error. In practice you wait till the Magnetic Compass is stationary whilst in flight and realign the DI if necessary. The Vertical Speed

Indicator (VSI) is located in the bottom right corner.

Beneath this panel is a line of switches, knobs and fuses. To the extreme left is the Primer. This is a plunger which can be locked shut and is used to inject fuel directly into the cylinders for cold starting. We don't have a choke. Next is the Master Switch. Then we have the Ignition Switch which has five positions and is key operated. Working clockwise we have the OFF position, then Left Magneto, Right Magneto, both Magnetos and the spring augmented Start Position. The Magnetos are powered by the engine and provide the electrical current to the plugs. You may wish to know that something in the order of 20,000 volts powers the spark across the electrodes.

There are few things less desirable than engine failure in flight. Wings falling off would be a good exception. Thousands of people have spent millions of hours trying to get aero-engines as simple and reliable as possible. Naturally the whole exercise ends up as a huge heap of compromises. One such is having two Magnetos supplying current to each sparking plug. There is a benefit. With two Magnetos working the fuel burns better and when each Magneto is tested by turning the key to Right or Left a drop in RPM is usually noticed. After the Magneto Switch is a line of fuses which pop out if they are in danger of being overloaded. These are known as Circuit Breakers. To the right of these we have the electrical switches for the Beacon, Navigation lights, Strobes, Pitot heat and other equipment as fitted.

The centre panel contains all the radio and radio-navigation aids and these vary from aircraft to aircraft. We have two VHF (Very High Frequency) radios, the frequencies of which range from 118.00 to 135.97. They are placed one on top of the other the upper being referred to as Comm 1. Each box is divided into two parts. On the left is a two part selector knob for the frequencies. We use these frequencies to talk to Air Traffic Controllers. For example, the frequency for Cambridge Approach is 123.60. We have a separate ON/OFF switch with volume control. The frequency selector knob has an inner and outer dial. Therefore we can dial up 123 first, then .60 afterwards. The right hand side looks almost identical but is used to select VOR (VHF omnidirectional radio range) frequencies. These range from 108.00 to 117.97 and this is known as the NAV side. Extremely simply there are a number of ground installations that broadcast radio beams with different signals throughout 360°. There is one beam for each degree throughout the circle.

When the appropriate VOR frequency for a particular ground station has been selected, the beam-bar (which is mounted vertically) in the circular instrument tells you how to get there. If the beam bar is right of centre then the nose must be steered right to centralise the bar. There are masses of extra considerations and I won't even attempt to enlarge on this subject as it delves into the lore of Instrument Flight which won't affect this project. Hopefully!! Beneath Comm 1 and Comm 2 is the ADF box, (Automatic Direction Finder). This operates on medium wave. Again very simply, when the correct frequency is dialled in, a needle on the instrument points to the beacon. ADFs can be affected by thunder-storms because they are medium wave. VORs are VHF and are usually far more reliable. Just for interest, if our aircraft was equipped for ILS (Instrument Landing System) we would have something closely resembling our VOR but with a horizontal beambar as well. This would tell us if our approach path was too high or low.

Looking down the panel even further we spot the Transponder. Yet again in the simplest terms, we can dial up a four digit number which eventually causes a matching number to mark our position when we appear on radar screens. We have a separate knob for each digit. Today we set 7000 as this is the standard Conspicuity Code. We will only set another number if directed to do so by Air Traffic Control services. An exception would be in an emergency with perhaps lack of radio communication. In these circumstances we dial in 7700. More advanced sets are equipped with Mode C. This gives out altitude information as well. It's plain to see how invaluable transponders are to people operating radar.

For the sake of clarity the radio navigation instruments are usually found in a vertical stack sandwiched between the flight instrument panel and the radios. Other instruments are found where space allows and are dotted all over the place. Examples are; fuel gauges, oil temperature, oil pressure, suction (for the vacuum pump), outside air temperature and so on.

Even on Cessna aircraft the position of supplementary instruments can vary, even on the same model type. A favourite moan of mine is the engine RPM counter. Pilots refer to this a great deal but it can often be found in different places. Below the radio stack we find three controls. On the left is the Carburetter Heat Control, then the Throttle and Mixture Control. I have always found them in the same order running from left to right on later models. The Throttle has a large Black knob and the Mixture is red.

The Throttle controls the amount of power required from the engine and the Mixture the amount of fuel. The mixture is 'leaned' off by screwing the Mixture Control knob outwards. It can be returned quickly to fully rich by pressing a plunger in the centre of the knob. Generally speaking, as the fuel in the cylinders also helps to cool the engine, the mixture is kept fully rich when climbing and flying in the circuit. We normally lean the mixture when flying steadily from one place to another. If the mixture is too lean the engine can easily overheat so as we will be manoeuvring around a lot whilst en route we shall keep the mixture fully rich. It's better to use some extra fuel rather than risk damage.

To stop the engine the Mixture control is fully extended and this strangles the fuel supply to the engine. To the right of the Mixture control we find the Flap Position Selector switch and glancing down and to the left the Trim wheel. Being able to trim control surfaces is very useful and most would say absolutely necessary. Changes in power setting affect the pitch of the aircraft substantially so we have an elevator trim tab. More advanced aircraft have rudder trim also. In fact, some even have aileron trim; super luxury! Between and just in front of the seats is a small lever which controls the fuel supply. As 150s are a popular training aircraft it has two positions only, OFF and ON rather than a more complicated selector for different fuel tanks.

Okay, having got through that lot, we are ready to commence. I run through the checks speaking out loud. This gives Aussie the opportunity to monitor the procedure and intervene if I leave something out.

"Seats, harnesses and hatches", we check adjustment and security.

"Instruments", we look for sensible readings and good conditions.

"Radio and Electric's OFF"

"Circuit breakers and fuses IN"

"Cabin Heat and Air", I check the movement and leave them closed.

"Throttle Nut loose".

"Mixture and Carb Heat". I check the movement and leave them both IN.

"Controls and Trimmer". The yoke is pushed and pulled and turned from side to side throughout all the possible combinations of movement. We also look at the actual control surfaces to make sure they correspond. Health Warning! When strapped in looking round to monitor the elevators and trim plus the rudder can easily rick the neck. Who said flying is safe?

I switch the Beacon or Anti-collision light ON and we are ready to start up. Having read through so many pages I hope you are not too excited.

"Brakes ON".

"Fuel Valve ON".

"Mixture RICH".

"Carb-heat COLD".

"Primer". I unlock the primer and give it three full depressions then re-lock it.

"Master Switch ON".

"Throttle", the knob is pushed in just a little, about a centimetre. I then put the ignition key into the switch. NOT BEFORE. Many serious accidents have occurred when the ignition or contact switches have either been left ON or have inadvertently been turned ON prematurely. The key is always removed prior to loading fuel and is invariably left on top of the coaming so that the refueller can see it.

I then open my window and we both look all around to make sure all is clear. In the unlikely event that someone is stooping close to the propeller I shout "Clear Prop". I wait for two seconds then turn the key to START. The propeller thumps round two or three times and the engine fires. Now it gets busy. The first task is to raise the engine RPM to 1200. As soon as this is done the 'Starter Engaged Light' and 'Low Voltage Warning Light' are monitored. If either stays on I will shut down the engine. Both are out so I watch the Oil Pressure Gauge. The pressure is rising. Good!

I quickly look round outside then adjust the engine RPM. It always rises a little. The suction gauge needle which shows if the vacuum pump is working and is in the 'green'. I now check that the gyroscopic instruments are erecting. They are. Next comes the 'Mag' check. I switch the Magneto or ignition switch to Left. Hardly any drop. Back to Both and then Right. Again, hardly any drop. Excellent. A drop of 100 rpm or so would be acceptable and barely 25 is registered. This tells me the 'Mags' are in very good condition. Next I switch the 'Mags' OFF and instantly put them back to Both. As soon as the switch goes to OFF the engine dies. If you leave it OFF for a fraction of a second too long there is a risk of detonation when the switch is returned to Both. Detonation is commonly known as 'backfire' and you can understand how much internal damage can be inflicted it this occurs. Consequently many flying schools don't teach the 'Dead Cut' procedure.

"Flaps", the flaps are withdrawn in ten degree stages and we visually check each stage.

"Instruments", a very quick scan is given to verify sensible readings and, as the coaming is clear, I set the DI (Direction Indicator). The compass shows we are pointing Nor-Nor-East on a

Above:
On short finals for Runway 25 at Wycombe Air Park.

heading of 030°. The DI shows 350°. I push in the 'slaving knob' and rotate the DI compass until 03 appears in the upright or twelve o'clock position. Incidentally, pilots are taught to think of the lateral plane around their aircraft in terms of the clock. Therefore three o'clock is ninety degrees to the right and six o'clock is directly behind. When flying along, if you spot another aircraft you might typically inform your colleague or co-pilot or passenger, (if carried), "Contact, ten o'clock high, five miles'.

The check list details "Avionics Fan' which we don't possess. It provides a signal to Aussie to switch everything ON regarding Radio and Nav equipment. We have Cambridge Approach selected on Comm 1 and the transponder set to 7000. Everything else is ON in case we need to use it quickly.

We are now ready to taxi out. A good look all around is the first step. It is clear so the brakes are released by applying top pressure to the rudder bar. From then on differential braking is applied by pushing your feet forward on the upper part of the rudder bar. It sounds complicated but is easily mastered. To stop straight equal pressure is applied to both sides. As soon

as the brakes are released I pull the yoke fully back. This relieves the load on the nosewheel, very important when taxiing on grass or rough surfaces. A quick burst of throttle to get the aircraft moving and I pull the throttle back and apply the brakes simultaneously. "Brakes checked my side". I push the throttle open, get rolling, and Aussie applies his brakes as I reduce the throttle setting. I should explain that before starting the engine we've both donned our headsets so we can talk normally through the intercom.

As there is no Control Tower here we turn the aircraft through 360° to check for approaching aircraft plus any other activity. None is seen so we taxi out towards the end of the runway. The take-off direction is generally determined by the direction of the wind. We have virtually no wind so environmental considerations come into play. Obviously we make the loudest noise on take-off so we select the direction that minimises the disturbance to the neighbours. In this case we take-off towards the west. Whilst taxiing we can check three of our six flight instruments. I dab the rudder and brake left. The Turn Indicator swings over left, the DI swings right and the Magnetic Compass swings left. Good. Next I swing the nose right. The Turn (and Bank) Indicator swings right, the DI swings left and the Magnetic Compass swings right. All in order.

Before reaching the end of the runway I steer the aircraft well clear of the edge of the strip to do the 'Power' and 'Take-off' checks. Normally I would face the aircraft into wind until the nose-wheel is centred. In this instance I point the aircraft back towards the West.

"Brakes ON".

"Temperatures and Pressures, Checked".

"Clear Behind", I look around both sides.

"Throttle, 1700", I push the throttle forwards to 1700 RPM.

"Carb-Heat, ON, no rise, OFF", should the engine RPM rise after selecting 'Carb-Heat' it will probably indicate icing. The RPM will only vary by about 100 so a keen watch is needed.

"Magnetos . . . Good". I check the left and right against Both. The maximum allowable is 125 RPM each and 50 RPM between the two.

"T's an P's within limits", the temperatures and pressures are quickly scanned as is the Suction to be between 4.6 and 5.4 (In the green band).

"Idle check". The throttle is slowly closed fully which should leave the engine idling between 500 and 700 rpm. The throttle is then returned to 1200 rpm. Aero-engines have a nasty habit of fouling their plugs at low rpm so 1200 is the recommended setting to avoid this problem.

Now we approach the nitty-gritty and I inform Aussie that I've started 'TAKE-OFF Checks'.

"Trim". The trim wheel is put on 'Take-Off' position. With full tanks and two people we don't adjust this until the climbout.

"Throttle Nut Tight". There is a screw that increases or decreases friction for this purpose. Keeping it tight ensures that during the take-off and climb if the right hand should leave the throttle, to adjust the flaps for example, the throttle remains in position.

"Mixture Rich".

"Carb-Heat Cold".

"Magnetos . . .Both".

"Primer . . . Locked".

"Fuel . . . ON . . . and sufficient". Aussie checks this also. The fuel tap is on and the gauges show sufficient fuel to allow ample endurance plus reserves for the intended flight. It seems a bit silly for a ten minute circuit but most aviation accidents occur because an 'obvious' check like this has been omitted.

"Flaps, ten degrees". I select the ten degree setting. Ten degrees is commonly known as 'lift-flap' on 150/152 types. It enables the aircraft to get airborne with a shorter take-off run. It must be borne in mind that each flap setting pitches the nose upwards. When the time comes I'll need a fairly hefty pull to 'unstick' the aircraft from the runway.

"Instruments and Gyros . . . Checked". The flight panel instruments are quickly checked for normal readings and I zero the altimeter. This gives us our QFE. Just to run through this, you need to remember that QFE gives us the pressure setting at the highest level of the aerodrome. This field is flat and 200ft above sea level. The QNH gives us the pressure indicated at sea level. Regional QNH gives us the lowest pressure in the ASR (Altimeter Setting Region). The country is divided up into several regions. Chatham, Portland and Cotswold are but a few. Above a certain altitude, normally 3000ft, we encounter the transition altitude. Above this all aircraft set 1013 millibars in their altimeter sub-scales and fly 'Flight-Levels'. QNH is needed when the first priority is terrain avoidance. Once well above the highest terrain obstacle all aircraft have their altimeters set to the same figure and collision avoidance is maximised.

When flying 'Flight Levels' the 'Quadrantal Rule' has to be obeyed. When flying a magnetic track of 000°M to 089°M you fly odd thousands of feet. FL30, FL50 and FL70 etc. When flying 090°M to 179°M you add five hundred feet. If you fly 180°M to 269°M the even thousands are adhered to. FL40, FL60 and FL80 for instance. Should you happen to have a magnetic track of 270°M to 359°M then you add 500 feet. Simple isn't it? In reality it's not very hard to remember but it goes a long way towards explaining why most private flights in the UK zoom around below 3000ft QNH.

I re-check the DI and then confirm that hatches and harnesses are secure and tight. The check-list maintains that I check the controls 'Full and Free'. A certain amount of shuffling of knees and knee-pads (the items we scribble our notes on) produces the desired result. Pitot Heat, Nav Lights and Strobes are selected as desired. All I want on this occasion is the Beacon and the Landing Light. I ask Aussie if he is happy with the checks and he confirms he is. I'm a great believer in involving the second pilot (if available) in the checking process. After so many years of commercial flying it has become almost a religion to Aussie.

I turn our Cessna throughout 360° yet again. This is achieved with a lot of power and the left brake fully ON. As expected there is no sign of aerial activity nearby. I taxi out to the full extent of the grass runway and align the aircraft to the west.

So here we are at last. The little Cessna is lined up and we are ready to go. Steadily and quickly I shove the throttle fully open. The engine bellows with power. We gradually move off. I correct with right rudder to keep straight. The speed builds up quickly. The whole air-frame is vibrating and shuddering. I've drawn the yoke back a little to give the nosewheel some respite. A quick check round the T's and P's. "T's and P's good" I inform Aussie. By now the Cessna is getting light and 50 knots is indicated on the ASI. We are bouncing now across the grass. I pull back and we're airborne! I relax the back pressure and increase speed to 60 knots. Barely ten feet above the ground I pull the yoke back and settle the ASI at 65 knots and trim.

Still with right rudder, T's and P's checked, the ground falling away, at 200ft I retract the flaps and pull the nose up and trim accordingly. We are flying now and I'm really starting to enjoy it. The visibility is totally naff at five kilometres but so what! At three hundred feet I bank the wing left-hand down fifteen degrees and start a climbing turn to the south. I steal a quick look at the farm buildings below. Great! We climb to five hundred feet and I initiate a turn to downwind parallel to the runway. The speed builds up quickly once levelled out so I draw the throttle back. We fly the downwind leg at 90 knots. I rush through the downwind checks, such as are applicable, "Fuel ON, Brakes OFF, Harnesses and Hatches Secure, Carb-Heat ON", pull the throttle back and bank into a descending left turn. Pulling back on the yoke to decrease airspeed below 80 knots, I select ten degrees of flap. This pitches the nose up so I push forward and trim. We are now on Base Leg and I select 20° of flap and steady the attitude at sixty five knots. Almost immediately I bank left onto finals. I select thirty degrees of flap, push the nose down and increase power to compensate.

This last bit needs a bit of explanation. Increasing the flap deflection angle increases drag so the nose is pushed down to maintain speed. Why increase power? It sounds as if a fast dive might result doesn't it? I thought so when first learning to fly. In practice you use the elevators to control speed and the throttle to control rate of descent. An aircraft behaves around two inter-related 'couples'. If you view the aircraft from the side the horizontal couple is thrust (from the propeller) versus drag. The second couple is in the vertical and has lift versus weight. It is complex matter to get to grips with but, once mastered, provides tremendous insight into how aeroplanes work. The two couples are completely interwoven and each part reacts against the other three. Consequently as I've produced more drag by lowering the flaps and compensated by pushing the nose down using weight to achieve speed, it follows that thrust will provide lift.

No doubt theorists are tearing their hair out with this explanation but it works. And, we're working right now. The boundary hedge is coming right up at us. The ASI reads sixty five knots. Good. I raise the nose slightly and give a tiny bit more throttle. We appear to be descending at a perilously steep angle. The boundary hedge has whipped by barely ten feet below the undercarriage and I pull the throttle right back hard to idle. At the same time I pull back in firm increments to hold the aircraft flaring above the grass. Our airspeed is dropping rapidly and I intend to get the wheels down just as the aircraft stalls. Yanking back on the control column, the nose pitched high, and with so much weight on board, the little Cessna drops firmly onto the grass. Not bad! We don't bounce and the airframe quivers with vibration and noise.

Up till now I've been keeping straight with judicious jabs of rudder and continue to do so

Below:
What started as a simple take off later became complicated as Charlie Lima was kept low to avoid a flock of birds.

during the first stages of the landing run. This is a very good grass runway but is still a bit lumpy when compared to tarmac or concrete. As the speed decays greater amounts of rudder are called for until it makes sense to transfer to the footbrakes. Whilst controlling this there are other duties to perform. The Carb-heat is returned to COLD. The flaps are fully retracted and the landing light is switched OFF. Back pressure on the yoke is gradually extended as the speed drops to relieve pressure on the nose-wheel. Taxiing should always be done on grass with the elevators fully up. See how many pilots remember when you next visit a grass aerodrome. I taxi back to the parking area and stop. Pulling ON the park brake, fully depressing the toe brakes and releasing the park brake knob I check they are holding with a burst of power.

I look across at Aussie and ask him 'what next?'

"Well done lad", he says, "I think I'll do a circuit from the right hand seat".

"You have control", I say and pull my feet and hands away from the controls. "I have control' says Aussie and sets about getting to grips with the Cessna. After twenty plus years flying all manner of twins from Titans to BAC 111s plus Viscounts it will not come as a surprise to learn that Aussie is also well acquainted with single-engined Cessnas as well. I know this of course and Aussie sets a fine example by running through all the checks item by item. I'm looking forward to the ride. Mind you, flying from the right seat is something I have very little experience of and, in the few opportunities I've had, I found it both strange and very demanding. Airline pilots get a lot of experience flying aircraft from the right hand seat. Private pilots on the other hand are trained in the left hand seat and spend most if not all their flying time in that position. It is unusual to find the flying instruments duplicated on the right side of the cockpit in light aircraft. Naturally I'm talking only of aircraft that have the pilots' seats in a side-by-side configuration. The main problems seems to stem from holding the control column in the left hand and steering the aircraft in the rolling and pitching planes whilst using the right hand for engine, propeller, trim, flap and other functions. When transferring to the right side most actions appear reversed, the control column is held in the right hand and the left hand does the rest. I've brought this up with several pilots and they nearly all readily admit to getting things all messed up especially during the busy, critical phases of flight when the brain has to work doubly hard.

Therefore I'm sitting here watching Aussie with avid interest. We are now lined up and ready to go. Aussie releases the brakes, firmly pushes the throttle fully open and we are moving off, speed building rapidly. After three hundred metres the aircraft is getting light and Aussie pulls back a little on the yoke. We are bouncing a little now as the wings develop lift. At 55 knots Aussie pulls back and we're airborne. David is standing on the parking area just past the halfway point watching us and I look down and give a wave. We're about fifty feet up and I can't resist checking the ASI and the rest of the panel. T's and P's (Temperature and Pressure) are good and I say so.

Despite the fact that I love looking down and enjoying the sights I can't avoid monitoring the flight. There is no criticism or insecurity in this, for I am very confident of Aussie's abilities. You can ask most, if not all, pilots, when the landing is imminent, they take a particular interest. I am sitting back but looking and learning. My gaze is flitting back and forth from the flight instrument panel to the view outside. I'm sizing up the situation with regard to attitude, placement, and speed. Despite the fact that I was doing the same some fifteen minutes before the scenario appears totally strange when you don't actually have 'hands-on' control.

Usually, the exact time when a reaction takes place doesn't coincide. In this instance I am very happy to realise that Aussie is making adjustments before I'm becoming aware, let alone concerned. I relax a little and settle back to enjoy the approach. The boundary hedge is looming large in the windscreen. Although we are flying barely in excess of sixty knots, it appears to rush up towards us. Aussie pulls back, the hedge zips by beneath and, with positive corrections, he flares the Cessna onto the runway. The inevitable noise of thumping and clanging at speed along grass announces our arrival on terra-firma. It has been an accomplished landing and I'm very happy. We taxi back to the parking area where Aussie commences the shut-down.

"Parking Brake, ON"

"Throttle, 1200 rpm".

"Magnetos, CHECK", Left. Right and Dead-check. "Good".

"Radios, OFF".

"Mixture", Idle Cut-Off. The engine sputters and dies.

"Magnetos, OFF", As the mags are on my side I turn the key and remove it, placing it on the coaming.

"Beacon OFF".

"Master Switch OFF", I lean forward and switch both segments OFF.

2.
Engine problems

It is now 14.15 local and we're taking stock. The visibility is 5 to 6 kilometres here which is just legal for VFR flight. VFR stands for Visual Flight Rules. The Visual Flight Rules are fairly complex to explain and have recently been changed. I expect that the majority of our flights will fall into categories D, F and G. In category D ATC (Air Traffic Control) provides separation for all aircraft and offers two forms of service; an Air Traffic Control Service and Traffic Information. For VFR our minima are the same in categories C, D and E. Below FL100 we must have 5kms

visibility, stay 1500 metres horizontally clear of cloud and remain 1000 feet clear of cloud vertically. Categories C, D and E refer to controlled airspace. In categories F and G there is a distinction for IFR (Instrument Flight Rules) but not for VFR. F and G refer to uncontrolled airspace. No traffic separation is provided but we will have access to a Flight Information Service. Below Flight Level 100 but above 3000ft AMSL (Above Mean Sea Level) we must have 5 kilometres visibility, must remain 1500 metres clear of cloud horizontally, and 1000ft clear of cloud, above or

List of international identification codes for airports or aerodromes visited and communicated with:

Aberdeen	EGPD	London (Stansted)	EGSS
Birmingham	EGBB	Luton	EGGW
Blackpool	EGNH	Lydd	EGMD
Bournemouth	EGHH	Manchester	EGCC
Bristol	EGGD	Montgomeryshire	
Cambridge	EGSC	(Welshpool)	EGCW
Cardiff	EGFF	Newcastle	EGNT
Coventry	EGBE	Norwich	EGSH
Dundee	EGPN	Perth (Scone)	EGPT
East Midlands	EGNX	Plymouth	EGHD
Edinburgh	EGPH	Prestwick	EGPK
Exeter	EGTE	Southampton	EGHI
Glasgow	EGPF	Southend	EGMC
Gloucestershire	EGBJ	Shoreham	EGKA
Humberside	EGNJ	Teesside	EGNV
Leeds/Bradford	EGNM	Woodford	EGCD
Liverpool	EGGP	Wycombe Air Park	EGTB

EXAMPLE DECODES OF A METAR AND TAF

I remember METARs as 'Meteorological Actual Reports'.
Example: SAUK301120 EGHH 25010KT 9999 3CU015 4CI250 17/13 1015
SAUK means Surface Actual, United Kingdom and 301120 = 30th day of month at 11.20 UTC. EGHH = Bournemouth. 25010KT = Wind direction 250° Magnetic at a ground speed of 10 knots. 9999 = Visibility more than 10km. 3CU015 = 3 OKTAs of cumulus cloud at 1,500ft. 4CI250 = 4 OKTAs of Cirrus at 25,000ft. 17/13 = Temperature 17° Celsius, Dewpoint 13° Celsius. 1015 = the QNH.

I remember TAFs as 'Terminal Area Forecasts'.
Example: FCUK300600 EGHI 1019 22007KT 9999 3CU015 6SC040 TEMPO 1015 5000 81XXSH 5ST010 PROB10 TEMPO 1015 95TS.
FCUK300600 means Forecast United Kingdom, 30th day of month issued at 06.00hrs UTC. EGHI = Southampton. 1019 = valid from 10.00 to 19.00hrs Zulu (UTC or GMT). 22007KT = Wind direction 220° Magnetic at a ground speed of 7 knots. 9999 = Visibility in excess of 10km. 3CU015 = 3 OKTAs of Cumulus at 1,500ft. 6SC040 = 6 OKTAs of Stratocumulus at 4,000ft. Tempo 1015 5000 = between 10.00 and 15.00hrs UTC, visibility will reduce to 5,000m for periods of less than 60 minutes. 81XXSH means 81 (which refers to a very precise table of weather classifications numbered 1-100) (XX) heavy (SH) showers and 5 OKTAs. PROB10 TEMPO 1015 95TS indicates a 10% probability of Thunderstorms between 10.00 and 15.00hrs UTC.

Very common meteorological abbreviations:
AC altocumulus; AS altostratus; BC patches; BL blowing; BR mist; CB cumulonimbus; CC cirrocumulus; CI cirrus; CS cirrostratus; CU cumulus; DZ drizzle; FG fog; FZ freezing; GR hail; HZ dust haze; MI shallow; NS nimbostratus; RA rain; RE recent; SC stratocumulus; SH showers; SN snow; SQ squall; ST stratus; TS thunderstorms; XX heavy;

METEREOLOGICAL DATA SHEETS

Sheet one (L) NAME: Faxed current actuals ETAFS for South Coast airports
Obtained from Brussels at Shoreham Airport at our request by Shoreham ATC

REMARKS: This is a FAX report containing meteorological information provided at 11.41 Zulu (12.41 local). The first line of each report or forecast gives the time it was compiled or is valid from. The airports here are EGHH (Bournemouth), EGHI (Southampton) and EGTE (Exeter). The first report starts SAUK; the SA stands for Surface Actual and are commonly known as 'actuals'. The proper name is METAR (Meteorological Actual Report) and the time of the observation is given first. For example SAUK 301120 shows that the report was compiled at 11.20 (Zulu) on the 30th. METARs are usually updated every 30 minutes. The following sections starting FCUK are TAFs or Aerodrome Forecasts.

Special points to note: The Southampton METAR shows very low cloud, 5 OKTAs of STRATUS at 700ft. The wind backs from 290° at Exeter to 250° at Bournemouth then backs dramatically to 160° at Southampton. Interestingly enough the wind speed drops at Southampton. TEMPO means for period of less than 60 minutes and PROB10 means 10% probability of less than 60 minutes. TEMPO and PROB are used in TAFs (forecasts).

At the time we received this at Shoreham the local conditions were appalling: low cloud, wind and heavy rain. As you can see, the 'actuals' and forecasts show considerable improvements approaching from the west. It was a case of sitting tight and waiting for the better weather to arrive.

```
92-09-30   11:41
ZCZC SRA100 301141
GG EGKAZBZX                                            Sheet L
301139 EBBRYZYX


SAUK301120
EGHH 25010KT 9999 3CU015 4CI250 17/13 1015=


SAUK301120
EGHI 16006KT 9999 5ST007 6SC015 15/// 1015=


SAUK301120
EGTE 29010KT 9999 5CU030 15/10 1016=


SAEGHD NIL=


FCUK300600
EGHH 1019 24007KT 9999 3CU015 7SC040 TEMPO 1015 5000 81XXSH 5ST008
        PROB10 TEMPO 1015 95TS=


FCUK300600
EGHI 1019 22007KT 9999 3CU015 6SC040 TEMPO 1015 5000 81XXSH 5ST010
        PROB10 TEMPO 1015 95TS=


FCUK300900
EGTE 1019 29008KT 9999 2CU020=


FCEGHD NIL=
```

below, vertically. Below 3000ft AMSL we must have 5 kilometres visibility, be clear of cloud and in sight of the ground.

We have just telephoned Ipswich for an 'Actual' – a Met. report at the time of enquiry. They have 5 kilometres. We then telephone Southend who have 9kms so we decide to fly down to Southend as they also expect an improvement. We load the baggage, trying to keep the heaviest gear forward. I've never seen so much clobber in a two-seater Cessna. With everything stowed, we again give the aircraft a quick pre-flight check. Fuel, oil, and control surfaces are the main priorities.

Satisfied we climb on board and strap ourselves in. I have already made notes on my kneepad giving direct track magnetic and en route radio frequencies. Aussie wants to fly the leg so I'm strapped into the right hand seat. We do our 'Internal Checks' and commence the 'Starting Check'. We have the engine started and all systems are 'GOOD'. We taxi out to the holding point having completed the Pre-Taxi checks and Taxi checks and at the holding point we run through the 'Power' check. Everything has been fine so far so we start the Take-Off Check.

"Trim", I suggest that we set the trim 50% forward of the normal take-off position with respect to the weight in the baggage compartment. Aussie readily agrees.

"Throttle Nut Tight", Aussie turns the collar clockwise to increase the friction.

"Mixture Rich".

"Carb-Heat Cold".

"Mags Both".

"Primer-Locked".

"Fuel, ON and sufficient". "Check?". I agree and say so. "Check"

"Flaps, ten degrees".

"Instruments and Gyros". Aussie and I look around the panel. Aussie winds the altimeter sub-scale round to 200 feet. This gives us a QNH of 1012. Now he turns the slaving knob on the DI to align it with the magnetic compass.

"Hatches and Harnesses' we both check that our straps are tight and that our doors are closed. "Check", I tell him.

"Controls", Aussie pushes, pulls and turns the yoke throughout all corners of the 'box', (the extremities of possible movement). Now Aussie checks the rudder travel. It's fine.

"Nav Lights and Strobes". This beacon is ON and Aussie turns the Landing Lights ON in deference to the impaired visibility.

We've turned all the radios and radio-Nav boxes ON and selected Stansted Approach on Box One using 125.55. Stansted has two alternative Approach/Radar frequencies of

Above:
Climbing out west of Southend.

126.95 and 123.80. We check the chart and decide to call Stansted when West abeam Royston. The ICAO chart shows that the Stansted CTA extends from 2000 to 3500 feet ALT and commences just 2nm (nautical miles) South-East of Royston on our intended track. A CTA is a Control Area and a CTR is a Control Zone. The Stansted CTR extends from the surface to 3500 feet ALT (Altitude) and will be intercepted approximately 7nm farther along our track after meeting the CTA.

Having completed all this, Aussie guns the throttle and turns November Delta throughout 360 degrees in order to check the approach and circuit. All is clear so we taxi out to the very end of the runway. We are lined up and Aussie opens the throttle fully. We both check quickly that T's and P's are correct and everything else appears normal. With the extra weight the little Cessna accelerates at a slower pace. At six hundred metres Aussie pulls back and we unstick. The VSI shows an initial rate of climb of 300fpm (feet per minute). Established in the climb Aussie checks the trim by carefully letting go of the yoke. We've judged it almost perfectly and November Delta continues climbing on the same path with no tendency to climb more steeply or descend.

At two hundred feet the flaps are withdrawn and the trim reset backwards to compensate. The ASI reads sixty knots. Lowering the nose slightly to increase speed, Aussie commences a left-hand turn onto a heading of 135°. There is very little wind and we expect that very little drift compensation will be required. T's and P's are checked and we both pay attention to the view below in order to ascertain whether our intended track is being correctly followed. The aerodrome at Bassingbourne appears just left of our nose and we can see Royston.

We now realise that our climb out and turn onto heading has been achieved sooner than expected and we will pass close to Royston just clipping the western side of the town. The Stansted CTR/CTA is Class 'D' Controlled Airspace so I give them a call.

"Stansted Approach, good afternoon, Golf Oscar Sierra November Delta".

"Golf November Delta, Stansted Approach, good afternoon, pass your message".

"Golf November Delta is a Cessna 150 out of Top Farm, VFR to Southend. One thousand five hundred feet, one zero one two, heading one three five, West abeam Royston, request clearance to transit your zone".

"Golf November Delta, Roger, can you accept Special VFR?".

I look across at Aussie who nods.

"Golf November Delta, affirmative".

"Golf November Delta, Roger, you are cleared

for direct track to Southend, not above two thousand feet, Stansted QFE one zero one six, squawk three four one six and call field in sight".

"Golf November Delta, Roger, cleared direct to Southend, not above two thousand on one zero one six, squawking three four one six, and call field in sight".

"That is correct Golf November Delta, you are identified ten miles Northwest of Stansted".

We turn our attention to the ground. We are looking for the town of Stansted Mountfitchet with the M11 motorway just beyond. A few minutes pass before we can see this. Almost as soon as we positively identify this location we see the complex of Stansted Airport emerging through the haze.

"Golf November Delta, field in sight".

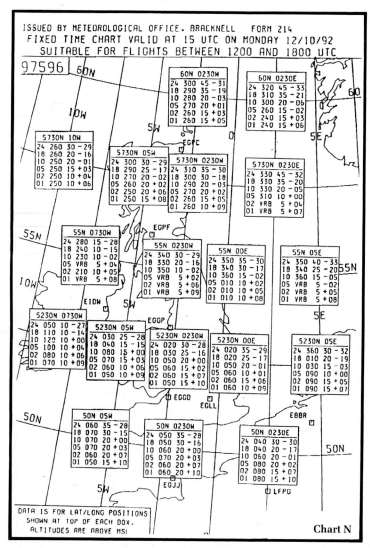

NAME: (N) UK low level forecast and (O) UK low level spot wind chart
Obtained from: Bracknell
At: Liverpool Airport

REMARKS: These are reproductions of charts sent by FAX originally. We wanted to ascertain the likely conditions for our flight from Blackpool to Carlisle. If you look at the box for 55N 0230W which covers the area to which we intended to transit on the SPOT WIND CHART it shows winds light and variable up to 5,000ft and above. Excellent. The LOW LEVEL FORECAST shows good visibility and a cloud-base of 2,500-3,000ft generally. The outlook expected little change so we could be confident of a calm comfortable flight with easy navigation by following the coast west past the Lake District. The only poor conditions are expected in the southwest and isolated.

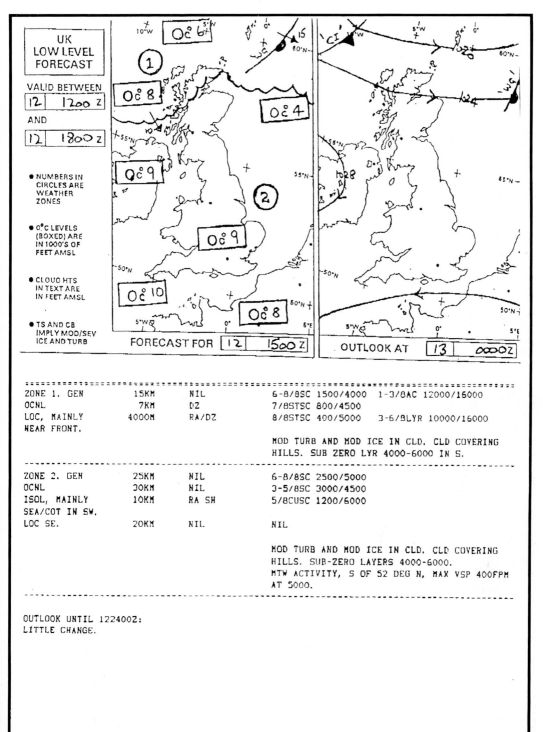

UK LOW LEVEL FORECAST

VALID BETWEEN

| 12 | 1200 Z |

AND

| 12 | 1800 Z |

- NUMBERS IN CIRCLES ARE WEATHER ZONES
- 0°C LEVELS (BOXED) ARE IN 1000'S OF FEET AMSL
- CLOUD HTS IN TEXT ARE IN FEET AMSL
- TS AND CB IMPLY MOD/SEV ICE AND TURB

FORECAST FOR | 12 | 1500 Z

OUTLOOK AT | 13 | 0000Z

```
==========================================================================================
ZONE 1. GEN        15KM      NIL        6-8/8SC 1500/4000   1-3/8AC 12000/16000
OCNL               7KM       DZ         7/8STSC 800/4500
LOC, MAINLY        4000M     RA/DZ      8/8STSC 400/5000    3-6/8LYR 10000/16000
NEAR FRONT.

                                        MOD TURB AND MOD ICE IN CLD. CLD COVERING
                                        HILLS. SUB ZERO LYR 4000-6000 IN S.
------------------------------------------------------------------------------------------
ZONE 2. GEN        25KM      NIL        6-8/8SC 2500/5000
OCNL               30KM      NIL        3-5/8SC 3000/4500
ISOL, MAINLY       10KM      RA SH      5/8CUSC 1200/6000
SEA/COT IN SW.
LOC SE.            20KM      NIL        NIL

                                        MOD TURB AND MOD ICE IN CLD. CLD COVERING
                                        HILLS. SUB-ZERO LAYERS 4000-6000.
                                        MTW ACTIVITY, S OF 52 DEG N, MAX VSP 400FPM
                                        AT 5000.
------------------------------------------------------------------------------------------


OUTLOOK UNTIL 122400Z:
LITTLE CHANGE.
```

Chart L

METFORM 215T: ISSUED BY MET OFFICE BRACKNELL AT

"Golf November Delta, Roger, continue as cleared, call overhead".

"Call overhead, Wilco, Golf November Delta".

We have picked a good time. We hear no other traffic on the Approach frequency and this has obviously helped us to obtain a clearance through the Stansted Zone. Our interest increases as we fly towards the overhead. The runway, taxiways, terminals, hangars and parked aircraft are all clearly visible. By now I'm looking directly down and taking special note of the Heavylift fleet spread around on the apron near their base.

Then I remember to call. "Golf November Delta is overhead".

"Golf November Delta, Roger", comes the laconic reply.

Despite all this I'm not very happy. Aussie virtually says as much. My RT is nowhere near as crisp as written and I've got a nagging doubt I can't pin down. Here we are, on the first leg of what to me is the experience of a lifetime. An opportunity to fly around many of the airports in Britain and getting a first class view into the bargain. I should be nigh on ecstatic, shouldn't I? The aircraft with its full load is wallowing through the air but this is fully expected. Anyway, I'm not flying it. Still the unease persists.

Stansted has disappeared behind and we are approaching the edge of the CTA. We receive a message.

"Golf November Delta, you are now leaving controlled airspace, resume own navigation and freecall Southend on one two eight decimal nine five".

"Golf November Delta, Roger, changing to one two eight decimal nine five, thanks for the help, bye".

"Our pleasure, Golf November Delta, cheerio".

I blip the transmit button twice as a final farewell.

I reach over and select 128.95 on the radio so we can monitor the frequency. We now have 12nm (nautical miles) of uncontrolled airspace in front of us before we reach the Southend CTR which is SFC (surface) to 3500'ALT. Chelmsford is emerging through the haze and the LTMA (London Terminal Manoeuvering Area) is above us from 2500'ALT to FL245. Just after Chelmsford the lower limit rises to 3500'ALT. You can see why very accurate navigation is so essential especially in South-East England. We are both working quite hard to be sure that our track is as accurate as possible. To do this we constantly refer to our charts and look around to confirm that the relationships of ground features coincide with those seen on the chart. It sounds easy, but, in practice takes concentration. I

expect that many of you, reading this, have experienced the sensation of taking-off on a commercial flight from a familiar airport in a familiar area and found that you've lost your bearings very quickly indeed. It all looks different from the air, doesn't it?

Obviously, we've both been trained in aerial navigation techniques but we still have to work at it when on an unfamiliar route. For example, the new Chelmsford bypass is an excellent feature. We get a positive ID on the road that leads south, passing below us, to intercept the A127 between Wickford and Rayleigh. Looking across in our two o'clock we spot a large lake. This is just as it should be. I recheck the T's and P's and immediately realise the cause of my earlier concern. The oil pressure gauge is on my side of the cockpit and it has definitely registered a drop from it's normal position.

"Aussie, we've got a drop in oil pressure".

"Are you sure? Are we looking for a field to land in?" says Aussie looking across at the gauge.

"No Aussie, we haven't got an emergency yet, we're still in the green, but we're slowly getting a drop. With less than ten miles to run shall we continue?" I ask.

"Yes", say Aussie, "Keep a constant eye on the gauge and watch the oil temperature too".

"Oil temperature is good and steady", I tell him.

Well, this has livened up the proceedings. Like most aero engines ours is described as air cooled. This is a slight misnomer because the oil plays a critical part in dispersing heat to areas where the air can cool it. Therefore the requirement for a healthy level of oil pressure to keep pumping the heat away is highly critical. Failure to do so can soon lead to engine seizure. Now you can see why we're sitting here, about 1500ft above the ground, taking a keen interest.

Just to keep us from getting too bored we've got a large, low and diffuse area of cloud immediately before us. In view of the low oil pressure we don't want to spend extra time attempting to fly round it. At the same time we'd rather not lose altitude. We've got to compromise and losing height is the lesser of two evils. Aussie puts November Delta into a shallow dive until we have visibility ahead below the cloud base.

We level out at 1100ft. "Give Southend a call", says Aussie.

"Southend Approach, good afternoon, Golf Oscar Sierra November Delta".

"Golf November Delta, good afternoon, Southend Approach, pass your message".

"Golf November Delta is a Cessna 150 inbound from Top Farm, VFR, one thousand one hundred feet, one zero one two, just past Wood-ham Ferrers (this is a VRP, Visual Reporting Point) and requesting joining instructions".

"Golf November Delta, Roger, runway in use two four, position for right base, QFE one zero one one, call field in sight".

"Position right base for two four, one zero one one, call field in sight, Golf November Delta".

We now pull out our map of the airfield, and check runway 24.

Referring back to the chart we decide to turn left onto a heading of 120° which should give us a good intercept for right base on runway 24. We spot the field and we're a bit too far West. Aussie turns further left onto a heading of 110°.

"Golf November Delta, field in sight".

"Golf November Delta, Roger, change to Tower on one two seven decimal seven two five.

"Changing to one two seven decimal seven two five".

I select 127.725.

"Southend Tower, good afternoon, Golf

November Delta is with you".

"Golf November Delta, Southend Tower, report established right base for two four, QFE one zero one one".

"Report right base, one zero one one, Golf November Delta".

Aussie pulls the power back to 2100prm, dips the right wing down to align with right base leg 90° from runway two four. We now have 30% oil pressure from normal. "You have control", say Aussie, "Try a right hand seat landing". As he has been a Line Training Captain I suppose I should have anticipated this. He is making me work for my money. Training Captains are like that. I haven't anticipated it and desperately try to spool my brain into overdrive.

"I have control". It sounds feeble.

Drawing the throttle back to 1700rpm the oil pressure drops yet further. It is now just in the green. Oil temperature is still good. I pull the nose back to bleed the speed off and thumb the transmit button.

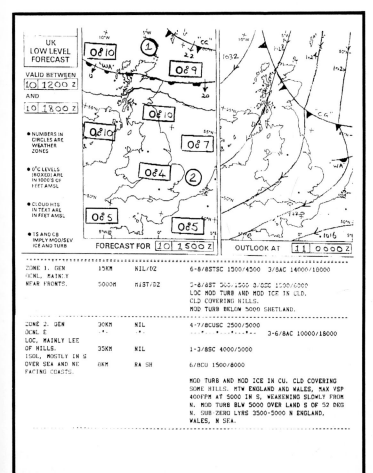

NAME: UK low level forecast
Obtained from: Bracknell
At: Bristol Airport

REMARKS: Reproduction of a FAX sent at 09.45 (Zulu or UTC). The warm front is approaching from the north but still fairly slowly. A cold front is coming in behind it faster from the northeast and will eventually occlude in the east. Looking at this we expect fine clear conditions in the south of England probably deteriorating quickly as we fly north later on. In fact this is just what happened. We encountered remains of the warm front as it crept across North Wales. The first signs appeared after passing Ludlow and quickly got worse as we flew on to Welshpool.

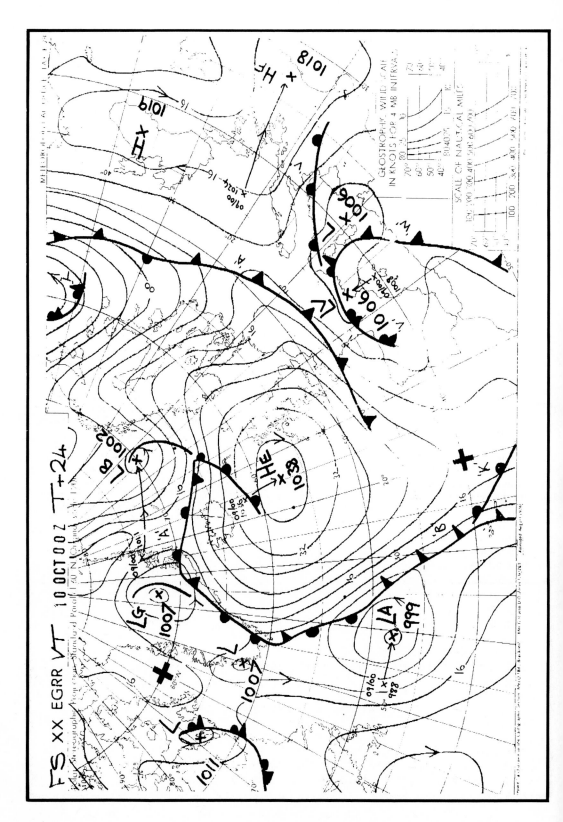

24

NAME: Surface T+24 chart
Obtained from: Bracknell
At: Aussie's office by Dial-A-Fax Metfax

REMARKS: Received by FAX. Area shows North Atlantic and Europe. Note the massive very HIGH pressure (1,038mb) area, the centre of which is approaching the UK. The WARM front coming in from the north will take some time to drift south in the light winds. We can probably look forward to two or three days that should be fairly clear if the breeze remains to keep the haze from building up.

If the LOW pressure areas out to the west continue in across the Atlantic we can expect a lot of low cloud, rain and poor visibility especially where WARM and COLD fronts meet forming an OCCLUDED front.

"Golf November Delta, established right base".

"Golf November Delta, Roger, report finals, number one".

"Report finals, Golf November Delta".

The ASI now reads 80kts so I select ten degrees of flap and push forward slightly on the control yoke. The ASI slowly reduces to 70kts at which point twenty degrees of flap is selected. Pushing further forward until the ASI remains steady I trim the aircraft to eliminate the pressure required. Now I run quickly through the pre-landing checks. Brakes OFF Hatches and Harnesses . . . Check. QFE . . . Set, Flaps . . .20°. Carb Heat . . . OUT, Mixture . . . RICH, Landing Light . . . ON.

It is now time to turn finals. Banking right, 15° bank angle, push nose down to maintain speed, runway centre-line coming up straight ahead. Level the wings. The approach angle lights situated on the left hand side at the start of the runway show four whites which means too high, This is fine for two reasons. First, should our engine fail, the propeller will probably stop and this will give a massive amount of extra drag. Consequently we need plenty of height to glide

in. Second, the runway is 1605 metres long and the taxiway to the apron is at the far end if the old cross runway has been well overshot. In our situation I prefer to approach high and land long. We only need four hundred metres to land in.

"Golf November Delta, finals to land".

"Golf November Delta, cleared to land, wind two six zero, five knots".

"Cleared to land, Golf November Delta".

You may now be wondering why we haven't announced our engine problem to the Air Traffic Controllers. Well, we had a brief discussion a few minutes back as to whether we should or shouldn't. Actually I brought the subject up as I was uncertain as to the correct procedure, if any, that applied to our circumstances. Aussie's

NAME: METARS (selected 'actual' reports)
Obtained from: Aberdeen Met Office
At: Aberdeen Airport

REMARKS: At this point we were ascertaining if flights further north than Aberdeen would be possible in the following day or so. The forecasts indicated that appalling conditions would prevail for at least another four days. In order to double-check the recent forecasts we applied for some METARs. (Also we wanted to see how things were further south and west.) EGPE (Inverness) isn't too bad in itself: a 10kt wind down runway 30; 1 OKTA of CB at 1,400ft and 3 OKTA at 2,200. However, a look at EGPB (Sumburgh) up in the Shetlands: 43kt winds! Further south EGPA (Kirkwall) on the Orkneys is giving 29kt with 2 OKTA CBs at 1,000ft. Thunderstorms are associated with CBs (Cumulonimbus) and we saw plenty of cells passing across Aberdeen complete with severe rain squalls and high localised winds. Many were combined cells. Also the unsettled squally conditions coming across the North Sea were reaching down to EGNJ (Humberside). Further enquiry revealed the west coast of Scotland to be far better off.

```
METAR   LABS57 151430
   LABS57 151430 MB
FF EGPDAAWX EGPDYFYB EGPDYMYX EGPDBHLX EGPHYMYX EGPFYMYX
151430 EGGYYBYB
   SAUK44 EGGY 151420
EGAC 35017KT 9999 4CU028 10/// 1007=
EGAE NIL=
EGNC NIL=
EGNJ 33013/27KT 9999 25RESH 2CU020 4SC025 06/02 1000=
EGNS 34014KT 9999 1CU025 5SC040 09/03 1006 NOSIG=
EGPA 01029KT 9999 27REGR 2CB010 3CU014 06/03 1004 INTER
   5CB010=
EGPB 02030/43KT 9999 1CB012 3CU015 07/M01 1001 NOSIG=
EGPE 33010KT 9999 25RESH 1CB014 3SC022 06/03 1006=
```

NAME: 48, 72, 96 and 120 hour forecasts
Obtained from: Met Briefing Office
At: Aberdeen Airport Control Tower

REMARKS: We requested these forecasts in order to ascertain the probable weather patterns affecting northern Scotland over the four days following 15 October. The area covered is very wide ranging from Canada and the Arctic land masses, the North Atlantic, Scandinavia, Europe and down to the North African coast. Of particular interest was the relatively large occluded front which was predicted to swing southerly. On the 48hr chart it is seen above Scotland, belling out from Iceland. On the 72hr chart it is predicted to reach Scotland. The southern sector of the front is shown as being a COLD front, becoming occluded along its northeastern side. It is this part which will, in all probability, continue to provide the strong multiple cells of large strong CBs that flowed across as we sat at Aberdeen. The 96hr chart predicts that the front will continue to turn and head east. Aberdeen and areas north will still be affected before clearing to the east as shown on the 120hr chart.

We sought local advice on this subject and the MET people at Aberdeen thought, from experience, that this would be the case. These conditions are frequently experienced towards the end of the year. In 1992, winter appeared to have arrived early and we were advised against continuing north in a small aircraft, especially as we intended to continue VFR.

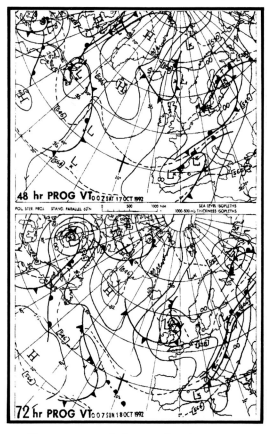

attitude was plain and practical, We still had oil pressure, the temperature was fine, and there were no indications that the engine was suffering. Even if we did bother ATC they couldn't do anything about it and we didn't actually have an emergency. Best to be aware and continue with caution.

Right then, here we are, established a bit high on the approach to Runway 24. We are five hundred metres from the runway threshold so I select 30° of flap, push the nose progressively forward to achieve 65 knots and re-trim. The wind is almost nonexistent and there is no turbulence. Damn good thing too. Taking things from the right-hand side gives me the impression that everything is back to front. I'm really working hard to maintain a reasonable approach. At fifteen feet above the runway I pull the power right back and flare the aircraft. With jerky rearward movements on the yoke the nose rises. Back a bit, forward a little, back a bit more.

We're down. Not bad, but not a greaser either. "Well done lad", announces Aussie over the intercom. I keep it straight with rudder and as the speed quickly decreases push the Carb Heat IN and retract the flaps. A quick glance at the oil pressure gauge shows it reading zero. I immediately give the engine a few more revs and a

small movement of the needle gives us a sign that we still have a small amount of pressure left.

"Golf November Delta, request taxi instructions".

"Golf November Delta, clear next left and continue across the main apron to the light aircraft park South of the tower".

"Golf November Delta, Roger, clear next left, and park South of Tower".

Picking up the 'Pooley's' Aussie checks the airport map. He tells me that we pass Hold Charlie, follow the Southern Taxiway, and route down to the far end of the apron. We taxi past several interesting aircraft including Vickers Viscounts and a Short Belfast which towers above our diminutive Cessna. On the South side of the main apron we see several rows of light aircraft. Getting closer I ask the Tower for parking directions.

"Golf November Delta, park on the third row next to the PA28".

I acknowledge and run beyond the third row to turn right then right again to taxi slowly up into position. I then apply the parking brakes and give the engine a burst of power. The oil

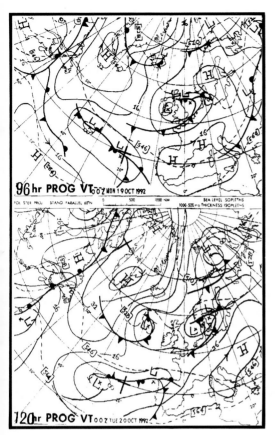

96 hr PROG VT 00Z MON 19 OCT 1992

POL STER PROJ. STAND PARALLEL 60°N   0   500   1000 NM   SEA LEVEL ISOPLETHS 1000-500 mb THICKNESS ISOPLETHS

120 hr PROG VT 00Z TUE 20 OCT 1992

pressure gauge doesn't even move. Pulling the Mixture knob fully lean stops the engine and the propeller thumps to a stop. "Looks like we just made it", I tell Aussie. He agrees. We tell the Tower we're shutting down and systematically turn all the electrics OFF. Aussie turns the Magnetos OFF, removes the key and places it on the coaming. Then we turn the Master Switch OFF. We remove our headsets and place them also on the coaming. Then we remove our kneepads and unfasten the harnesses. Checking that the aircraft is secure, we clamber out and walk across to the Control Point where we Book In. The place where this is done is identified by looking for a large black 'C' on a yellow background.

Entering the office we Book In and explain our mission. Aussie has sent a fax message to all the airport managers in advance of our initial departure, and, wherever possible, we intend to telephone prior to take-off. As you can easily imagine it is almost impossible to predict our arrival time more than a few hours before our take-off from the preceding airport due to weather and other considerations. Phone calls are made and we're invited to meet the airport manager. At the same time we inform the opera-

tions staff of our oil pressure problem but nothing can be done before the following morning.

The airport manager kindly grants us permission to photograph on the airport and issues the necessary clearances with security etc. Southend has few scheduled movements this evening so we retreat to the departure lounge for coffee and wait for nightfall when a 737 is expected. Aussie wants to take some night shots of the turnaround.

Ten minutes prior to arrival we make our way out through security and position ourselves on the apron. Aussie makes a quick check that he has all his equipment at hand. We both look out to the East to spot the approaching Boeing 737. It has had a long flight in from a Mediterranean island but the landing lights appear way out on the approach, spot on time.

The runway at Southend is not very long for this class of aircraft and the crew have an additional problem. Just before the runway there is a railway with overhead pylons. Therefore I am watching this landing with particular interest. The 737 comes in at a searing pace compared to smaller aircraft. The pilot drops it down far too quickly to my eye after the railway and it bounces back up in a most alarming way accompanied with the left wing dropping. It puts the wind up me just watching. The 737 crunches back down and reverse thrust is slammed on almost immediately. The whole affair reminds me of an aircraft carrier landing. A very brutal affair. I've experienced just such landings in 737s on much longer runways, as a passenger, with much kinder approaches. It serves to remind me just how strongly these aircraft are built.

The 737 taxis in and Aussie sets himself up to take photographs. I assist with the tripod and sorting out extra film. The speed with which all the service vehicles descend into position is most impressive. Passengers are disembarked and re-boarded in double quick time. Refuellers recharge the tanks and food and duty-free items are loaded on in what seems an instant. We are repositioning ourselves for different angles constantly but still seem to be behind the pace of the ground-crews. In what feels like five minutes but is probably in excess of thirty the 737 restarts its engines and prepares to taxi out, bound for the Mediterranean. With the photographic gear stowed safely by the terminal wall we stand aside and watch the departure. As the 737 lifts off in a crescendo of noise and fades into the night I feel a sense of emptiness as the silence encroaches.

We hijack an empty baggage trolley and make our way to the taxi rank.

3.
Southern England

It is now 09.00 Tuesday morning. I have just met the engineers who have removed the cowling and are taking the oil pressure relief valve out. They tell me that this is a common problem with these Continental engines because the valve is situated upstream of the oil filter. Upstream? That sounds like a naff design feature. The engineer holds out the valve for me to see. Sure enough there is a large piece of grit or carbon lodged on the valve seat. It must be nearly one millimetre in diameter. "That's enough to cause the problem", the engineer tells me. "What's more the seat has been scored as it has moved around. Where are you flying to?" I tell him we intend flying down to Cornwall and back via several airports. They advise against it unless the valve is changed.

It turns out that it may take some time to locate a valve and get it delivered. The sun is out now so Aussie sets about hiring another Cessna to take the aerial shots of the airport. He can get one in a couple of hours with an instructor so we take some ground shots on the apron. Since we are both pilots, it has been decided that we can move about the apron areas unsupervised. As a young lad and serious aircraft spotter I'd have given almost anything to be able to do this.

After further thought we decide to hire another aircraft. Armed with our 'little black books' of contact numbers we set about phoning around from the airport terminal. After thirty minutes of enquiring and pleading our cause, Shari Peyami, a director of Wycombe Air Centre, offers to provide a 172 at very reasonable rates. Not only that, he'll deliver the aircraft for a discounted figure too. It does help that I'm a member of his flying club.

We sit down with a cup of coffee and the ICAO half-mil chart of Southern England. We look at where we intend to go and where the aircraft will have to be returned to. It doesn't take long to see that the Wycombe Air Centre deal is by far the best. I ring Shari and accept his offer. It is now 12.30. How soon can he deliver and

can he remove the side window stays to enable clear photography? The stays are no problem he says and he will get the aircraft despatched immediately. We're to expect arrival around 14.00 to 14.30. This is great news. Maybe we can get Manston and Lydd covered before nightfall which, by looking up the table at the back of my Pooley's Flight Guide, was 18.51 on 25th September, four days before. Therefore we're looking at being on the ground before 18.40.

Aussie is up in a hired 152 taking the aerials and I set about planning the next leg. Special

Above:
G-OSND at Southend having the oil pressure problem investigated.

Above:
Engine run-up after cleaning the pressure release valve.

note is taken of the departure route from Runway 24 at Southend. All propeller aircraft must climb straight ahead to at least 600 feet AAL (above aerodrome level) before turning. If requiring a left turn, which we shall, we must maintain a track of 190° to the north bank of the Thames before resuming own navigation. From there to Manston will require a track of 110°. As there is still little wind this will also be our heading. Using this course will take us one mile (nautical of course!) south of danger area D138/35 OCNL/60 after six miles tracking 110°. This chart information tells me that D138/35 extends from the surface to 3500 feet being occasionally extended to 6000ft. I can refer to the notes at the bottom of the chart for extra information. Let's see. Well D138, D138A and D138B are not listed in the notable variation section, so I look down the general list. Here we are. The contact frequency is Southend Approach. That's simple enough, we'll be talking to them anyway.

Shortly before crossing south of D138 we'll be in the Cross-Channel CTA 1000′ to 3500′ALT. About four miles further on the CTA changes to 500′ to 6000′ALT until we reach the Manston Cross-Channel CTR which is surface to 6000′ALT. We will enter this ten miles out from Manston. When entering the Cross-Channel CTA we will transfer from Southend Approach to Kent Radar on 129.45. I make notes of all the en route frequencies on my photocopied kneepad log-sheet. The chart also tells me that 129.45 is the LARS frequency (Lower Airspace Radar Service). On top of this the FIS (Flight Information Service) is provided East of Airway A1 by London Information on 124.6. It sounds incredibly complex but, when you break it down bit by bit, it is really quite simple. Foreign pilot friends of mine extol the virtues of British

Air Traffic Control Services. They think our system is wonderful. Not only do we cover almost all the conceivable requirements of pilots flying in our airspace, ATC are both very professional and tolerant of private pilots. They don't expect, usually, first class radio telephony procedure, and certainly don't get it. Unlike commercial pilots who use their radios constantly, many private pilots only fly occasionally. In consequence our radio patter is often rusty. Despite this, my experience has been that ATC people are invariably incredibly helpful in allowing private pilots to do what they want to do, and go where they want to go, whenever possible. The only thing they appear to ask, quite reasonably, is talk to us. If you have an opportunity, listen in on a busy frequency in the summer. These ATC men and women barely get time to draw breath.

Turning the pages to Manston in my Flight Guide I notice they state PPR (Prior Permission Required). I ring them up, get a weather actual and I'm given my PPR number 1402. Runway in use is 11. Odd! They have an easterly wind whereas Southend has a westerly. In a straight line they're only 27/28nm apart.

In telling this story it is impossible to give a minute by minute, blow by blow, account of everything we do. I shall try to give you the interesting bits. Please bear in mind that we will be following a set procedure for each leg of the journey. The first part is to pre-plan the flight using all the information available and double-check wherever possible. We shall consult the ICAO chart plus our flight guides. We shall visit the briefing room at each airport and check the copious amounts of information contained within to see what applies to our intended flight. Then we shall telephone the airport we intend to land at and inform them of our intentions. We will then confirm vital points regarding procedure and ask for an 'actual' weather report. Having checked the aircraft we will load fuel to maximum capacity whenever our expected flight time needs more than 50% of the capacity in the tanks. Having completed preflight checks, taxi checks, pre-take-off checks we will regularly carry out in-flight checks covering the aircraft plus navigation and radio frequency checks. We have various checks when approaching our intended destination right the way down to the landing and taxi through to our parking spot. To cover every aspect of each fight would make repetitive, boring reading. Please bear this in mind.

It is just after 14.00 and we've informed the Tower at Southend that we expect a Wycombe Air Centre aircraft to arrive. Could they please direct it to park next to November Delta? No problem they tell us. A few minutes later, standing beside November Delta we spot a 172 on the approach sporting the distinctive colours of my flying club. It lands and starts taxiing across. Hello! There is another 172 from Wycombe Air Centre on the approach. We aren't expecting this. Nigel Huxtable has ferried our Cessna down to Southend. He is a engineer at Wycombe Air Centre. Wayne Spurge having heard of our plight has volunteered to fly the second 172 down to retrieve Nigel. Wayne is undertaking a BCPL (Basic Commercial Pilots Licence) course at Wycombe. It is a very generous gesture and we extend our sincere thanks.

I am delighted. Our aircraft is G-WACL. Charlie Lima is my favourite 172. It is the most basic 172 on the Wycombe fleet but I've spent many happy hours flying Charlie Lima and it has never let me down. It is a very simple reliable airplane. We load our luggage and equipment on board. Then we return to the Control Point and settle our account. David, the owner of November Delta has agreed to fly down to Southend and retrieve his aircraft. He is obviously very unhappy and extends his apologies for the way things have turned out. It is not his fault. These things do happen from time to time and he manfully accepts this.

As I'm currently checked out with Wycombe Air Centre I assume control of Charlie Lima. Aussie remarks on my change of attitude. I've checked the aircraft thoroughly and found no faults. I'm happy. One reason is that the 172, being a nominal four seater, can accept our load with ease. We are nowhere near the limits with regard to the weight and balance calculations. It is now 15.30. We're strapped in and have engine start clearance from Southend Tower on 127.725. We've checked the departure information on ATIS 121.8 (Automatic Terminal Information Services) and informed the Tower that we have copied this information. We are cleared to taxi through Hold Echo via the Eastern Taxiway to Hold Alpha for Runway Two Four. Having read back the clearance we proceed to Hold Alpha where we turn the aircraft into wind, such as it is, for our Power and Pre-Take-Off checks.

Checks complete, all systems A Okay, we tell Southend Tower we are ready for departure. G-WACW, the other 172 is just lining up and we hear their departure clearance. They need a right turn after 600' to take them North of the London TMA.

"Golf Charlie Lima, line up after the departing Cessna".

"Line up, Golf Charlie Lima".

The ATIS frequency provides all the informa-tion we require and takes the load off the ATC personnel in the Tower. We have the QNH, temperature, dewpoint, wind direction and strength. It is a beautiful afternoon, and I'm keen to get airborne. We line up on the runway centre line with 1600 metres of runway stretching ahead and give the instruments a quick final check.

"Golf Charlie Lima is cleared for Take-Off".

"Take-Off, Golf Charlie Lima".

I push the throttle fully open, not too quickly, and we start our run. With the power of the pro-peller backwash the rudder is effective almost immediately and I use it to keep straight. Easing back on the yoke takes the strain off the nose-wheel. At 55 knots I start easing back. At 60 I pull back and we're airborne. The speed quickly rises to 75 and I ease back still further to main-tain 75 in the climb and trim. The ground is falling away rapidly. I check the T's and P's All Good. Stealing a quick look at the terminal area below out to my left I then check the ASI, DI and Altimeter. I'm looking for 650 feet before turning as Southend is listed as 48ft AMSL (Above Mean Sea Level). Then I check the Turn and Slip indicator to make sure the aircraft is climbing 'in balance'. During the climb a bit of right rudder has to be applied continuously to counteract the torque effect and full power pro-peller backwash.

Whilst climbing on a track which is a continu-ation of the runway centreline Aussie calls the Tower as we pass through 500'. "Golf Charlie Lima is approaching six hundred feet to turn left heading one nine zero".

"Golf Charlie Lima, that's approved, contact Approach, one two eight decimal nine five".

"Changing to one two eight decimal nine five, Golf Charlie Lima, cheerio".

Aussie reaches across and changes the fre-quency by selecting Box Two. In a little while he will put Kent Radar on Box One, then, once we're with Kent Radar, Manston Approach will be dialled up on Box Two. We don't always bother with the two radios. On quieter legs we may well change frequency on the radio in use as it only takes a couple of seconds. Whoever changes the frequency, the second pilot will check that the correct numbers have been dialled in.

"Southend Approach, Golf Whiskey Alpha Charlie Lima is with you".

"Roger, Golf Charlie Lima, I have your details, continue on track of one nine zero degrees until past the North bank then resume own naviga-tion to Manston".

Aussie reads the message back. It barely takes an extra minute before the North bank of the Thames estuary slips by beneath. I bank over

Above:
On the approach to the massive runway at Manston, direction 110 degrees. The closest view gives an excellent impression of the width of the emergency strip.

left until our heading of 110° comes around on the DI. It is very smooth. We level out at 1300' QNH and I check the DI and Magnetic Compass are aligned. They are.

Aussie is sitting back, most relaxed, but I won't kid myself that his eyes aren't flitting about monitoring our progress. I've got into a frame of mind where I positively like this. I often fly with instructors because they keep you on your toes and are quick to arrest any bad habits that may start developing.

Aussie is doing the radio and generally keeping a eye on my flying and navigation. Levelled off in the cruise, RPM 2400, ASI 105 knots, I now have time to appreciate the view. The haze has reduced substantially and we can see clear across to the North Kent coast beyond Whitstable. We get a grand view of Southend pier and the seafront. The sun is glinting off the water looking South and the various boats look very picturesque. As we head into Manston we are initially given a downwind join for runway One One. We can hear that Manston has another aircraft in the circuit but request a straight in approach. We're told that this should be possible and to keep heading in. As we pass just North of Herne Bay we get a clearance for a straight in approach. The preceding aircraft has landed and taken-off again for another circuit.

The runway is seven miles ahead but we still can't see the aerodrome. We've worked out where it should appear and start slowly descending. At five miles out we spot the runway. My task now is to descend slowly and select the right point for getting the aircraft into landing configuration. I run through the pre-landing checks. At two miles out, passing through 800 feet I pull the power back, bleed off the speed and start bringing the flaps down in stages. The runway at Manston is immense. It is 2752 metres long and 61 metres wide. In addition there are vast concrete areas to either side. This is mainly because Manston was (still is?) a master diversion field for aircraft in serious trouble like undercarriage failure. They have arrester gear, normally derigged, positioned 457 metres from each end of Runway 11/29. For pilots used to flying from small aerodromes this size of runway does present various perceptual problems. Our aircraft is so small and slow it is quite tricky working out the correct height to pull the power back and flare for landing.

Most pilots, unfamiliar with the situation flare too soon and this can result in a very heavy landing if not corrected. I've landed at Manston before and know the problem. Also the Eastern Taxiway to the terminal area is two thirds of the way down the runway to the left. Being a bit cocky I arrest the descent at thirty feet, push the throttle forward and fly down the runway at 65 to 70 knots. Particular attention has to be paid to the airspeed because the runway, being so immense, gives the impression that you're flying much slower. If the speed is increased you will get a hell of a lot of float before landing. If careless the flap limiting speed could be exceeded. I can see the taxiway approaching and reduce power. Letting Charlie Lima descend I pull the nose back barely ten feet off. The speed settles down. Despite being very aware of the problem I'm concentrating hard to get the touchdown right. Back a bit, back a bit more, back even further. The nose is quite high now but we still haven't touched down. The stall warner sounds and I give a final yank on the yoke.

We're down. A little harder than intended but there's no bounce. I push the Carb-heat in and retract the flaps. Using the brakes I steer left to the taxiway. Again, having been into Manston before, I already know that you need to slow the taxiing speed before entering the taxiway proper because it goes downhill after the concrete apron is passed. Ever vigilant the ATCO (Air Traffic Control Officer) gives us a warning. Light aircraft park on a grass area West of the main apron. As we park a Boeing 707 starts moving up the taxiway. Aussie is justifiably worried. If it turns on the taxiway we are liable to be blown away in the blast. Aussie sets the control surfaces to expect a blast from the right rear quarter. We both watch the Boeing taxi straight ahead, Whew! no problem. Obviously we, unlike the other light aircraft nearby have not been tied down.

There are certain airports that have evolved into centres for various types of aircraft, mostly types which are out of production and common usage. For example, if you want to see a Vickers Viscount go to Southend. If you want to see a Boeing 707 go to Manston. We are surrounded by these magnificent Boeings. In their heyday they brought about a new era in jet travel. Immensely strong, and dependable, the 707 was the classic aircraft that started the popular jet transport age. As a lad, I clearly remember spending hours by the perimeter fence at Heathrow awaiting the first arrival of a 707 in new airline colours. On the apron at Manston we see a classic combination. A Boeing 707 parked in front of an Ilyushin Il-76. I had flown into Le Touquet at the beginning of August and been confronted with two Il-76's towering over everything on the apron in front of the tower. What a sight! These ex-USSR aircraft now compete for freight work around the world. A clear sign of the fast changing times we are living in.

Whilst I'm telephoning ahead to Lydd and Shoreham and making route and frequency notes, Aussie has been invited on board the Il-76 to have a looksee round the crew compartments. Lucky devil!

Time is getting on. I'm looking to depart Manston by 17.00. I've phoned the tower asking for a clearance to fly a tight right-hand circuit in order to photograph the airfield and this has been provisionally granted subject to traffic considerations. The 707 that taxied past so close is doing some kind of training exercise and, having completed the approach, climbs out, lightly loaded, at a spectacular angle of climb. I find this demonstration of what these old Boeings are capable of very exciting. Having got things under control we strap ourselves back into Charlie Lima at 17.05. Completing the checks we get start-up clearance at 17.10 and taxi out towards Runway 11/29. At the top of the taxiway I find a suitable area for our Power and Pre-Take-Off checks.

Having announced 'Ready for departure' we are cleared to line up on Runway One One. Due to the length of this runway we have no need to back-track. We simply taxi out to the centre-line and turn towards the East. We get our take-off clearance and accelerate down the runway. Well before the end I pull back and we climb out. I'm looking to achieve the best angle of climb this time. The check list gives this as 55 knots but I settle for 60. Climbing steeply we get a clearance for a close right-hand circuit. With such slow speed I delay the turn until we've exceeded 800 feet. Then, banking cautiously at ten degrees we come around to face just South of the runway still climbing. Manston is so large we need 1500 feet to get satisfactory shots. Aussie has his window wide open and I relish this opportunity to fly precisely, slow and safe. With the window open two things happen. I need to put right rudder on to counteract drag and, I definitely didn't expect this, need to trim nose down. With the window open below the wing we are getting increased lift. Very odd!

One pass is all we need. Aussie is quite happy with the results and I set course to the South-West. Tracking towards the coast we spot the Channel Tunnel Terminal at Folkestone. We've just been handed over to Lydd Approach on 120.70. Aussie requests clearance to orbit West of Folkestone to take photographs and this is immediately forthcoming. We fly back and forth a couple of times to get the results. We don't intend to land at Lydd. We just want to shoot the approach and take photographs. We get clearance from Lydd Approach to complete this project. Now we have a problem. Lydd is

Above:
The terminal and main apron at Lydd, seen as we climb out from Runway 22.

renowned for being the invisible airport. I have flown past it before and not seen the runway or airfield until East abeam Runway 22. This evening we are cleared for Runway 22 and the sun is right in our eyes. Checking our position to right and left as best we can, we still approach 500 feet too high. I pull the power back and push the nose down. Even at such a steep angle we're probably not going to get a result.

We fly down the runway at Lydd at 150 feet, ten degrees of flap, 75 knots on the ASI. The low sun is blinding us through the windscreen even wearing sunglasses. Visibility to either side is excellent, however, so I constantly monitor my flight instrument panel and look out away from sun. At the end of the runway I push the throttle fully open, retract the flaps and climb out. This is proving to be a great day. I'm in my element here and loving every minute of it.

At eight hundred feet I level Charlie Lima and select a heading for Brighton. Measuring off the

chart we reckon this to be 255°. Navigation is simplicity itself and we settle back to enjoy a low level flight. We pass by Rye, Hastings, Bexhill and Eastbourne. We circle overhead Herstmonceaux Observatory for photographs. This really is what flying in small aeroplanes is all about as far as I'm concerned and I can tell that Aussie is very enthusiastic too. Approaching the South Downs we climb a bit higher then descend north of Newhaven to fly low (but legal) over Peacehaven until we're over the sea. The scenery we've just passed is breathtaking in the evening light. To fly like this is a great privilege, worth all the expense and countless hours studying. When you have a prize like this the price is irrelevant. We fly past Brighton close to the seafront. The marina and piers slide past on our right. Aussie is already talking to Shoreham on 123.15, the approach frequency and we are passed over to the tower. We've been cleared for a left base approach to Runway 21, QFE 1015. It is time to get serious. The Flight Guide is out and we re-check our approach course to the runway. Shoreham is a busy aerodrome and we monitor other radio calls to get a precise mental picture of the position of other traffic in the area. As we're cleared left base it is essential we make our turn inland at the correct point. If we overshoot this point I will be too close to the end of the runway and may conflict with downwind traffic. Therefore Aussie gives the tower very precise position reports.

Runway 21/03 is the only 'hard' runway at Shoreham. They have three. 07/25 is the main grass runway being 909 by 50 metres. In very high winds they have 13/31 which is 425 by 30 metres. Very short! Runway 21/03 is 824 by 18 metres and is typical of runways I'm used to. I did most of my training at Wycombe Air Park and their only 'hard' runway is 07/25 which is

Below:
The coastline just south of Shoreham aerodrome looking east toward Brighton. CL on left base for Runway 21.

Below:
The author and Charlie Lima by Shoreham Terminal.

732 by 23 metres. 23 metres can be considered as pretty thin. Shoreham is longer but only 18 metres wide. From a left base position half a mile out and six or seven hundred feet high it looks little wider than a railway line. I'm pretty fortunate this evening because the wind is calm and almost in line with the runway. I decide to maximise Aussie's opportunity to get a shot of the approach by staying high on left base and using a glide approach which entails a very nose down attitude when coupled with 40° of flap. The light is very poor at the moment and I can't hold out much hope photographically. Even so Aussie decides to give it a go.

Managing to achieve a workmanlike touchdown, (more luck than judgement?), we fast taxi to a departure point from the 'active' which is grass. Traversing the grass runaway 07/25 we reach a hard taxiway and turn left. Shoreham Tower gives us parking instructions for a spot on the grass to the east of the main apron. Slotting into line and with shutdown checks complete we undo our harness and walk across to the Control Point. Shoreham is the home of the PFA (Popular Flying Association) and I make a quip to the effect that Shoreham is a base for 'real' pilots. The bar is barely thirty metres from the Control Point. Even able bodied pilots should be able to cover this distance without assistance. The men manning the Control Point couldn't be more helpful. We require lodgings for the night without incurring great expense. They know just the number to ring. There is a place in Lancing, prepared not only to accept pilots but also willing to come out and fetch us. And they will drive us back to the aerodrome in the morning.

Having 'Booked In', we secure Charlie Lima for the night and transfer our baggage to the terminal building. This is a wonderful example of 1930s architecture as applied to airports. When our landlady arrives Aussie is lying on his back in the middle of the foyer of the terminal building, flash equipped, endeavouring to get a 'shot' of the domed roof painted with a couple of circling aircraft. Immediately she decides we are suitable visitors – Aussie on the floor and me sitting nearby clutching the remains of a pint of lager and laughing. We are driven 'home' and find we're in a beautiful cottage with oak beams on the ceiling and are accorded a most convivial welcome.

Getting back to the flying, I now want to explain some of the low flying rules (principally as they apply to single-engined, fixed wing aircraft). Without copying the entire regulations it will serve as a reminder of how difficult it is, for the pilot already in flight, to interpret. We can

Above:
Charlie Lima and the traditional style of the Shoreham main building.

start with the 500 foot rule. An aircraft must not fly closer than 500 feet to any person, vessel, vehicle or structure. This can be envisaged as a sphere surrounding the aircraft. Helicopters have other considerations. There is a general requirement of all pilots, no matter what their machine is, to land clear in the event of engine failure. Thereafter there is the consideration of flight over congested areas. An aircraft, other than a helicopter, must not fly over a congested area below a height sufficient to allow it to land clear of the area and without danger to people or property if an engine fails.

The next part of the regulation states that you must not fly less than 1500 feet above the highest fixed object within 2000 feet of the aircraft. There are also rules about flying near large open-air gatherings. If more than 1000 people are gathered you may not fly within 3000 feet without written permission from the CAA and the organisers. These are only a few of a collection of very specific requirements. They can be quite tricky to judge as you fly along at over 100 mph so, as I've said before, constant vigilance is required. If in doubt, I increase the margin substantially because contraventions are dealt with very severely. The best defence is to be able to prove that contravention was unwitting and couldn't reasonably have been foreseen.

No doubt you are now wondering how the devil we get off the ground in the first place let alone back down? We have exceptions for this of course but there are still pitfalls to be avoided. For example, if an ATC clearance is granted for a flight over a city centre at, say, 1000 feet, the pilot of a single-engined aircraft should not accept it.

Different rules apply to multi-engined aircraft. That is why you can regularly spot twin-engined aircraft flying quite low over towns and cities. Sometimes they might be taking photographs but there's a better chance they'll be providing traffic information for a radio station. Or alternatively they may simply be taking advantage of their multi-engine status to transit busy airspace by flying below approach and departure routes surrounding a major airport. Lucky aren't they?

14.00 hrs. Wednesday afternoon. Shoreham. We got up this morning to find a glorious day. Sunshine and clear skies. Aussie took the opportunity to get some decent snaps and we also made an interesting visit to the control tower when we explained our intentions after take-off to photograph both overhead Lancing and around the aerodrome.

The ATCOs couldn't see any problems for us and as expected the clearance was subject to traffic conditions. We had intended to depart at 11.00 and Charlie Lima was fully fuelled well before. I had checked the chart and flight guide for restrictions and frequencies. Southampton, like Southend was also Class 'D' controlled airspace. I had thought of routing direct to the Bishops Waltham or Botley VRP but decided to fly along the coast, over the sea, to Littlehampton then turn inland passing south of Arundel and Chichester. Goodwood aerodrome is north of Chichester so I'd made a note of their approach frequency 122.45. Goodwood should be able to tell us if gliding was taking place at Thorney Island as we would pass close by. Then there is Danger Area DO30/10 which covers a large part of the Solent to the south and east of Portsmouth harbour. The northern extremity is over the town and harbour of Southsea. We would be flying above according to plan. Next, we will plan to fly across the military aerodrome of Lee-on-Solent (Fleetlands) which unusually doesn't have its own MATZ (Military Aerodrome Traffic Zone). A typical MATZ will have a diameter of 10 nautical miles and extend up to 3000ft. It will also have a 'panhandle' sticking out to one side, along the main runway's extended centre-line, 4 nm wide and extending from 1000ft to 3000ft. I said typical because there are variations. The combined MATZ at Boscombe Down/Middle Wallop is a good example. As Fleetlands is very close to Southampton, and as Goodwood will probably hand us over to Southampton, it will probably be they who will advise whether or not we should have a little natter before passing overhead. I'd made a note, Lee-on-Solent Tower 135.70. Odd, no approach frequency. Probably not a busy place. Over Calshot where a wartime Short Sunderland flying boat is based (not many of those old birds around) and up Southampton Water past Fawley to the airport. That was my plan, with stacks of snap potential there. I checked the weather and found that an appalling bad weather front was making its way eastward and it was due to arrive just after 11.00 hrs local. It did and it was. Cloudbase maybe 500 feet or less and torrential rain.

We had sat in the restaurant, enjoying a very nice lunch, watching the rain pour down and not enjoying that. At 13.30 as quickly as it had arrived, it cleared up with brilliant sunshine gleaming off the dripping aircraft. It was too good to miss so we dashed around getting a few more 'effect' shots before returning to the Briefing Point for TAFs and METARs for Southampton and Bournemouth. Great, both are CAVOK. A TAF is an aerodrome forecast usually issued for a nine hour period. A METAR is a routine aerodrome weather report compiled on the hour and half hour. CAVOK means visibility 10 km or more, no cloud below 5000 ft AAL (Above Aerodrome Level) or below the minimum sector altitude whichever is higher and no Cumulonimbus. No precipitation reaching the ground, no thunderstorms, no shallow fog or low drifting snow. It doesn't mean clear skies and it doesn't indicate the wind. It is easy to mistake CAVOK

Below:
Heading west from Shoreham. Note the glare from the haze out to sea.

Above:
Overhead Southampton docks with the runway just visible in the distance in the top centre of the photograph.

Above:
Approaching Runway 20 to land at Southampton. Salt deposits on the windscreen can be seen following the coastal flight.

for great flying conditions even though this is usually the case. We return to our 172, give her another preflight check, strap in, start the engine, switch the radios, NAV and transponder to standby and make our call.

"Shoreham Tower, good afternoon, Golf Whiskey Alpha Charlie Lima, request preflight radio and taxi".

"Golf Charlie Lima, readability five, taxi to holding point for runway two one, left hand, QNH 1015".

"Golf Charlie Lima, Roger, taxi to holding point, two one left hand, one zero one five".

We taxi out doing our Taxi Checks, find the holding point and turn into wind, nosewheel centred for the Power Checks followed by the Pre-Take-Off Checks. Everything is functioning normally and controls, instruments and radio gear are all set up. We set 7000 on the transponder.

"Golf Charlie Lima is ready for departure".

"Golf Charlie Lima, line up after landing Cessna, surface wind two seven zero, fifteen knots".

We have spotted the inbound Cessna turning finals and make another call. "Shoreham Tower, Golf Charlie Lima would like a normal circuit with a right-hand climb out after the approach to pass south of Lancing at five hundred feet, then climb to fifteen hundred feet to position south of the field".

"That is approved Golf Charlie Lima, no conflicting traffic, call downwind initially".

"Golf Charlie Lima, Roger, call downwind".

The incoming Cessna calls finals to land. As he slows down after a successful crosswind landing we taxi out and line-up on the centreline. For a crosswind take-off I shall push the yoke forward and right for into-wind aileron. Having reached 60 knots I will pull the yoke

back smartly to unstick quickly and sort out the climb once airborne. We're off. I level the wings a bit, right hand down slightly and use the rudder to stay straight. Then I level the wings with a bit more rudder applied hoping to stay on the extended centreline from the runway. The brisk wind gives us a noticeable amount of drift. The closer to the ground the more evident drift becomes. Fixed wing circuits are flown at 1100 feet. At six hundred feet I bank onto a heading of 300°. As the altimeter passes 1000ft I turn left onto a heading of 045° which should give us a track of 030° parallel to the runway. When directly opposite the runway we call downwind and do the normal checks even though we don't intend actually to land. The Tower tells us to proceed as planned so I stay very high on base leg. Slowing the airspeed to 70 knots, at 800 feet I pull the power right back, select full flap of 40° and turn left pushing the nose down very steeply. This has the advantage of getting the nose out of the way to provide a better view for

Below:
Safely on the centre line of Runway 20.

36

photographing the runway. At 200 feet I push the throttle fully forward, carb-heat IN, pull the nose up, retract 10° of flap, check we have a positive rate of climb and retract the flaps in 10° stages. It is demanding because a lot is happening quickly, but it's great fun.

We climb out turning right towards Lancing and pass by close to the south. This is a nice touch. The people we'd stayed with were so hospitable that we offered, over breakfast, itself a memorable feast, to take an aerial view if the sun was out. Climbing away, circling Lancing to the north we have a particularly pleasing view of the college. Aussie calls the Tower and we get clearance to climb to 1500ft to shoot the aerodrome from the southern edge. We circle round for another go then depart to the west over the sea. Our flight is going as planned and we admire the unfolding vista. Aussie handles the radio and I do the stick and rudder bit. Not that I have much to do. The harbours leading to and past Portsmouth look superb. I have a notion to stay circling till our fuel runs low but we press on. Overhead Calshot we spot the Sunderland very white and imposing sitting at the top of the slipway. We are only on our second day and already I know I'm running out of superlatives. Just imagine the view, flying at 1700ft up Southampton Water, the city and docks spread before us. The radio is very quiet. Why aren't more people committing aviation? We don't get many days as clear as this. Approaching the airport we get an unusual clearance It is so quiet we have a choice of circuit direction. Our choice! Aussie asks for a right-hand circuit as runway 20 is in use and he will have a splendid opportunity to get the field aerial photographs from his seat. I stay high and passing West abeam the terminal start our descent. The runway is 1723 metres long and 37 wide. There is, however, a brisk crosswind verging on the approved limit for our aircraft.

We turn finals and receive clearance to land. Aussie advises me to stay high on the approach as turbulence is usually generated from the sheds in the railway marshalling yard just before the runway. I crab down the approach path, into-wind wing down, compensating with left rudder. This is known as crossed-controls. It takes some thinking about but is a very effective way of dealing with crosswinds.

Low over the runway I prepare for the flare while the wind is giving me problems with gusts and eddies. I juggle the controls faster than a fiddler's elbow but I'm not getting on top of the job. We come down the last couple of feet with a bit of a thump. No bounce. Good. Well, it's far from my best cross-wind landing but I'm not ashamed

of it either. Even the professionals struggle to get their touchdowns right. I've had a few rough landings when on commercial flights around Europe. I apologise to Aussie and he says it was fine. When flying commercially, he says, you soon get a thicker hide. You can't win 'em all. A good landing is one you walk away from. I've heard it before but feel a lot better. We're given directions to park amongst the private aircraft on the apron north of the tower. It is a poor time of day for Aussie. There isn't much on the apron to photograph. He decides we'll have a quick turn-round and make tracks for Bournemouth. While he books in, makes his introductions and

Below:
Aerial view of Bournemouth airport looking south to the coast.

Bottom:
On base leg at Bournemouth for Runway 26.

arranges permission to work on the apron, I set about checking Charlie Lima and planning the short flight to Bournemouth.

We departed Shoreham at 14.50 and landed Southampton at 15.50. I'm looking to get away on our 5th leg by 16.30 local. This isn't much time so we're both busy. Incidentally, the reason I give the time in 'local' is because in aviation it is normal to work in UTC (Co-ordinated Universal Time) which was formerly GMT (Greenwich Mean Time) which was referred to as Zulu Time (Zone Time). Aircraft operating internationally obviously cross many time zones. This doesn't apply to us so I'll use local time, the time you would see on your watch if you spotted us making our way round the country. Aussie clambers in at 16.25 and I give him the en route frequencies and ATIS information. This means that Aussie is working very hard and I'm getting the best part of the deal just having to fly the aircraft. We haven't got time to arrange things in a fairer fashion.

It may easily be supposed that the pilot, stick and rudder mover, has the big job when flying. I used to think so. The reality is that navigation and radio (proper and intelligent use of) often becomes the more demanding part of the job in hand. When learning to fly my instructors and instruction manuals often made a particular point of emphasising that, whatever else is happening, flying the aircraft safely and correctly is the number one priority. Then attend to navigation and radio etc. They are absolutely right. Of course, real life does tend to interfere. When flying passengers on a pleasure trip as sole 'Pilot in Command', the combination can make for very high work loads at specific times. This is when paying for first class instruction pays dividends. I haven't yet had a problem with getting my priorities right, but, I won't take credit for this. I've been very fortunate and have flown with some terrific instructors.

I feel we are beginning to get a crew together here. I know very well that the work-load will swing quite wide at times. In this case, having concentrated on the photographic aspects, Aussie has to adjust instantaneously to commanding the radio and flight-director role. We get engine-start and taxi for Hold Two Zero. This is half way down the runway. Although we have stacks of room we back-track three hundred metres before turning 180° for line-up. There is a hill beyond the end of the runway and we want to be well clear of it. Having received clearance to take off, just as at Shoreham I use the cross-wind technique. It works well and we set course for Bournemouth.

Bournemouth and Southampton airports are interesting because they have their own CTRs combined into a single CTA which is 1500ft ALT to FL55 on frequency 120.55. The distance apart is only 22nm and our track is 244° magnetic. Allowing for a small degree of drift we agree that 245° should set us up well for a 2000ft orbit from the south if clearance is obtained. We pass just north of Lyndhurst and are passed from Southampton to Bournemouth Approach on 119.625. Their QFE is 1015 and we're cleared to orbit at 2000ft. I know Bournemouth well, having spent a couple of years there in my misspent youth. In fact my family lived nearby and my sister has since moved back. It looks very different now, commencing to circle overhead the airport, which is situated comfortably to the north of the urban conglomeration that extends from Poole in the west to Christchurch in the east without so much as a 'by-your-leave'. The light is beginning to fade so Aussie decides that one semicircular pass is enough. He calls downwind high for 26 (the active), announces we've completed our task, and we get a clearance to land. This is interesting. Charlie Lima has the 40° flap facility, which many 172 models don't have, being restricted to 30°. The wind has dropped as might be expected in the early evening and is almost straight down the runway. I decide to commence a glide-approach from 2000ft using the full flap range.

Warming the engine at five hundred feet intervals gives a lot of back pressure on the yoke as power is applied. It is working out well. Towards the end, because of the amazing nose-down attitude. I need some power to take us over the 'piano-keys', the 'Zebra-Crossing' marked at the start of each runway. The touchdown is nice and we've slowed down sufficiently to taxi left via Hold Echo which is not very far down runway 26/08, a long 1838 x 46 metre. Our landing run is barely 250 metres. Carb-heat IN, flaps RETRACT, strobes OFF, we concentrate on finding our way to the parking area, West Apron, which is south of the Tower. Small aeroplanes are low and finding the way can be quite tricky at large airports.

We're arrived to find Bournemouth virtually deserted. A lone Herald sits forlorn and empty. Walking across the large apron we make enquiries. Are there any movements scheduled to arrive soon? Well, there's a couple after dark. You might think that we could have planned our trip better but, after trying the exercise a couple of weeks before it soon became clear that there will be so many variables especially with the weather and light that we would just have to take our chances. Of course, we couldn't possibly foresee if or when technical problems might arise. For this book it didn't matter and in fact quiet periods assist our purpose. For Aussie it is proving rather difficult. Airports look better when they are full of activity. He is having to apply all his creative ingenuity to get any worthwhile shots at all! We decide to take advantage of the weather and fly down to Exeter before nightfall.

I have just rung my sister, and, having found her at home, suggest that she takes her children down the road to the cliff top at Alum Chine where we would give them a flypast. Returning to Charlie Lima we run through the normal checks, start-up and taxi out to Hold Golf at the end of runway 26. The circuit is right-hand but we get cleared for a left hand turn after take-off. QFE 1015/QNH 1017. I open my check-list to confirm the Best Rate of climb speed. It is 65 knots which also happens to be the Normal climb speed recommended. The 172 is a very straightforward aircraft. For take-off and landing, if in doubt use 65 knots and this speed will be fine for most operations. For extreme short-field work 55 knots is recommended. The close QFE/QNH figures show that Bournemouth airport is built on low land. The flight guide gives 36ft AMSL. I want to get as close to 1500 feet as possible before flying over the built-up area. Therefore, after lifting off, I continue climbing out on the runway heading. The surface wind is 15 knots so our ground speed is 50 knots. There is little sensation of speed. At eight hundred feet I bank left and head 180°, due South.

Right. We're almost spot-on. I have recognised Alum Chine and Aussie gives Bournemouth Approach a call. We ask for one orbit at 1500ft then descent to 500ft over the sea departing West, climbing to 1200ft passing Sandbanks and Wareham. This is approved. Circling I point out the family house. Large trees nearby put the house in shadow. Wouldn't you know it? Coming around full circle, carb-heat OUT, throttle pulled back I shove the nose down until VNO is reached. Most ASIs have colour-coded segments marked round the rim of the dial. White extends from VSO which is Stall Speed (full flap) to VFE Maximum Flaps Extended Speed. Overlapping this is a green sector which shows VSI Stall Speed Clean (no flaps) to VNO Normal Operating Limit Speed. Then the green turns to yellow which goes round to VNE Never Exceed Speed where a red block reinforces the message. It is advisable not to enter the yellow segment unless the air is calm and smooth. VNO on Charlie Lima is 127 knots. Maximum manoeuvering speed is 104 knots. Notice the distinction. The lower manoeuvering speed indicates the limits of full control deflection. Diving down I aim to pull out just opposite Alum Chine. Aussie thinks it would be a nice touch to open the window and wave. Therefore I keep the power right back and ease the dive to slow down. At 110 knots Aussie opens the window and waves his arms out in the airstream. Three tiny figures can be seen waving back, the two smaller figures going totally bananas. Carb-heat IN, full power applied to roar away, climb and waggle the wings vigorously as a departing salute. Climbing out we absorb the view. It is enthralling. The low autumnal sun bathes the harbour, island and the Purbeck hills with an orange sheen. Thousands of tiny boats speckle the water. We spot the large Truckline ferry berthed near Poole town centre. Wareham, astride the rivers Piddle and Frome eases past. I want to cross the coast near Kimmeridge Bay to get a first class look at Lulworth Cove and Durdle Door which will be superb in the setting sun. But there is work to be done.

We are fast approaching the Portland AIAA (Area of Intense Aerial Activity) with a gaggle of Danger Zones plus the Portland MATZ. Bournemouth Approach think Portland is closed and suggest we call them on 124.15 the LARS (Lower Airspace Radar Service) frequency. We do this but there is no response. We call again. This time another light aircraft out of Compton Abbas and approaching Weymouth gives us his details and intentions and confirms that Portland is closed. This is expected at this time of day. Operating hours vary but the LARS controllers offer an invaluable service. Based at military aerodromes they provide traffic separations and navigation assistance for civil aircraft across large areas of the UK. Bidding our fellow aviators a friendly farewell Aussie dials up the Flight Information Service on 124.75 so they can monitor our progress towards Exeter which we calculate by a simple rule-of-thumb method, distance divided by speed plus a bit for headwind, giving, EAT (Expected Approach Time) 19.45 local.

We are now over the sea, ticking off the points of particular interest. We fly past Weymouth with the distinctive Isle of Portland rising dramatically beyond. It's not really an island being connected to the mainland by a thin link of rocks and gravel upon which the road runs. The unusual Chesil Beach comes clearly into view ahead and left so I start looking out for the famous swan haven at Abbotsbury. The swans look so small I initially mistake them for gulls. The Dorset coastline is renowned for its beauty whether seen from land, sea or air and this evening puts on a gala performance. Aussie

Above:
Overhead Poole harbour, superb in the evening light.

Below:
Sunset along the Dorset coast, just beautiful.

Bottom:
Charlie Lima on the grass at Exeter.

dials up 337.0 to find the Exeter NDB (Non-directional Radio Beacon) which is 4.1nm from the threshold of Runway 26, which we expect to get. The sun is very low now and makes navigation inland tricky as it pierces our windscreen.

The NDB needle swings round and gives us a heading which comes close to our predicted course ruling off the chart. Aussie has flown for years into Exeter and suggests that I practice using the ILS (Instrument Landing System). Why not? We call Exeter Approach having said cheerio to the FIS controller and get the QFE with a direct approach for runway 26. We're coming up to the NDB so Aussie sets up the ILS on 109.90. The needles start swinging into place. What I need to remember is that the aircraft has to be flown towards the bar. If the vertical bar is right of centre you steer right until it centres. If the horizontal bar is low you descend. Having set up the approach, power setting controls height. This is all highly simplified but it gives an idea of the basics. Getting closer I use the rudder for slight directional changes. I'm cheating of course and keep looking out of the windscreen to judge the situation visually. At half a mile out I check the PAPIS. These are lights placed close to the near end of the runway on the left side. PAPIS stands for Precision Approach Path Indicating System. They are ingenious devices comprising lights placed in tubes set at varying angles. The pilot sees four lights placed in a line horizontally. If too high four white lights show. If too low four red lights show. When just right two reds and two whites show. The angle of the approach is shown in our Pooley's Flight Guide. For instance, the PAPIS for 26 are set at 3.5°. If we were approaching from the other end the PAPIS, pronounced Papee, is set at 3°. Obstacle and terrain clearance are major consideration in setting this angle. We've got two reds and two whites. Disregarding the ILS the approach is continued visually. Runway 26 is a whopping 2083 metres by 46 wide. Wycombe Air Park where I did most of my training measures a diminutive 735 x 23 metres for comparison. Judging the right height to flare is difficult because of the sun and the runway surface is hard to make out. Happily I get it just about right and we settle gently. We then receive instructions to depart via the grass taxiway.

This would lead us towards the grass parking area where we're instructed to stop for the night. The taxiway leads directly south from the intersection of runways 08/26 and 13/31 so it should be easy to find but we can't see it. I point the nose towards where it should be and we just spot it as we taxi towards the edge of the runway. Having completed the shutdown I notice something familiar about the Grumman AA5B Tiger next to us. The registration is G-BLLT. Reaching back into my flight case, to extract my log book, I find the entry I'm looking for. I show it to Aussie. "There you are, Lima Lima Tango, I flew it from Dunkeswell doing a bit of type conversion in December 1990." Dunkeswell is situated 10nm north-west of Exeter and is notable for its height above sea level, 850 feet!

With Charlie Lima secured we make our way over to the terminal to book in. Exeter was a base for Aussie and he sets about enquiring after old friends. It is a sign of the times. So many people have left and moved on in the last couple of years that the news is a bit depressing. We check with ATC to see if any notable movements are expected soon. They might provide fodder for night shots. There aren't any known but we fall into conversation with two very enterprising aviators also in the office. Trevor Loveday and Don Bowtell have flown an Auster J/1 Autocrat G-AIBX out of Gransden near St Neots to tour the grass strips of Southern England. This makes an interesting parallel to our round of the airports. We've been operating at the two extremes so to speak. Later on, having found accommodation nearby, we meet for dinner and swop tales. They have had some real adventures. For example they landed in one field only to discover they should have used the field next door. The point was that their choice was a much better field! On another site the runway passed through a gap in a stone wall. By comparison to the Auster our simple Cessna seemed positively high-tech.

The elderly Auster could fly rings around our Cessna when it comes to the nitty-gritty of rough grass strip operation as Trevor is quick to point out. In fact it is an ideal machine for this work and can out-perform many later STOL types hailed as being state-of-the-art. This is very interesting. Alan Bramson, the well known aviation writer wrote an article a little while ago comparing old British aircraft of the thirties with post-war and recent American types. The prop may have to be swung to get the donkey going but usually the oldies out-paced their modern rivals in ranges, rate of climb, cruise speed etc. Is this progress? I felt like returning to Charlie Lima to give a consoling pat on the cowling.

08.00 Thursday 1st October. We have fog. Not only that but after it clears the weather coming in from the west stays pretty awful. Initially we get a bright spell, though the airport apron is almost empty. Apart from a bright red RAF Hawk, Aussie has to try to make a Jersey European Short 360 look glamorous. These ubiqui-

Above:
Low cloud on the hills en route Exeter-Plymouth.

tous flying sheds provide the backbone of feeder-liner work in the UK. By following Aussie around and watching his camera angles I find that it is possible to enhance this buxom beastie. As someone once said, they'll look great when the packing case is removed.

We now settle into a quiet period of mutual dejection. The front is coming through and we've just got actuals from Culdrose, Lands End and St Marys on the Isles of Scilly. It couldn't possibly be worse for VFR flight. Heavy rain beneath a cloud base of 2-400 feet containing embedded CBs (cumulonimbus) which spell out the possibility of thunder-storms. Winds are gusting up to 25 knots. What to do? Shall we sit it out or give up and try for Cardiff or Bristol? We can still make Plymouth but the low, dull eight oktas cloud cover with intermittent rain spells a dismal prospect.

Seeing that we've got little better to do I shall tell you about OKTAs. The amount of cloud in the sky is usually measured in eighths or OKTA. When consulting a Met Forecast you will find four categories of cloud coverage and these are reduced to three letter designations. Therefore SKC = 0 OKTAs (Sky Clear). SCT = 1-4 OKTAs (SCaTtered). BKN = 5-7 OKTAs (BroKeN) and OVC, you guessed it, 8 OKTAs (OVerCast). When studying Meteorology for my PPL I found the subject fluctuated maddeningly between items of keen interest and complete boredom. For pilots, getting the Met right can literally mean the difference between life and death. It is a stark reality that weather has killed and will kill again. I don't trust my judgement even now when the picture turns from rosy to murky and prefer to consult a higher authority. Local knowledge often provides the best key to safe flying as even a good general forecast can hide unpleasant surprises. This is especially true for non-instrument rated nerks like me.

It is now 13.00 and we are still flaying our intellects willing a decision to be born. We have the same scenario further west but a flight down to Plymouth is still feasible. I spot a bright area approaching from the south-west and suggest, (read insist), that we take a chance and get airborne to shoot the field. Aussie wearily agrees. Charlie Lima has been fuelled and fettled and I'm eager to do something. We taxi out to the holding point and find our way barred by two Cessna 152s training student pilots, going methodically and very slowly through their checks. On top of this a RAF C130 Hercules picks this time to practice ILS approaches. Frustration! The last of the bright patch slides past as we get clearance to line up. Aussie calls mission abandoned and we return to the grass parking area.

There is an expression that Sir John Harvey-Jones uses on occasion which really appeals to me and it applies right now. We have to get our ducks in a row. Both our instincts tell us to abort and return to Bristol but it's not that easy. We're under obligation to cover UK airports and, although small, both Lands End and St Marys are significant because they are on an extremity. Personally, I want to go there. Professionally, Aussie want to go there. The main problem lies in interpreting the Atlantic forecasts. At this time we see a series of fronts coming in. Between the fronts are areas of clear sky. What we can't predict is whether these fronts will catch each other up. A bit earlier St Marys reported sunshine whilst Lands End had tractors out mowing the runway. We decide to fly down to Plymouth and see what tomorrow offers. There is a choice of route. We can fly round the coast which is longer or follow the A38 through the hills which is shorter. Getting yet another 'actual' from Plymouth we plump for the A38. Low cloud is still the major hazard. Our 172, can, however, turn around in a relatively small amount of space and the distance between the hills is more than adequate. Checking the hilltop height we find that we can follow the route and still remain well above 500 feet over the small towns encountered on the way.

Exeter airport is listed at 102ft AMSL and Plymouth is 474 AMSL, being situated on top of a hill north-north-west of the city. The cloud-base at Plymouth is 1300ft AAL. It could easily drop lower within five minutes. It is now 14.25 and

Top:
Turning onto finals for Runway 13, Plymouth.

Centre:
Air Traffic Control Officers in the tower at Plymouth.

Above:
Departing Plymouth, note the low cloud base.

we 'book-out' on the radio. The wind is 270° at 10kts. We have engine start logged 14.30, and we taxi back to the intermediate hold for Runway 26. This positions us just over half-way down the runway allowing a take-off distance approximating 900 plus metres. Estimating a run of 350 metres I'm more than satisfied. The take-off is uneventful and we climb out heading 215° looking for the A38 south of Exeter. It transpires that the dual-carriageway is easy to identify. Looking down I see a line of trucks toiling up the steep hill out of Exeter. Our next staging point is Buckfastleigh Abbey. Our estimate for Plymouth is 15.05. As predicted the clouds are firmly clamped to the tops of the hills on either side. We get some rain. A careful eye is kept peering forward looking for signs that the cloud-base may be dropping. We lose contact with Exeter so Aussie dials up Plymouth Approach on 133.55. No response. The hills still shield our transmission. We spot a clump of low cloud so I drop down until we can see clearly beyond it. We estimate our altitude at 6-700ft AGL (Above Ground Level). Aussie calls again, this time successfully and we are cleared for a dead-side join for Runway 13. Checking the Flight Guide we see that circuits are left-handed on 13 and 06. Right-handed on 24 and 31. As we shall be approaching from the south-east I will want to keep the airport on our right. Ivybridge has just been passed and the ground levels out around us (a bit). We can't see the airport so an estimated position has to be determined. "I think we steer 300°, agree?" No response. "Aussie, I think we steer 300° now". I look at Aussie and see his mouth moving but the intercom has gone dead. Aussie starts pushing and pulling the connections and flicking the switches. Still dead. I shout across, "Can you hear the tower?". "Yes", he shouts back. I can too so it's no big deal. I turn the nose onto 300° and Aussie gives me a thumbs up. We spot the airport so I call "field in sight".

"Golf Charlie Lima, Roger, change to Tower 122.60".

"Change to tower 122.60, Golf Charlie Lima".

Aussie reaches over and selects 122.60.

"Plymouth Tower, Golf Charlie Lima is with you".

"Roger, Golf Charlie Lima, join downwind left-hand for Runway 13, QFE 1000, call established".

I'm not expecting this as I'm set up for a dead-side join. Dead-side is self explanatory really, it's the opposite side of the runway to the active circuit.

"Golf Charlie Lima, can you confirm join downwind LEFT-HAND?"

"That is correct, Golf Charlie Lima".

I thumb the transmit switch twice which is a shorthand way of saying understood or goodbye etc. without tying up the frequency with laboured repeats. So, now we want to be on the other side . The airport is quite close, about two miles to run (nautical miles, naturally) so the nose is brought round to track just before the end of Runway 31. As we close on the runway extended centre-line Aussie gives the Tower our position. Established downwind I give the Tower the downwind call as part of the pre-landing checks.

"Roger, Golf Charlie Lima, call finals, you are number one".

"Call finals number one. Golf Charlie Lima". Due to the low cloud-base which we estimate at 800ft AAL I keep the circuit fairly tight. With 1000 set on the altimeter subscale our altitude is 600ft.

We are so close to the runway I don't fly a base leg. Instead I fly a continuous turn during which the runway is out of sight while we descend at a steady rate. As we come round I see that I've turned a little tight so cut the turn short heading right to intercept the threshold.

"Finals to land, Golf Charlie Lima".

"Golf Charlie Lima, cleared for land, surface wind 180, 10 knots". We have a crosswind. Right wing down, steer straight with rudder. The runways at Plymouth drop away from the intersection. This produces a long flare and the stall warner is bleating away.

Our wheels are so close to the ground I do nothing about it except haul the yoke back in little stages. I'm very worried that I don't pull back too much into a 'balloon'. If this happens, with the aircraft climbing on the last vestige of lift over the wings, we could crash back onto the ground most ignominiously. It would probably write the aircraft off as I'm not at all sure it would be possible to go around from such a slow speed. Either way the aircraft would be on the verge of entering an incipient spin with the result that a wing would drop and probably hit the ground first maybe causing us to cartwheel. With nearly full tanks, need I go on? We actually flop down, wobble, tidy up the dangley bits and back-track to the intersection where we turn left onto Runway 24/06 then left again onto the apron. The Tower asks us to park in the far left corner.

After booking in we go in search of a 'sparks' to fix the intercom. Someone recommends Plymouth Executive Aviation. We enter the hangar and our jaws drop in unison. Standing proudly at the back of the hanger, in a great state of refurbishment is an English Electric Lightning complete with personalised number plate G-LTNG. What a surprise! They provide an engineer with electrical expertise and soon fix our problem. A connection has come adrift and a spot of solder is all that is needed. We are invited up to meet the MD who tells us all about the Lightning restoration project. We get permission to look around and photograph. It is an awesome machine. The design parameters seem to have been, work out what is required and double it. The performance was staggering in its day and I wonder if anything could beat it now. One thousand five hundred miles per hour in second gear. I believe nobody ever found out how fast it could really go.

In the UK at the very least it will be the hottest item around for a PPL with a twin rating. Fast jets leave me fairly cold on the whole but the Lightning is a classic. I still remember a squadron taking off in formation at the Farnborough show and climbing vertically from the end of the runway. I'll never forget it and have a soft spot for this type. Every last nut and bolt is being fully restored and they believe it'll fly out of Plymouth one day. Should that happy event occur they have no plans to take it supersonic. Before departing we wish them every success. Walking outside, the din of an Air-Sea-Rescue Wessex taxiing by draws my attention. It is near Charlie Lima and I rush across fearful that the down-draught from its rotors could blow our plane over. The Wessex turns round and taxis away for take-off. I set about searching for tie-down weights as strong winds are forecast. It is raining and I almost miss the fact that fuel is syphoning out of the fuel-tank breather on the port wing. This is caused by the considerable slope of the apron. I find Aussie and we turn Charlie Lima to face uphill. Fortunately we haven't lost much fuel.

We find a small hotel on Plymouth Hoe and in the morning step outside to do our own 'actual'. There is a small island nearby, not very high, and the top is in cloud. We experiment with the sound of some naughty words. Returning to the airport we find the situation is worse than yesterday afternoon. Watching the satellite pictures on television it is clear that the fronts coming in across the Atlantic have indeed closed together. The 24 and 48 hour forecasts offer little hope of getting down to Lands End and the Scillies. We have promised to station Charlie Lima back at Wycombe for Sunday bookings. But, can we get back? Up in the Tower ATC prove immensely helpful. They provide us with 'actuals' and forecasts for Cardiff, Bristol, Exeter, Bournemouth and Southampton. Aussie studies the situation in depth.

So near and yet so far. Just another 65 miles. At 11.00 the cloud-base was 200 feet here. It is now 14.00 and it has lifted a bit. We want at least 500 feet to get out. We've also monitored the Met reports from Culdrose because we can gain a picture by comparing what they had with what we have as we know the wind speed and direction. The general cloud-base does lift as it moves eastwards but not enough to fly inland. Our only option is to hug the coast where there is a slim chance we can fly inland from Bournemouth or Southampton following low terrain to White Waltham perhaps which is 130ft AMSL. Wycombe is 520ft AMSL and they tell us that have a 300ft cloud-base. We shall have to cover some very nautical miles.

Right then. We're going for it. Charlie Lima has been tanked up to the brimful and I've given her a very thorough inspection. With life-jackets donned we get cleared for engine start, still Runway 13, QFE 997, and taxi to the CAT Hold. The point is, if you taxi beyond the CAT Hold your aeroplane may disturb the ILS system which could have dangerous consequences. Quite frankly, I'm still in awe of the limits to which commercial flights can operate. Invariably the pilots tend to be over modest and berate their abilities. Highly paid bus drivers, computer watch-dogs etc. I remember a very funny piece concerning this aspect. The flight deck of the future will be staffed by a pilot and a dog. The dog is there to bite the pilot if he touches anything. There is a common misconception regarding auto-pilot systems. People neglect to remember that it is the pilot who tells the auto-pilot system what to do!

ATC give us clearance to line up on 13. There is no need to backtrack since, from the intersection of the two runways, we have in the region of 800 metres in front of us. Runway 13 is pointing in the direction we want, almost. When climbing out we shall turn onto a heading of 150° until we reach the coast. Clearance to take-off is given, I open the throttle fully and check Ts and Ps and RPM. Full RPM is not developed at the start of the run but gradually builds up as airspeed increases. The margin isn't large, in the order of 200 RPM. As 13 slopes downhill our speed increases faster than usual and we're soon off. The cloud-base is between 700 and 1000 ft on the QFE. With the QNH set we find that we can fly at 1200ft. Keeping close in to the coast, regular look-outs are made for suitable places to land or ditch. The estuary to Salcombe passes and we cut the corner at Start Point having made sure the masts which rise to 875ft AMSL 450ft AGL are clearly seen. Our heading is 030° as we point towards Brixham. Plymouth

Approach starts getting intermittent so, saying goodbye, Exeter Approach on 128.15 is selected. We pass Dartmouth and fly over land briefly to cut a corner between Brixham and Paignton. Aussie has requested Exeter and Southampton actuals and is busily copying the details down. Exeter has 300/10 (surface wind) 17k RA (visibility 17 kms in rain) 2/08, 4/12, 6/25 (OKTAs and altitude, the last being 6 OKTAs at 2500ft), +14 (temperature), 1012 (the QNH) and Squawk 7207. Aussie reads this back. "Read-back correct Golf Charlie Lima, are you ready to copy the Southampton actual?"

"Ready to copy, Golf Charlie Lima".

Aussie's pen races across the paper, I can't actually write this fast but suppose it takes a 'pro' to know one. 280/7 18k Ra 1/10 5/14 7/18 +16 1010. Not good but still acceptable for Class D airspace. We decide to continue following the coast towards Bournemouth.

Exmouth, Sidmouth and Seaton are behind now and we're waiting for Lyme Regis to appear. The cloud-base has dropped, forcing us down to 800ft, and more rain is being encountered. Exeter Approach has been changed to London Information 124.75 for a Flight Information Service. Portland is closed. As conditions continue to deteriorate I step up the FREDA checks. FREDA is the popular nmemonic for Fuel, Radio, Engine, Direction and Altitude. Passing along Chesil Beach even lower cloud appears and we drop down to 500ft. Fortunately the view ahead clears and Portland Bill is seen through the mist and rain. Banking steeply I turn Charlie Lima around to fly past the front at Weymouth. What a difference to our evening flight down two days earlier! Heavy rain clatters on the windscreen so I pull the Carb-heat fully out. It clears after a couple of minutes and the cloud is higher. Pushing Carb-heat back in, I increase the power and climb back up to 800ft. Visibility improves now. Durdle Door, Lulworth Cove and Kimmeridge slip past on the left. Banking round Durlston Head, we change our frequency to Bournemouth Approach who approve a low-level course round the bay to Hengistbury Head, one of the VRPs in the CTA. Getting into Bournemouth would not present a problem so, aware that we can return, we pass on towards Southampton.

At Hengistbury Head Bournemouth pass us over to Southampton Zone on 120.225. Our VFR flight to Wycombe is approved through the Zone via the Solent, Southampton Water, Totton and Romsey, calling initially abeam Lymington. When we do call abeam Lymington we find our path ahead is obscured by cloud down to sea level. The north coast of the Isle of Wight is visi-ble so we cross the Solent to take a look. It is very murky but landmarks 5 miles away can still be made out by descending to 500 feet. From Cowes the huge chimney near Calshot (662ft AMSL) is visible. We set course to track up past Fawley to Totton. Southampton now has 4 OKTAs at 700ft. We don't even see Totton. Coming up towards the docks Totton is hidden by more low cloud. I put Charlie Lima into a steep turn through 180°.

We both agree that there is nowhere left to go and with conditions becoming close to IMC (Instrument Meteorological Conditions), Aussie calls Southampton requesting a landing there.

"Southampton Approach' (we'd been passed from Zone to Approach when opposite Fawley) "Golf Charlie Lima has turned back heading 160° as it is not possible to maintain Victor Mike Charlie in the Totton area. Request approach and landing clearance for Southampton.

"That is approved Golf Charlie Lima, confirm your present position and conditions".

"Golf Charlie Lima is Victor Mike Charlie, 600 ft, QNH 1011, estimate 5 miles South-East of field".

"Golf Charlie Lima, Roger, we have you identified 5 miles South-East of the field, continue present heading and follow the river North towards the field. Runway in use is 20, QFE 1010, call field in sight".

Aussie reads these details back.

"Read-back correct, Golf Charlie Lima".

We have no problem finding the river, in fact we're almost on top of it. I bank over and pull Charlie Lima around once more. As I straighten out heading 010° Aussie advises me to slow down. As I was just about to do this I'm very pleased because right the way through the trip, by far the worst conditions I've ever encountered, we have managed to work very well together without a single disagreement. I slow Charlie Lima down to 75 knots with 10° of flap. After an mile or so we spot the field.

"Golf Charlie Lima, field in sight".

"Roger, Golf Charlie Lima, change to Tower 118.20".

The Tower approves a low level circuit at 500ft, 1010 to join down-wind for 20, calling down-wind. Aussie acknowledges. I concentrate on flying, running through the checks as we pass abeam the terminal. Our flight path is barely beyond the airport boundary.

Now comes the interesting bit. Passing beyond the end of the runway I slow back to 70 knots and bring the flaps down to 40° in fairly quick stages. Shoving the nose down, I bank steeply over to the left. "Steady lad", cautions Aussie. I must not let the speed drop below 65 knots. As we come round Aussie calls finals to land.

"Golf Charlie Lima is cleared to land, surface wind two three zero, eight knots".

"Cleared to land Golf Charlie Lima".

We are pointing down at the runway with the VSI virtually off the clock. Speed steady, musn't round out too late. My aiming point is one-third of the way down 20. The throttle has been drawn back as far as possible. The glide gives a strange impression of floating down almost vertically. Steady, steady, NOW! I pull back the yoke. The nose rears up away from the concrete ahead. Whew, just about right, our dive is transformed into the flare. I touch down crisply and beam with appreciation as I hear Aussie's voice in my headset. "Very well done, congratulations".

The landing run, short though it is, takes us past the first taxiway some 800 metres from the displaced threshold. The Tower instructs us to continue and depart next right. This leads us back onto the main apron. We are allocated parking on the light aircraft apron north of the control tower. It is a tight squeeze getting into position. The disc brakes are fitted to the main undercarriage only and are operated by forward pressure on either rudder pedal plus use of the rudder bar which applies spring pressure to the nose-wheel. By juggling these two factors and using power applied by the propeller it is possible to taxi quite exactly. You must remember the wings sticking out on both sides! Seems obvious, but beware. I cut the engine during the shut-down checks and with all systems OFF log the time, 17.05 local. One hour 35 minutes from Plymouth. What an experience! At no point en route did I consider we were pushing our luck nor have we infringed regulations. A lesson and a half.

I'm writing this sitting on a train home from Eastleigh which reminds me that I am old enough to remember most of the UK airports by their 'proper' names. Southampton Airport was once Eastleigh. Bournemouth was Hurn, Plymouth was Roborough. Later on we hope to see Bristol which was Lulsgate and Cardiff which was Rhoose. I remember Manchester as Ringway, Gloucester as Staverton, Edinburgh as Turnhouse, Leeds/Bradford as Yeadon, Liverpool as Speke, Aberdeen as Dyce. I suppose I'm getting sentimental because it seems that the old names carried a piece of magic; an acknowledgement of events which formed the history of aviation; heroic attempts to land which ended in disaster and foolish attempts that succeeded or even inaugural flights of a type or of a service. This rich tapestry of aviation history seems diminished when the name disappears.

We did make another attempt to get out of Southampton. Our only chance had been to depart north but, once airborne, we had to hold while airliners approached on the ILS. We were still hemmed in by low cloud to the east and west. There was a chance, but, years of commercial flying told Aussie that circumstances would probably conspire against us. I'd said, "let's give it a go". In fact, by the time a gap occurred it would have been dark at White Waltham, our prime destination. We landed back at Southampton and tied Charlie Lima down.

We travelled by train back to Southampton on the following Sunday and flew back to Wycombe. The flight time was logged as 12.10 to 12.55 local.

Below:
Southampton airport in the kinder conditions for our return.

4.
Wycombe to Scotland

16.10 hrs local. 9th October. 1880 ft QNH 1020. Heading towards the overhead at Oxford Airport (which was known as Kidlington). En route to Gloucestershire Airport (once known as Staverton). This makes a change. I'm sitting in the right-hand seat. The reason is that Aussie has now had an opportunity to be checked-out by a club instructor. Most flying clubs insist that you are checked on their aircraft before they allow you to fly off. This applies no matter how many hours' experience have been logged. At Wycombe Air Centre there is also a stipulation, which is primarily an insurance requirement, that pilots must be checked if they have not flown a club aircraft in the previous month. Whereas I agree that to check pilots who haven't flown for a month or more is very sensible, it can be a little frustrating to be checked-out after flying elsewhere quite extensively during the preceding week. I believe other clubs have this restriction imposed. It makes an interesting comparison with the CAA requirement for keeping your licence valid. This simply states that you must fly at least five hours per annum. Not a lot is it? To make sure the CAA regulation is complied with you have to get a Certificate of Experience stamped in your log-book and signed by an authorised person. Having done so it is valid for thirteen months. Why thirteen? I've no idea.

Still, the formalities have been complied with and we now have very pleasant VFR flying weather above 1000ft. We started at 15.45 and took-off on the hard runway 07, QFE 1003, wind 10-15 knots and gusting higher from the North. Climbing out, we turned onto 030° at the end of the runway to avoid the noise abatement area, at 600ft we changed heading to 360° up to 1000ft. Then 305° to the Stokenchurch telecommunications tower upon reaching which we changed frequency from Wycombe Tower on 126.55 to Benson Radar 120.90. We requested a Flight Information Service, plus as we would pass through their zone, a MATZ penetration. These were granted.

After the Stokenchurch tower we continued on a heading of 305° which gave us a track of 300° because there is a cross-wind component and a small tail-wind. Having cleared through the Benson MATZ we were advised to change to Oxford Approach on 125.325. I've just spoken to them and we must pass over the top at 2300ft on their QNH 1020. Oxford is 270ft AMSL and this would subtract 9 millibars to give their QFE. Aussie checks the QNH and continues to climb to 2300ft. I report level at 2300 to Oxford Approach. As we pass overhead I report this also. At this point we can check our drift estimate accurately. We should pass just south of the runways, in fact we pass over the top which means we're half a mile north of track. Excellent. There is a splendid view of Blenheim Palace approaching just left of our nose. Aussie gets the grandstand seat as we pass by. A mile past Blenheim I say goodbye to Oxford and dial up 119.0 for Brize Radar, request a Flight Information Service, and tell them we're turning onto a heading of 290°. They have little to offer us except the Cotswold QNH

Below:
Charlie Lima frames the control tower at Gloucester airport.

which is also 1020. A call to a LARS (Lower Airspace Radar Service) will typically go out as follows after their acknowledgement of your call-sign. Call-sign, aircraft type, position, heading, altitude with pressure setting, flight status (VFR for example) and destination plus the service required. Obviously we have made, and will make, a great many transmissions of this nature. To prevent it getting too boring I'll mainly ring the changes.

The frequency is very quiet and we can appreciate the Cotswold countryside spread out beneath. Quaint clusters of stone buildings without a hint of brick to be seen. Our track takes us directly overhead Little Rissington aerodrome, a RAF base that has gliding and parachuting activity from time to time. Brize confirms they are closed today. We're still in Charlie Lima I'm glad to say. I notice Aussie was pleased too. The club has four Cessna 172s, one of which, Charlie Yankee, is reserved for instrument flight training.

With Cheltenham visible in the distance we change-over from Brize to Gloucester Approach Tower on 125.65. It is an interesting airport because they still retain three runways, all long enough for most light singles and twins. This is an airport where you have a reasonable chance of landing into wind. What went wrong? Most airports abandoned this eminently safe and sensible idea years ago. Today we are mainly into single runway operation presumably on the basic premise that these 'so-called' pilots should work for a living.

Years ago, even long before my time, aerodromes were mainly 'all-over' grass fields. The pilot could then ascertain the direction of the wind usually by reference to a wind-sock and land, or take off, in that direction. Later on, when the desirability for hard runways became a necessity, usually three, sometimes more, were built in the direction of the prevailing winds. In those days most, very nearly all, aircraft were of a tail-wheel configuration. To this type of aeroplane cross-wind landings presented a major problem. Since the adoption of tricycle undercarriage types, to which cross-winds are less of a problem, many airports and aerodromes have reduced the options. The majority have two runways at most.

Maintaining 'hard' runways is a problem. Maintaining 'all-over' grass fields is a problem. One point is clear. On the whole it is not 'cost-effective' to keep multi-directional runways serviceable. It is, however, a great deal safer. During the last 'unpleasantness' when resources were distinctly limited, people in the know didn't squander resources on the classic 'A' con-figuration aerodrome because it was just a good idea. Today I fear, we have lost sight of that simple 'common-sense' rule. We spend many hours training our pilots more effectively, usually at their expense, but, would it not make more sense if we provided more runways?

Having got that off my chest I'll get back to the job in hand. I call Gloucestershire Airport with their call-sign 'Gloster'.

"Gloster Approach, good afternoon, Golf Whiskey Alpha Charlie Lima".

"Golf Charlie Lima, good afternoon, pass your message".

"Golf Charlie Lima is a Cessna 172, North abeam Andoversford, inbound VFR from Wycombe Air Park, 2300 feet, 1020, request joining and landing".

"Golf Charlie Lima, Roger, join overhead at 2000 feet for runway 04 left-hand, QFE 1020".

As I read these details back, Aussie starts running through his checks. A PA.28 has just taken-off on a circuit detail. As it climbs cross-wind we get redirected to join cross-wind as number two. As we are approaching runway 04 from the

Below:
Ready for departure from Gloucester.

Above:
**The author planning the next leg of the trip with
flight guide and half mil chart.**

east Aussie steers right to intercept the cross-wind line. Having turned down-wind I call the Tower when abeam the centre of the runway and get an instruction to call finals, number two. The PA.28 has descended on base-leg and we have lost sight of it. This is a common problem. A light aircraft two or three miles away, flying at a lower level, especially against a complex and varied background can be very hard to identify. Aussie spots it turning finals so he banks left onto base.

Aussie has just landed very nicely and we're parked on the apron behind the control-tower. For it's size 'Gloster' has the most complicated network of aprons and taxiways I've ever come across. There are several interesting aircraft here but one type in particular grabs our attention. It is a rare Scottish Aviation Twin Pioneer. A very rugged high-wing, twin radial engined, triple-finned tail-dragger! I don't know if it has a current C of A but it certainly looks airworthy. Built at Prestwick, most were supplied to the RAF for transport and communications duties in remote areas. For their day they had impressive STOL capability. This one is probably thirty plus years old.

Aussie is scooting around and I've just checked Charlie Lima. There is plenty of fuel on board for our intended flight down to Bristol in the evening before dusk. I have some time to spare so I'll tell you about a couple of features of our trip. You will remember that Brize Radar gave us the Cotswold QNH. Cotswold refers to

the ASR (Altimeter Setting Region). The UK and large areas of surrounding sea are divided up in a patchwork quilt of ASRs. The Regional QNH is the lowest pressure reading in the ASR and this should be set when cruising below the Transition Altitude. Having the lowest pressure set maximises safety for obstacle clearance and terrain avoidance especially when flying on instruments. Having aircraft operating on the same QNH makes life easier for ATSUs (Air Traffic Service Units) providing Flight Information Services. You might well be wondering if there is an end to the amount of abbreviations used in the pursuit of flight. The short answer is yes. The long answer is no. As aviation develops new terms come into existence and as there are only twenty-four hours in a day, (so far!), the need to abbreviate will remain as strong as ever.

The next item is the Oxford AIAA SFC-5000ft ALT which we have just flown across. Looking at the 1:500,000 chart I doubt you will spot another area so complex. As you have seen, in practice our flight was quite straight-forward. This was largely due to taking a course deliberately calculated to offer the least resistance. To our south we passed the Combined MATZ of Benson and Abingdon which itself butts up against the Brize Norton CTR. Brize doesn't have a MATZ. To the west the Brize CTR overlaps the Fairford MATZ which is NOTAM activated. NOTAMs are Notices to Airman issued by the CAA and posted at briefing points as well as in most flying clubs. The Fairford MATZ is intermittent in other words and anyone wishing to fly through it should check if it's active before take-off in case entry is prohibited.

To our north we had the UHMRA. This is a beauty! It stands for Upper Heyford Mandatory Radio Area the largest part of which extends from the surface to 3500ft ALT. I could write a small book just on this one subject, but I won't. Very simply, if you wish to enter this area you call Upper Heyford on 128.55. Doing so will give you one of the few opportunities to speak to a real 'Stars and Stripes' American. Upper Heyford is one of the few American bases left in the UK and they control the airspace. Generally they are closed at week-ends and on public holidays but, especially in the summer, they have aircraft departing from, or arriving back to the base, usually in connection with an air display. For this contingency they operate a separate frequency, (don't ask why).

I have joined up with Aussie because in the few minutes left before our intended departure we are treated to a spectacular sun effect. A thin gap is allowing a spread of rays slowly to traverse an area just west of the airport. A less cynical soul than myself might describe it as 'biblical', mainly because Renaissance painters often employed this effect to add drama to their compositions.

We depart on runway 04 and set course down the Severn Estuary. There is no need to draw

Below:
Refuelling from the tanker at Bristol.

chinagraph lines on a chart. The unfolding vista before us is quite breathtaking. Imagine, if you can, an unfolding pattern of splendiferous sunsets. One after another. Aussie is taking total control, flying and looking after the radio and navigation. I'm sitting back and relishing the experience. This is great. Absolutely great. Aussie is into home territory so I sit back and enjoy. I feel the same way coming back into Wycombe. The warm pleasure of familiarity.

Fifteen miles out from "Gloster" we change over to Bristol Approach 132.40 who also offer LARS. This is very convenient for us and Aussie requests the Bristol weather. Here it comes: 040/12 25km NIL 1/30 3/60 +11/+3 QNH 1023 QFE1001. So, there is a reasonable cross-wind. Visibility is excellent at 25kms, no rain and 1 OKTA at 3000ft. We are expecting this and appreciate that it hasn't changed much in the last couple of hours. Just past the Severn Bridge, which is lit to perfection by the setting sun, we have the Filton MATZ ahead. Bristol inform us it is closed for the day. We hear two airliners, a Dash 7 and a Saab calling in also. To enable them to land we are told to hold over the Portishead VRP. The runway in use is 09, QFE 1001. The QNH has been set 1023 on the way down and the large difference shows that Bristol Airport is quite high, 620ft AMSL in fact. Watching the second airliner turn finals, our clearance for a base-leg join for 09 is received. Bristol (once Lulsgate) has long since closed its shorter crossed runways and 09/27 has been lengthened to 2011 metres. That should be long enough for most large airliners but there is a potential difficulty for larger machines in that the runway dips down in the middle. It doesn't present the slightest problem to Aussie as he flares Charlie Lima into a nicely set up cross-wind touchdown. It did present an insurmountable problem to the crew of a Spanish A300 Airbus a few years ago. After flaring long down the incline, they came speeding up the slope to realise, too late, that the runway finishes at the top of the rise. They came to rest in the field at the end of 27. Our landing run is miniscule and we have to taxi a couple of hundred metres before departing via Taxiway 3 for the light aircraft apron near the Bristol Flight Centre. I set about tying down for the night while Aussie arranges accommodation. We're in luck. Bristol Airport is a few miles out of the City centre and we are offered a lift in by a young lady from the Flight Centre who hopes to become a flying instructor before too long.

11.00. Saturday 10th. There is still a brisk north-easterly wind which makes it feel pretty cold out on the apron despite the sunshine

Above:
Charlie Lima ranked up with the Bristol Flying Centre Cessnas.

to shoot the terminal as it passes by on our left. For the last hour or so a steady stream of jets plus a few turbo-props have landed, been turned around with amazing speed, and departed. Bristol is not just busy, it is successful. In '85 they handled 44,701 movements. By 1990 this had nearly doubled to 72,134. It is interesting to note that during the same period the tonnage of freight also doubled from 4402 to 8744 tonnes.

We start up at 11.30 and taxi out to Taxiway One which runs parallel with the runway for almost its entire length. At Hold Foxtrot we do the power and pre-take-off checks. Reporting ready for departure we're cleared on to Hold Golf right at the end of 09. Lining up, I get ready for my first cross-wind take-off from the right seat. It goes well enough but I notice the extra effort required.

For starters the air is reasonably turbulent. Coupled with an open window and Aussie's directions to raise the wing or lower it as required, I have plenty to do keeping Charlie Lima on a straight heading. As we pass the terminal the Tower gives us clearance for a low level left-hand orbit. This is good stuff and I start enjoying the experience. Having finished we head off north, climbing up to 1500 feet. For the next half hour we circle around shooting various sites ending up near the Severn Bridge. I've put Charlie Lima into the most ungainly attitudes endeavouring to provide Aussie with clear views of the target area. At last we've finished. It is surprisingly hard work and I've enjoyed every minute.

We set course for Cardiff, the next destination. With Cardiff coming up into view we ask Cardiff

which blazes down through a 3 OKTA cloudbase at 2500ft QFE. In fact it is a classic sharp autumn day where you see a steady stream of broken fluffy cloud cruising across the land. Charlie Lima is fully fuelled and all the checks are good. I bring the aircraft log up to date prior to each departure and often after landing. Aussie has been taking every opportunity the sun allows to shoot the airliners and terminal area. It's a pity but it looks as if the apron will be virtually deserted by the time we take-off for the aerial shots.

We have a lot to do. I've met up with Aussie in the Bristol Flight Centre to snatch a cup of coffee and quickly run through the next leg, the 10th so far. Aussie has a lot of photography work to do between Portishead and the M4/M5 junction. We decide it is better if Aussie stays in the left-hand seat. For a start, with runway 09 still being used, if we get clearance to back-track to the very end we'll be nicely set on the climb

Below:
Ten degrees of flap and getting ready to turn base leg for Runway 03 at Cardiff.

Above:
Established on left base leg for 03, Cardiff.

Below:
Turning onto finals for 03.

Bottom:
Happily at rest on the Cardiff apron.

Approach on 125.85 if an overhead orbit is permissible. The ATCO says it is and what altitude do we require. We request 2000 feet and this is approved. Coming into the overhead Approach hand us over to Tower on 125.00. Cardiff (once Rhoose) is now dominated by a huge new hangar on the northwest quadrant of the airport. It will be used to service large wide-bodied jets, for British Airways. Finishing off, the Tower clears us for a down-wind join for 03.

This is 1119 metres long and is used mainly by small single-engined aircraft like ours. It also means a landing almost into wind. The big boys have to put up with a cross-wind on 12/30, 2354 metres long.

We have the QFE 1018 set on the altimeter so I set Charlie Lima up to dive off 1000 feet pretty sharply to arrive down-wind at 1000 feet. Aussie decides to let me bring Charlie Lima in. There is a small temptation to take time off to admire the setting, Cardiff being so close to the Bristol Channel. Fleeting glances are the most I dare afford as I judge the descent onto 03. Due to the wind a shortish down-wind leg is flown and the drift is very noticeable on base. Everything goes well until the flare which is really an interconnected series of minor balloons interspersed with prodigious bursts of power. I'm too busy to see if Aussie is covering his face in embarrassment. I suspect he'll put eye slits in a sick bag and wear this as we taxi up to the terminal as most people will think he's the pilot. To be fair to myself I do eventually get down softly enough to prevent a bounce. It's a shame the crazy flying pilots from the Tiger Club weren't there. I might have been offered a job on the spot. Still, it must have brightened up the day for the ATCOs who, to their credit, don't laugh as they direct us towards the parking area for general aviation.

Once parked up Aussie dashes off to make his introductions and arrange permission to photograph on the apron. I settle down to plan the next leg, up the Bristol Channel via Newport to Gloucestershire Airport, (we hope to get some aerial shots today), then on to Welshpool for our overnight stop. Aussie has a friend in that vicinity who owns a rare biplane which Aussie hopes to photograph one day for 'Flyer' magazine for whom he is the Chief Photographer. Having noted the en route frequencies and having studied the chart I set about giving Charlie Lima another thorough external and internal check. While doing this I hear an odd familiar sound. Looking round I see a Tiger Moth climbing away from runway 03. This is most unusual. Tiger Moths don't have brakes, relying instead on the tail-skid digging into grass. Taxing on hard surfaces is quite an accomplishment. I imagine the

Above:
Charlie Lima dwarfed by the tower and admin building at Cardiff.

Above:
CL watching a F.27 get started up for departure.

pilot used the grass until reaching the runway edge.

Those of you who drive cars might find the price of our fuel, AVGAS 100LL (Low Lead), of interest. Just as at filling stations it does vary. For the type of work we're doing we expect a fuel burn rate averaging out at around 7 imperial gallons per hour. Shoreham charged us 54p per litre (all prices are plus VAT). Exeter wanted 54.5p per litre. Plymouth asked a very reasonable 51p per litre. Bristol settled for an intermediate 53p per litre. Oil will set us back somewhere between £2.00p and £2.50p a litre or quart, oil still being dispensed in either quantity. Our oil burn and loss is working out at one litre per three hours maximum. Not bad for an aero-engine of this type for this work.

Landing fees have varied a great deal. Some airports offered us a discount because of the nature of our flight. A few, bless 'em, decided to waive the charges. We paid £11.75 at Southend, £11.97 at Manston. Southampton charged £18.49 close to Bournemouth at £17.68. Gloucester asked £10.00. In France I've never been asked for much more than £2.50 for landing a small single even at large regional airports. 'Vive la difference'. Despite this, private flying is more popular in the UK than anywhere in Europe. I wonder why? We are not at the top of the economic tree. Far from it. But we love to get our bums into the air. One thing I do know. From a small aeroplane the constant change in the nature of the terrain which we enjoy in this island makes for fascinating low level flight. Those embarking on airliners get but a brief glimpse as they roar off to Flight Levels above the clouds. Also our airspace is more complex and more congested than anywhere in Europe.

According to foreign pilots I've spoken to, the British Air Traffic Control Services are second to none. This, of course, does cost a bob or two. A lot of regional airports abroad don't even possess a radar facility, Extraordinary, isn't it? As a PPL flying VFR I don't usually need these services in order to fly from A to B, but they certainly enhance safety and peace of mind.

It is interesting to search through the statistics relating to British airports as this seems to provide pointers to the relative prosperity, or lack of it, as fortunes change in different areas. Cardiff has done well it seems, adopting the major regional airports status. It seems odd to me being so close to Bristol. In '86 Cardiff logged 40,000 movements increasing to 64,000 in 1990. Passengers handled increased by 131,000 during the same period whilst freight went from 4573 to 7353 metric tonnes. The South and South-East present a more confused picture. Bournemouth, so quiet when we arrived, showed an increase from 76,578 to 106,519 movements between '86 and 1990. Passenger and freight volumes show healthy increases. Shoreham, without airlines, shows an increase in movements from 50,893 in '85 to 61,526 in 1990. Southend shows an increase in movements from 80,000 in '86 to 91,054 in 1990. Oddly passengers handled dropped from 165,991 in '86 to 120,022 in 1990 peaking at 173,642 in '87. Freight went from 24,772 tonnes in '86 dropping slightly to 22,923 in 1990. Freight tonnage peaked at 28,225 in 1988, however. Obviously, none of these statistics reflect the profitability of the operation. More throughput doesn't necessarily increase profits. It does, however, always increase costs. I imagine airport managers must spend hours reaching into days and weeks fathoming the murky statistical depths in order to distil a clear picture. Considering the calamitous effects of the recession in the past two years I wouldn't mind seeing up to date figures.

We are having lunch in the terminal and I'm slightly pushing Aussie for a departure around 14.30 to 15.00. Cardiff is busy now and there are many photo-opportunities. Although our separate tasks should complement each other, at times like this we have to compromise. It boils down to interpreting the changeable weather. Aussie is much better at this than I am. He agrees that poor conditions appear to be forthcoming, edging towards the Welshpool area. Considering the terrain we decide to leave sooner rather than later.

Back in the left-hand seat I get engine start at 14.45. We have quite a long taxi to the Holding Point for Runway 03. Emerging from the general aviation apron we have to taxi across the southern part of the main apron to Hold 4. We wait for clearance to cross the main Runway 12/30. When clear we taxi across heading south-west, past the hangars and buildings occupied by flying clubs and general aviation companies before turning into the taxiway that runs parallel East of runway 03. Before reaching the end of the taxiway we join a queue of light aircraft waiting to take-off. There isn't room to get past the student pilots so we just have to be patient, watching the Datcom meter register the charges at over a pound a minute. It takes over a quarter of an hour before we get lined up on Runway 03. Even then we have to hold while a powerful twin lands on 12. When cleared for take-off I climb out on the extended centre-line for two miles then turn right onto a heading of 060°. This takes us directly over Cardiff and on towards Newport. The docks are virtually empty in both cities. Another sign of the times. Passing over Newport, Aussie asks me to 'dog-leg' past the 'Transporter Bridge' so he can take a few photographs. Squeaking 'one-for-me' over the intercom I happily comply. The 'Transporter Bridge' is indeed a novelty, with I believe, only two such constructions in England.

Soon after this we pass close by the steelworks at Llanwern. It is an abysmal blight across the landscape. Unless you've flown close by I find it hard to believe you might comprehend just how awful such a massive works appears. It looks like a scene from Dante's *Inferno* dumped regardless into a vista of pastoral tranquillity. Coming up we see the Severn Bridge, appearing incredibly fragile as it spans the estuary between its two slender supports.

The cloud is thickening as we fly towards Gloucester. We hope it will be worthwhile coming back up here because we are flying two sides of a triangle, adding many more miles than a direct track. However, a direct track route might have been ruled out by the high terrain between Cardiff and Welshpool. There are three spot heights on the chart over 2000 feet, the highest being 2524 north of Merthyr Tydfil. That top could actually be covered in cloud right now. It's one thing to fly through a valley which you know is wide and doesn't rise much. Its quite another to fly up a narrow valley which climbs continuously and may be shrouded in cloud near the top. Bristol has asked us to call Gloucester Approach. This we do explaining our intentions. We get approval subject to traffic and not below 1500ft QFE. As we fly by Gloucester City we notice that our target area is covered by shade. I fly five orbits while Aussie takes the best shots he can get. We are surrounded by large patches of sun but the clouds keep merging and overlapping in such a way that the area we want stays in shade. Would you believe it! We thank the ATCO and depart north-west on a heading of 340° to allow for drift, saying we'll stay on his frequency. I reset the Regional QNH which is still 1020.

We have to be more careful with our navigation now. There are very few distinctive features along the route and it's not a part of the country either of us knows well. The first waypoint is the M50 with Ledbury coming up 4 miles beyond. And added feature shown on the chart is a multiple track railway heading east-west beyond the town. We spot it. We now have few features until Leominster 15 miles ahead. As we approach it starts getting murky and the cloud-base lowers. We decide to leave our direct track route and follow the railway to Ludlow taking care to skirt the restricted area at Woofferton half way between the two towns. We say goodbye to 'Gloster' and call up Welshpool Radio on 123.25. We tell them we shall be routing from Ludlow to Craven Arms and Bishops Castle.

This is the first time we've encountered a 'Radio' service on this trip and it feels just right for me because I'm usually flying between smallish aerodromes. There are three main levels of service concerning aviation telecommunications. First you have ATC (Air Traffic Control Service) which is manned by licensed air traffic controllers and controls the kind of airports we've encountered so far. Basically the pilot obeys instructions unless safety or legal considerations dictate otherwise. The second level is AFIS (Aerodrome Flight Information Service) which is manned by licensed personnel trained to at least AFIS level. In law it is an information service and the pilot's decision is final. In practice, as AFIS is usually provided at busy aerodromes, it is better to treat it as an ATC service. The third level is A/G (Aerodrome air/ground radio service) and no ATC qualifications are required, the operator having an 'Authority to Operate'. In text books this type of facility provides the most basic information. In real life a great deal of sensible directions and advice are provided in addition to information and most operators achieve a very professional standard of conduct. I tend to treat A/G as AFIS in as much as it will be very stupid to ignore advice or information given.

We hear another aircraft departing Welshpool and turning in our direction. Aussie steps in straight away to get their altitude. Communicating through Welshpool we descend to allow a three hundred feet space and I steer across to the right of the valley. Both aircraft confirm they have the QNH set and I switch the landing light ON. We spot the low-wing single coming down the valley above our level passing roughly half a mile to our left. I climb up towards the cloud-base as Aussie wants to dial up 323.0 to find the NDB which is situated on the aerodrome. It is now very dull indeed but we can see main features for up to five miles easily. In these conditions the field will be hard to spot even if we know exactly where to look. They have one runway, asphalt, 830 x 18 metres, direction 04/22.

We are asked to join overhead not below 2000ft for Runway 04 left-hand QFE 1013. Welshpool is 233ft AMSL so the pressure has not dropped since leaving Gloucester. Due to high terrain close to the aerodrome, circuits are flown at 1500ft QFE and pilots are advised not to descend below safety height, *before* final approach, *after* positively identifying the runway. With the QFE set we cannot remain clear of cloud at 2000ft and report this. The best we can achieve is 1700ft. The radio operator calls another aircraft practising touch and goes for its position. It is downwind. By following the ADF needle we eventually spot the aerodrome. We have no more than two miles to run. We pass overhead at 1700ft just below the cloud-base and bank round sharply to join downwind descending to 1500ft. I run through the prelanding checks and start slowing Charlie Lima to 80 knots. Where is the other traffic? We heard him call base so he should be on finals by now. Aussie cautions "Don't turn till we see him". I say "No way Aus", just as he calls finals. We still don't see him. I look back over my shoulder towards the aerodrome. Nothing "I have him", calls Aussie, "eleven o'clock about 700 feet".

Where? I still don't see him. "Ten o'clock" chimes Aussie. Now I have him! "Well spotted Aussie". As he speeds past I swing round onto base. Aussie calls our position. We're about three miles out so I fly round onto finals only bringing in the flaps towards the end. Even so I touch down smoothly about a third into the runway leaving quite a long taxi to the buildings on the left near the top of the aerodrome. Aussie's friend has already arrived and waves as we taxi past to park. We shut down, clamber out and make our greetings. Our shut-down time is 16.50, 2.1 hours after start-up at Cardiff. What a difference!

Welshpool is just like coming home. It is small and friendly. A short walk of fifty metres across the grass gets us booked in and clasping a mug of coffee. People are interested in where

Below:
How did we get it all in? Unpacking at Welshpool.

Above:
The author checking the fuel tanks (top) and refuelling at Welshpool.

we've come from and where we're going. I often think they don't believe the answers we give them. Round Britain? Really? Yes, really, we assure them.

12th leg. 16.10 Sunday 11th October. I have just refuelled Charlie Lima after making the initial checks and we're going to get away soon. We had a great time yesterday. The aircraft we came to see is actually an Oldfield "Baby" Lakes designed by Barney Oldfield in Needham, Massachusetts. I must tell you about it because it is the antithesis of most aircraft we shall be looking at during our trip. Apparently is wasn't actually "designed," and if it was, Mr Oldfield threw the fag packet away years ago. For the oldies amongst you here's a smile. His company is BOAC; Barney Oldfield Aircraft Company. Aussie and I can't understand why his friend Julian hangars it. Surely it would be cheaper

kept in the glove compartment of his car? This little lady of the sky has intriguing statistics. Span= 16'8", Length= 13'9". Height= 4'6". Yes, that is correct. And, wait for it, her weight is 215 kgs! It is tiny and I soon realise that Julian is my kind of person when he describes flying. Normal flight, he says, shrinks his brain to the size of a lemon. Aerobatics down to a pea. I know that feeling so well!

We woke this morning to find clouds in the tree-tops. The improvement has been a long time coming. We now have 1200ft AAL. Seven miles out on our intended track north are masts 720ft AGL. We are rather concerned that the cloud doesn't drop further up the valley. Somebody has just come in and assured us it is fine, actually lifting the further north you go. Certainly the Liverpool actual looks good with 4 OKTA at 2300ft AAL. Aussie climbs in, we extend heartfelt thanks to Julian and Sue, and start up.

Runway in use is still 04. QFE 1017, QNH 1024. We wait for the circuit to clear and backtrack. We run briskly through our checks having done the majority back up the other end. I'm in the left seat. As we climb past the aerodrome buildings we wave down to Julian who has stayed to watch our departure. As 500 feet I turn onto a heading of 020°. The visibility soon improves and we spot the field where the "Baby" is kept. There is another strip close by to the west and we spot this too. A Cessna 172 like ours is based there but frankly, I wouldn't fancy tackling that strip without a very thorough briefing beforehand. We aim towards Oswestry. Aussie has a natter with Manchester on 119.4 as we shall enter their CTA (1500 to 3500ft ALT) near Hawarden aerodrome. They have no conflicting traffic shown and ask us to contact Hawarden Approach on 123.35. Hawarden, near Chester, is owned by British Aerospace and they build the 125 business jet there. To prove it they have one about to take-off. We scarcely catch a glimpse as it zooms up like a missile into the clouds. Closer in, they have another light aircraft crossing their ATZ from west to east. It is higher than us but should cross fairly close by. Despite cocking a wing up periodically we never catch sight of it. Hawarden pass us over to Liverpool Approach on 119.85. Aussie requests the weather. I glance across as he writes it down at a furious pace. 060/10-15 20km 4/23 6/40, I've seen enough. It's fine. Liverpool is 81ft AMSL but you wouldn't believe it to look at. The new runway, 2286 metres long, runs along the banks of the river Mersey.

We are cleared for a right-base join for runway 09, QFE 1021. Oh wow! There is a real treat.

The approach lights, gleaming beneath an overcast sky march out into the Mersey on huge gantries. It makes for a spectacular approach path. Putting Charlie Lima back onto terra-firma in a workmanlike way, Aussie says I'm getting like an airline pilot. Not too fussy, just do the job. Well, I'm certainly getting some practice. We turn back on ourselves to taxi up the 27 High Speed Turn Off, an angled taxiway which allows airliners a quick exit from the runway.

12.10. Monday 12th October. Still overcast but getting brighter. Either way we've spent enough time here. I try, probably not very well, to hide my impatience from Aussie. I sense it is getting him down as well. Monday mornings

aren't when it happens at Liverpool. There have been a few movements but the light is simply awful. The forecast doesn't show any sign of improving till this evening if at all. It's a shame because the re-developed Liverpool Airport is actually quite nicely designed and situated. The old airport, Speke, has a terminal with a preservation order on it and is connected to the new airport by an umbilical taxiway. I think one runway is still used by light aircraft to avoid strong cross-winds. Its axis is roughly 33/15. It is the only runway not listed as disused in my Flight Guide.

At 12.30 we get "start approved" and taxi to Hold Delta which is downhill from the main apron. In order to save the disc brakes I reduce the RPM from 1200 for short periods. While doing the Power check we notice a Mag drop on the right. Fortunately a longer run at 1900 RPM clears the problem but it does show why the manufacturer states that the engine should idle at 1200 RPM to prevent plugs fouling. We wish to photograph the approach to 09 and ATC give us clearance to take-off with a right turn over the Mersey. They slot us in to cross at 90° to the approach after a landing light aircraft. Then we climb steeply north of the airport to shoot the terminal area. Following this we request a departure route up the Mersey at 1200ft QNH. This is also approved. The sight of the approach to 09 has livened up my spirits no end. Aussie gets ready to shoot the centre of Liverpool as we fly past. It is impressive. The two main cathedrals stand out proud of their surroundings and we have the superb sight of the Mersey waterfront with the Liver building jutting out foursquare amongst its neighbours. Yet again, what a privilege. This is why I wanted to do this project.

Bloody hell! The cockpit has filled with white smoke! Has the engine exploded? White smoke means oil. I pull the throttle back and select Carb-heat. I can hardly see the instruments. I shove the nose down. If we have a fire I want to put Charlie Lima into the Mersey as soon as possible. A dive might put the fire out. Standard drill. Fly the aircraft first and foremost. No smell. Odd? Aussie has gone into hyper-drive. I open my window to try and clear the air as I'm positive we have no fire. Open windows could fan the flames. Aussie confirms we don't have fire. I can now see the instruments. I maintain a steady fast dive. The VSI is unwinding altitude at a phenomenal rate. Aussie finds the problem. The fire extinguisher has gone off. I shove the throttle in and cancel the Carb-heat control. We climb back up as the cockpit clears.

Above:
Loading our baggage on Liverpool apron having finished the pre-flight checks.

It has taken a paragraph to describe. In real time it took maybe five seconds. We've lost 300 feet. The retaining pin had fallen out of the fire extinguisher mounted between our seats. As Aussie twisted round to photograph the Liver building his heel pressed against the trigger. It has covered everything in dry powder. What kind of dry powder? Have we inhaled a toxic chemical? We feel fine. We can continue to Blackpool or return to Liverpool. We could put down at Woodvale south of Southport. We take stock and check. We both agree the drama is over. We shall continue to Blackpool. We pass by Woodvale, over the sea, giving them a quick call on 121.00. They pass us on to Warton 124.45. We shall pass through their MATZ before reaching Blackpool. Warton provides the LARS for the area. We are now in the Holyhead ASR. Liverpool is in the Barnsley ASR. Odd? I

think it is. We are also using a different ICAO chart since leaving Liverpool. We are now referring to Sheet 2171AB Northern England and Northern Ireland, Edition 14. Crossing the Ribble estuary, Warton asks us to contact Blackpool Approach on 135.95.

Aussie requests a high overhead join so we can snatch some aerial shots before landing. This is approved. Oh yes, before I forget we have turned our transponder back to 7000. Warton has us squawking 7062. After our orbit we are cleared for a down-wind join for 07 right-hand, QFE 1026. Blackpool formerly had four runways and still use three arranged in an unusual way to fan out from the west side of the aerodrome. These are 07/25, 10/28 and 13/31. Our runway is the shortest at 870 metres. I imagine this indicates that severe westerly winds are commonplace here. The light is a bit brighter up here and I've never flown in this region before. Apart from spotting the Blackpool Tower (not the one on the aerodrome) at 2000ft we are treated to splendid views around the coast as we circle.

Below:
On the way north from Liverpool with Blackpool shortly to come abeam.

Below:
Lining up on Blackpool's Runway 07.

Above:
A new perspective on an unmistakeable landmark, Blackpool's famous tower.

Below:
The cause of our sudden alarm, the floor of Charlie Lima covered in what proved to be baking powder after our fire extinguisher accidentally discharged.

I've got myself orientated now for 07 and let Charlie Lima down. Our base leg takes us out over the sea. This is lovely. Plenty of time. I steal a few glances along the shore as we drop towards the threshold. Another good one! Is it possible I'm getting the hang of this? A little care has to be taken not to land long. There is a large part of the runway that is disused at the 25 end. Parking on the grass, and having shut down, we clamber out and dust ourselves off. What a mess. The interior of the cabin is coated in white dust. I could murder a soft drink. We make enquiries and A.N.T. can hoover us out immediately. Can they do our throats first? It turns out that the material in the extinguishers is baking powder and we are assured it won't do us any harm. It will harm Charlie Lima, however, as it is highly corrosive. The engineers set about the cabin with powerful vacuum cleaners and are soon able to declare Charlie Lima fit and well. We hear an opinion that more damage is done to aircraft by extinguishers inadvertently set off then will ever be done by fire. I'm sure this is true. Fire in the air is indeed a very rare occurrence, especially in small aeroplanes. Having got proceedings under way we make a dash for the bar. Whew! What sweet relief.

Our next night stop will be Carlisle and I've plotted a course following the coast to Maryport where we shall turn inland. Most of the flight will be over water so we don our life-jackets. I'm really looking forward to this leg. We taxi to the hold for 07 and, with the QNH set at 1027 (Blackpool is a mere 34ft AMSL), get our take-off clearance. Our start-up time was 15.20, we have been on the ground just over 2 hours. Well done A.N.T. After clearing the circuit our course takes us along the front at Blackpool looking out for a

Below:
Passing Walney Island aerodrome, Barrow-in-Furness.

Above:
Hilpsford Point, south of Barrow.

knotted handkerchief on a bare head. What is this country coming to? Not one in sight. Leaving the Blackpool ATZ we go back to Warton on 124.45 for LARS as the Tower slides past Aussie's window. The foundations are made of cotton bales washed ashore from a wreck I'm told. Can this be true?

We fly up to Fleetwood then turn north-west on a heading of 330°. The easterly wind has died down so we have little drift to compensate for. Ahead is a huge expanse of sea before we reach Barrow-in-Furness. 13 nautical miles. How apt. There is an operational aerodrome just beyond Barrow and I have made a note of the Tower frequency but it is not needed as Warton inform us it is closed at this time. We now get our first sight of the towering hills and mountains of the Lake District. We pass a hightec windmill farm built upon the disused aerodrome at Millom. Ahead is a large Danger Zone D406/50 OCNL/80 extending from the coast way out to sea in a large fan shape. Luckily this is closed also. Beyond is R413/2.2, the atomic plant at Sellafield. We decide to stay out over the sea. Even so we are close enough to get a good look. A plume of steam out of Sellafield thrusts upwards to merge with the cloud-base. I'm not at all keen on nuclear power and find the spectacle of the vast plant with the beauty of the Lake District beyond both awesome and forbidding. We fly on, the trustworthy Lycoming mounted inches in front of our toes performing its pounding duties without complaints. Our instruments all show normal and sensible readings. I'm developing even more regard for this aeroplane and I'm known for respecting machines without developing sentimental attachments. I reach out and pat the coaming. We fly on past Whitehaven and Workington. A silver sheen appears on the sea as a weak sun struggles to pierce the thin overcast. Our heading is now 020°. I had turned before reaching St Bees Head just south of Whitehaven. At Maryport I bank the right wing down and straighten-up heading 060° direct for Carlisle Airport. I feel a slight tinge of sadness having left the coast, perhaps accentuated as we return to more practical matters of precise overland navigation. We both pay much more attention to the chart.

Below:
The high-tech windmill farm at the disused aerodrome at Millom.

We are looking for a multi-track railway which should be on our right. Okay, there it is. The town of Aspatria should appear over the nose as the railway bends slightly left to pass through it. It does. Straight ahead we look for a 325 foot mast at Wigton, a VRP for Carlisle. Spotting this we sign off with the Flight Information Service that has followed our path since leaving the Warton frequency and dial in Carlisle on 123.60. They respond and we are cleared to continue in on track. The disused aerodrome of Great Orton is identified and slips by one mile to the north. Shortly after the conurbation of Carlisle is clearly seen. The Tower clears us in for a direct approach to runway 07, QFE 1021. I adjust our heading slightly south to 065° as I want to pass over the northern part of the town. Our track should take us over the M6 motorway just before it bends to the west. Flying across Carlisle I put Charlie Lima into a descent, reducing power on the throttle to leave it nudging the lower part of the green segment. Below this I will pull the Carb-heat out fully. Passing over the motorway we sight the runway dead ahead. Excellent. We have three miles to run and Aussie reports this to the Tower. They acknowledge and ask us to report short finals number one. There is other traffic on the frequency RAF traffic. Two C.130 Hercules have taxied out and are occupying both the holds near the middle of 07. We are instructed to land and continue past both taxiways. With the RAF watching I want to put in a good performance and really flare Charlie Lima out to touch down very smoothly. It's pretty good. With almost nil wind and no turbulence my task, it has to be said, is made very easy. Passing by the two Her-

cules, our instruction is to turn around and wait whilst they back-track for a formation take-off. As they enter the runway we are cleared to taxi to the apron to park on stand One Delta. Having shut-down we stand beside Charlie Lima and avidly watch the two Hercules perform a formation low level pass back down the runway towards the west. An impressive sight. We learn that we're arrived at the tail-end of a major French/British military exercise on the airport.

The exercise was probably the most unusual photo opportunity to occur at Carlisle since Watt invented the steam powered light bulb and we've just missed it. The trouble with military matters is that they are not widely publicised. It seems the airport was piled up with Transalls and well as Hercules. We learn that at present there are no scheduled services operating from Carlisle, (previously know as Crosby on Eden), and after our arrival at 16.25 there are very few movements. Most of these are local training flights. We had thought about getting into Prestwick way back in Liverpool, (was that really only this morning), but the Prestwick 'actual' is very poor. The light has gone completely so we decide to stay the night. The staff here are super friendly and Charlie Lima gets hangared for the night. Whilst in the process of doing this we get a real jaw dropper of a surprise. At the back of the hangar is a privately owned Fairey Gannet!

11.00hrs/13th October 1992. 15th leg. We have decided to make a decisive decision and we are going to Edinburgh. Prestwick and Glasgow are out. The en route weather isn't very good in places as far as we can tell so I shall plot a course using as many valleys as possible. I have been walking around the airport in search

Below:
Long, long finals to Carlisle!

Below:
Short finals to Carlisle. Note the Hercules holding for take off.

of local advice on potential weather problems and in my travels have spotted some very nice aeroplanes. Apart from a couple of beautiful classic De Havillands in immaculate condition, a Moth Minor and Hornet Moth, there is a superb example of another classic aeroplane for sale. It is a high-wing Stinson called, I think, the 'Gullwing' Reliant. This is in mouth-watering condition and has my chequebook twitching even though I can't possibly afford to buy it, let alone keep it airworthy. Together with the Gannet which towers over everything. this has been an interesting visit.

Aussie will fly this leg and my job in the last hour or so has been to furnish him with as much information as possible. He, of course, has been busy with his cameras. I have never flown north of the Midlands before so I'm very cautious in evaluating the information. I have driven very extensively across all of the UK in the last twenty plus years so that is a great help but Scotland has a lot of hills and mountains. At 09.00 we had a 4000ft cloud base here. Fresh winds bringing rain from the west were forecast. They haven't even started to appear and it is almost calm now. The pressure settings are exactly the same as yesterday. Edinburgh has 2500ft cloudbase and 15-20 miles visibility. By checking Prestwick and Glasgow I can see that the very poor conditions have already reached them and the front is moving easterly. We would not wish to get cut off midway. Looking at the chart there are spot heights listed at 2287, 2268, 2403 and 2028 feet west of the A74. To the east 2257, 2697 and 2455 feet occur. With 2500ft cloudbase given at Edinburgh it would be very stupid to attempt to fly direct and a route via Newcastle up the east coast would be a very long way round. Over a coffee Aussie considers my findings. The route I suggest is to follow the A74 to Abington. Then the valley towards Biggar using the railway as a guide path up to Livingstone. The A74 follows a valley through the hills and by closely inspecting the 1500ft contour line on the chart we see that we can remain 500ft AGL without climbing much above 2000ft if required. Aussie agrees with my suggestion.

Next he pays a visit to the Tower to double-check the time the front arrived at Prestwick and the wind direction and speed. If we leave now (11.30) there should be a comfortable gap. I have already fuelled Charlie Lima to full tanks and made the pre-flight inspection. We start up at 11.40 and take-off on runway 25 climbing and circling to get some shots of the airport from above. This complete, Aussie sets the nose on 295° to intercept the A74 near Gretna Green.

I wish you were up here with us. It is really very nice flying weather. Who could suspect that such vile conditions are creeping towards us not more than 50 miles away? This of course is the danger and there is no substitute for careful pre-flight planning. To our north is the Spadeadam WRDA (Weapon Range Danger Area) listed as D510/5.5 OCNL/20. We would know it's active even if the ATC hadn't told us because the rumble of powerful jets could be heard on the ground at Carlisle. At Gretna we pass from the London FIR to the Scottish FIR and switch from Carlisle 123.60 to 119.875 to request a Flight Information Service. Both Aussie and I are concerned that the low flying jets may appear near us. Even though they won't be supersonic, if the worst happens, it is doubtful we would have time to blink let alone take evasive action. In a mid-air crash between a Cessna and a Jaguar recently the rear crew member ejected instantly after the impact. The front seat pilot was three quarters of a second behind and this delay killed him. The Cessna came down in bits.

It is now 12.30 and we have just called Edinburgh Approach. 121.2 to tell them we've arrived at the Kirknewton VRP. We entered the CTR SFC-6000ft ALT seven miles back. We have been fairly lucky I would say. The flight up to Abington was very pleasant indeed. I know the A74 very well and really enjoyed picking out all the familiar landmarks as we passed by. The cloud-base stayed high too, probably never getting lower than 2500ft AMSL which meant we could stay well above 500ft AGL. It got lower to the north-west of Biggar but we still managed to squeeze through following the railway just as in the good old days. Conditions improved quickly and we stayed fairly low (about 800ft AGL) until climbing up to 1500ft near Livingstone. Aussie thinks we should buy a ticket from British Rail due to the service offered.

As we get closer, heading 045° we are handed over to the Tower frequency 118.70. They in turn instruct us to join down-wind for runway 26 left-hand QFE 1025, call established downwind. With the field in sight Aussie sets himself up for the join. Runway 26/08 looks rather short. In fact it is 909 metres long but the generous width of 46 metres helps conceal the length. There is another factor. Edinburgh is a most unusual airport. The old airport survives almost intact with only a shortish runway approximately 02/20 being disused. A new runway and terminal has been built to the west and the new runway (2560 metres long) extends north across the top of the old airport. A third runway on the old airport is still useful for airliners when the

Above:
Ground controllers hard at work at Edinburgh

Above:
Hold Golf and runway direction signs, Edinburgh

Below:
Airliners and business jets demonstrating how busy Edinburgh is.

Bottom:
Detail of the 'Direction to Stands' signs at Edinburgh.

wind gets up as it still has 1829 metres in the direction 13/31. The runway layout at the old airport is atypical too. Rather than the normal arrangement looking like a cross between the letter 'A' and a teepee, these are arranged crossed upon a more central point.

I'm pleased it is a long wide runway for our Cessna. The wind has got up and provides plenty of turbulence. Aussie is having to work quite hard using large control inputs to keep Charlie Lima descending towards the runway centre-line. The Tower has given the wind strength as 20 to 25 knots (23 to 29 miles per hours). Fortunately it is blowing almost straight along the runway. There is nothing for me to do now. Just sit back and watch Aussie get on with it, keeping my knees and feet as clear of the yoke and rudder bar as possible. The gusts slam into us like a large unseen fist and Charlie Lima reels with the impact. The stall warner blips as the airflow over our wings becomes ruptured. Doggedly Aussie pursues his chosen line of approach and doesn't attempt much of a flare. There is no need, our ground speed is barely 40 knots (46 mph) when we touch down. "Well done Aussie", I call across the intercom as we retract the flaps and restore the carb-heat IN after landing.

It was a nice touch-down too. Our shut-down time is 12.50 so the total time was one hour ten minutes. We are now being well received. The operations manager and assistant manager have come across to meet us. We have lunch and discuss the possibilities. An hour after landing the front comes through with torrential rain and probably higher winds. This hasn't stopped the airliners from continuing as normal but we certainly made our flight at the right time. For now

west abeam the long new runway to shoot the airport 'out-of-sun' then continue to the bridges. There is a lot of scheduled airliner activity and even though I position Charlie Lima to cross quickly between these arrivals and departures we just can't get our clearance. I circle again and again, varying the size of the circle in an attempt to position just south and west of the terminal as each succeeding airliner departs but each time there is another lining up and the controller can't see enough space to let us through to cross. Obviously our requirements don't stack very high against the operating costs of the big boys and their schedules have priority.

At last there is a gap. It makes a change to bank to the right. We have been holding for over twenty minutes which gives a good idea just how busy Edinburgh can get. It only takes a couple of minutes to reach the bridges which present quite a spectacle as we circle in the early evening light. The newer road bridge looks slender and frail against the huge girder mass of the much earlier rail bridge. This is most certainly another notable milestone on our trip. Returning to the airport our luck has changed and we get a clearance to pass overhead as a Boeing 737 turns onto finals beyond the city centre. We can see it

Below:
The Forth Rail Bridge not quite showing its best side in the gloomy weather but spectacular nonetheless.

Top:
Dismal weather racing at us across the fuel farm at Edinburgh airport.

Above:
The BAA airside crew bus kindly delivers us back to Charlie Lima for our trip to Perth.

there is not much for us to do except sit it out. Not being one to miss an opportunity, Aussie takes shots inside the terminal building, transferring later to the control tower of ground operations.

By 14.30 the worst has passed and a bright sky with lots of sun has appeared by 15.00. This presents excellent light for Aussie and I follow in his wake trying for some detail shots of apron activity. We decide to get airborne for some aerial photography, taking Peter Sands the airport assistant operations manager with us. This provides us with a opportunity to show our thanks for the help he has extended. I am taking this flight leaving Aussie free for his cameras. I start up at 16.45 and take-off on 26 again. By climbing above circuit height we can circle to the south of the airport. The Forth bridges are clearly visible to the north and we wish to pass

Top:
Aussie lines up CL for landing on Perth's Runway 21 in the pouring rain.

Above and Below:
CL and the Flying College's aircraft all submitting to the downpour at Perth.

clearly. As before our runway is 26 left-hand and, with the wind now much reduced I have an opportunity to make a smooth approach and landing. Whilst descending on base leg, and just about to turn finals, a flock of twenty or more geese in a 'Vee' formation pass beneath our path just fifty feet below. After landing I am instructed to turn left onto Runway 13 and then right onto the Southern Link Taxiway which takes us back to our previous parking space on the South Apron close to the GA (General Aviation) Terminal. For those of you who have a particular interest we take down our predeparture information from the ATIS frequency on 132.075 and our ground movements were controlled on 121.75. We shall stop here for the night as Aussie has some business to attend to in the city tomorrow morning.

12.30hrs 14th November. 16th leg. We have the weather copied off ATIS. 260/15 15km NIL WX 3/16 6/25 QNH 1005. Good, wind still down the runway but the lower cloud 3 OKTAs at 1600ft is rather low. We are also on another chart, Sheet 2150ABCD Scotland, Orkney and Shetland, Edition 14. The highest spot heights either side of our track which follows the M90 motorway to Perth are 1168ft to the east and 1243ft to the west so we don't expect any problems with comfortable terrain clearances. As we taxi out I re-check our VFR flight details given by Ground Control after start-up was approved.

We are to proceed VFR, not above 2000ft QNH 1005, taxi to Hold Oscar, Runway 26. This will take us back up the Southern Link, across Runway 13/31 and along the quaintly named 'Lazy Lane' taxiway to the Hold. Aussie is flying this leg for sentimental reasons. Perth (previously Scone) was the base for his Commercial Pilot's License course and a lot of water has been passed since his last visit there. With the customary checks complete we line up and take off cleared for a right-hand turn towards the Forth bridges. Although much duller than yesterday evening the two vast structures still present an awe inspiring spectacle. Edinburgh Tower hands us over to Approach who want us to report passing the VRP at Kelty just north of a stipulated Entry/Exit point into the CTR. A bit of close chart reading satisfies us that identifying Kelty is straightforward and indeed we soon have the VRP in sight. Passing over this waypoint we hear a Bell Jet Ranger contact Edinburgh Approach heading towards us but we fail to catch his altitude. A quick call informs us that he is 800ft and we are now 1500ft on the QNH. Rule 19 in Aviation Law states that aircraft following a line feature, the motorway in our case, shall keep the feature on the left. This

Above.
The Stevenson Box for recording Met data. This example is at Perth.

Left:
An elderly Bedford fuel tanker and fuel pump at Perth.

Below left:
Another hazard of light aircraft operation, areas of grass coned off because of boggy conditions.

goes way back to the 1920s when at least one mid-air collision resulted when opposing aircraft were on the same side of a railway for example. We spot the Jet Ranger lower down on the far side of the motorway. Edinburgh now inform us that there is intense gliding activity to our right operating out of Portmoak. We spot several aircraft apparently ridge soaring north of the gliding centre. None are seen nearby. We now encounter rain which isn't very heavy. Visibility beneath is still good. A few minutes later the rain passes and we catch our first sight of Perth with its distinctive golf course set on an island in the middle of the River Tay. The aerodrome lies beyond and 10 to 15° east. We say goodbye to Edinburgh and already have Perth Approach 122.3 selected on Box Two, Unexpectedly we are asked to contact Perth Tower on 119.8 instead. Cut out the middle man?

Perth Tower gives us instructions to join down-wind for Runway 21 left-hand, QFE 991, number four. Perth is a very busy place with intensive training operations sometimes using all three of the runways virtually simultaneously. The twin-engined aircraft will mainly use 03/21 at 853 metres with the two shorter runways, 10/28 (asphalt) 609 metres, and 16/34 (grass) 620 metres, being used on the whole by singles. (As well as 03/21 of course). Very high winds have been forecast but these have not yet occurred I'm glad to say. Aussie has a reasonable cross-wind component to cope with and although not his best landing to date, I would be well satisfied with it in these blustery conditions. We are led up 21 to the end, turn left onto 10 then first right to a parking spot on the main apron close to the Tower. Fifteen minutes after parking a terrific squall, more like an airborne mobile waterfall, crashes belligerently across the aerodrome. It has not taken us by surprise as we could see it coming when we joined to land. One poor student gets caught out and is instructed to make his way to Dundee and land there. Dundee is our next stop barely 12nm away. Our total time from Edinburgh was 30 minutes (Chock to chock as it were).

We haven't too much time to spend here. The squall passes by as quickly as it arrived and bright blazing sunshine glitters off dripping aeroplanes. We rush around with our cameras to capture the effect before it dries off, take a quick look in the hangars, and climb aboard Charlie Lima once more. I take the P.1 left seat this time and discover that the wind has turned around so that we are instructed to taxi for the Hold to Runway 34, the grass runway. It's our first time on grass throughout the trip since the very first departure for Southend. Once airborne after a typically bumpy take-off run we are cleared to climb out in a wide right-hand circuit up to 2000ft QFE before making an orbit overhead to photograph the field. This complete we can actually see Dundee so I point the nose towards the airport which has a single runway 10/28 parallel and close to the north bank of the Firth of Tay.

We ask Dundee, which has a single Approach/Tower frequency on 122.90, if we can orbit overhead for photographic reasons. The answer is affirmative, 2000ft on the QFE 1002. Notice the reluctance to allow us to operate within the ATZ, a factor which has cropped up several times previously. I'm not carping. It shows that the ATCOs are on top of their job, making quick decisions that keep their airspace 'clean' and allowing visiting 'missions' to cavort about, while all the time providing meaningful information in one form or another. Just circling over Dundee Airport in an incomplete 'figure eight' to establish ourselves down-wind for Runway 28 presents some superb views. At times

like this I seriously question whether I would rather be pilot or passenger. As a pilot attempting the approach for the first time coupled with the preceding consideration I would definitely not want to relinquish this experience. As a passenger I could really appreciate the view.

Honestly, I'm trying to do both. The primary duty is to fly Charlie Lima accurately and safely. At the same time I'm stealing quick glances at the unfolding vista. I will say it again; this is what flying small highly manoeuvrable aircraft is all about. We are flying slowly enough to appreciate the scenery and at the same time there is enough going on to provide a high 'work-load' for the pilot. Established on finals at 150 feet, approaching the threshold, I get a severe shock. We plunge almost vertically fifty feet before I can shove the throttle forward to arrest the drop. Before the threshold there are playing fields full of people eagerly in pursuit of some fashionable ball game. Our nose is pointed pretty much straight at their haircuts. Although thoroughly occupied with aiming at a point just beyond the 'zebra-crossing' marked on the runway I cannot help seeing, in almost peripheral vision, some faces swinging around towards me.

It is hard to understand what is going on, and I haven't got time to work it out. We are getting buffeted left, right and centre. The air is in turmoil. And we have a substantial crosswind. Terrific, all my least favourite landing conditions thrown together at once. We are still on line for the runway and I shall make a determined effort to get Charlie Lima down. Kicking the rudder left then right then left again. Great big bootfuls. Yanking the yoke left and right, trying to keep straight with the into wind wing down, pushing and pulling, struggling to maintain the descent. This is awful. Crossing the threshold I cut the power. By a miracle, it seems, we are still above the runway centre-line. As if exhausted, Charlie Lima collapses onto the runway. I hear the screech as the right wheel makes contact. We veer off to the right and the left wheel drops heavily. I slam the rudder even further over to the left and we straighten up. I'm still trying to fly the aircraft even though we're on the ground. I turn the yoke hard right. I should have done this as soon as we touched. A stupid mistake. We slow down and I start dabbing the brakes. Whew! We've made it. My nerves are severely frayed and I'm sweating with the effort. The Tower tells us to back-track to the apron.

We discover that when the wind is roughly northerly it is normal to encounter difficult conditions as the air tumbles downhill across the buildings then over the trees beyond the airport. We watch a student pilot in a 152 having a terri-

Above:
The Air Traffic Control officers at Dundee look out over the apron toward the Tay.

ble time. A little later, up in the Tower, I follow the landing path of a small twin-engined airliner. They end up touching down nose-wheel first, the mains hitting very heavily. This makes me feel a lot better. After all, if the pros are struggling, then my efforts weren't quite as bad as they seemed at the time. I had expected Aussie to be critical but he isn't. His opinion is that obviously I was struggling but, credit is due, mainly because the actual landing really wasn't too bad and I managed to hang on and control the situation. By now I feel that my self-esteem is almost restored.

With the QFE and QNH reading being the same, and just by looking at the site, it seems that Dundee might be the lowest airport we will visit at 13ft AMSL. Liverpool, which lies alongside the Mersey looked very low but was surprisingly high at 81ft AMSL. Southend, much further inland was 48ft AMSL. Blackpool, just in from the coast was 34ft AMSL. The winner so far, and it will probably remain so, is Shoreham which is a bare 6ft above mean sea level

Dundee has a seasonal problem with birds. Being large and flat with abundant grass areas, airports inevitably attract birds, and it is ironic that invariably our powered metal machines have to deny nature's feathered creatures a suitable landing spot because their superior aerial accomplishments conflict with our clumsy, fast, ungainly and brutal attempts at flight. For centuries, as I understand it, the small flatland now occupied by the airport has been used by migrating birds, and they arrive in thousands. In consequence, especially during the migratory periods, ingenious methods have been devised to disperse the birds. One such method is to broadcast distress calls over a loudspeaker mounted on a vehicle equipped with tapes pertinent to the various species arriving. I find it sad that it is necessary to inflict such measures in order to provide us with the privilege of flight. Indeed, the inestimable rewards of powered flight are always counterbalanced by the nuisance created, be it noise, cost, or danger. Glider pilots, by comparison, are much more in accordance with natural forces, are invariably better 'real' pilots, and inflict negligible environmental damage. Science has failed to provide an alternative to fossil-fuelled, metal, fabric, wood and various plastic, fibreglass, or composite material machines, to achieve speedy, reachable, safe, and comfortable transportation over substantial distances. This is a price we have to pay. Many people question the cost and I will admit to considerable sympathy. Even with these misgivings, while the opportunity exists, I want to fly despite the costs, and accept that it is a very self-indulgent exercise.

Aussie has just returned from his photographic explorations and it's time to cut the chatter and decide on our next step. We have planned to overnight in Aberdeen. The surface wind there is strong and gusty but straight down the runway. Atrocious conditions are speeding down from the far north along the east coast. The distance from airport to airport is 55nm. If we make a quick getaway, we should be able to get in. Strapped in and started up we get taxi clearance to the Hold for Runway 28, QNH 1001. It is the shortest taxi distance so far. Our departure instructions are to turn left over the Tay and route to Broughty Castle east of Dundee before turning onto track for Aberdeen. Our initial track from the Broughty Castle VRP is 030°. With 20 to 30 knots winds from roughly 340° there will be substantial drift to allow for. Clearance to line-up is received so I taxi out to the centre-line using right brake and right rudder to swing the nose west. A quick check round the panel, T's and P's good, D.I. agrees with runway heading, take-off clearance is given, open the throttle firmly forward to full-power, yoke fully forward to keep the nosewheel firmly on the asphalt, and right aileron down. As the speed increases the turbulent wind effect gets stronger and a lot of rudder has to be used to keep straight. At sixty knots Charlie Lima is distinctly skittish. I yank the control column back, hauling us into the air then almost immediately relax the pressure which allows the nose to drop and airspeed to increase. Due to the very bumpy conditions I climb out at a higher speed than usual and try to keep the ASI between 75 and 80 knots. Even so the stall warner sounds frequently as we claw and buffet our way slowly upwards. At 500ft a left turn is commenced with 15 degrees of bank. The 225° turn onto track for Broughty has taken us across the Tay almost to the south bank. In the air I have actually turned onto 240° to compensate for drift. Our path just clips the northern limits of the Leuchars MATZ and as we pass over Broughly Castle we say cheerio to Dundee and dial up Leuchars for a Flight Information Service on 126.5.

Visibility is superb in the evening light and the terrain below is bathed in warm sunlight with an orange tinge. Only the clouds over the high ground to the north give a visual clue as to the behaviour of the air as they are torn apart into very dramatic shapes. It is bumpy. Very bloody bumpy and after twenty minutes my arms and shoulders are aching with the effort of keeping Charlie Lima on the straight and level. We seem to be the only people in the area as Leuchars is silent. We are flying at 1800ft and normally I would expect smoother conditions. Undoubtedly the high hills reaching up to 3000ft are to blame. At times we have 30 degrees of drift angle. It is so accentuated it looks comical and our ground speed must be down to 80 knots at times. We are now following the A94 which is the main road from Perth to Aberdeen. The disused aerodrome at Edzell is seen covered in aerials. Aussie asks Leuchars for the Aberdeen weather. A couple of minutes later Leuchars asks if we are ready to copy. It is amusing to me to watch Aussie bouncing in his seat, his fist tightly clenching the pen, struggling to maintain contact with his knee-pad. "What have we got Aussie?" "It's not very good, he announces and reads it out. 330/19, 7kms, RA SN, SH 1 OKTA CB at 600, 8 OKTA at 1500, +2/+1, 1001/995. "Showers, rain and snow as well as CBs, what do you think we do now?" "Well", say Aussie, "We're most of the way there now and the cloudbase is basically 1500 feet; the rain and snow will probably be very localised so let's have a look". I agree and tell him I'd rather have 19 knots almost down the runway than turn back and have another go at Dundee unless we have to. We dial up the Aberdeen ATIS on 121.85 and copy Information Zulu. The significant elements are runway very wet and surface turbulence. As Aussie says goodbye to Leuchars and selects Aberdeen Approach on 120.4. I switch the pitot heater ON and the landing light ON.

We are still in the clear but can see the massed banks of cumulus cloud forming a line just north of Stonehaven. They look very angry and very intimidating and tower heaped together high into the heavens. The tops will be well over twenty thousand feet. Beneath it is pitch black from our standpoint and looks impenetrable. We are 5nm south-west of Stonehaven which is a VRP. There is an Entry/Exit point just south of the town but Aberdeen Approach instructs us to descend to 1000ft and hold. The reason soon becomes clear as we hear a Kittyhawk call-sign announced. This signifies a Royal Flight and we soon spot the BAe 146 just before it disappeared into the solid cloud. As the front rushes south the air before it seems to be boiling and we are now right in it. What we'd had before was just the prelude. At times I have the controls at full deflection and shove the rudder over to help us remain level. Charlie Lima is being tossed around like a small boat on a rough ocean. Aberdeen instructs us to position over the sea east of Stonehaven not above 1000ft on the QNH. The front is now upon us and we are forced down as we orbit. At 500 feet we can see along the coast. We are still in VMC. Aberdeen Approach instruct us to follow the coast to Bridge of Don which is north-east of the city. The airport lies to the north-west. We accept and plunge deeper into the murk. Snow flurries alternate with pounding rain. I select the carb-heat fully out, fearful of icing in the carburettor. Aussie asks for another weather check. It is still basically the same. This is hard to believe as we battle our way north through what are by far the worst conditions I have ever encountered. This is very personal now. It is us against the elements and I'm not flying any more, I'm fighting. I can feel the controls trying to wrench themselves away from my grip. It is both frightening and immensely exhilarating. I'm just so aware of the awesome fundamental forces that are being unleashed against us. Aussie gives me encouragement as I twist Charlie Lima through another violent gust.

We have no windscreen wiper and I'm really thankful we have the rain-repellent applied. Sheets of torrential rain smash into us but the water skids off instantaneously. It is amazing, we can still see quite clearly through all this for up to five miles. The lights are on in Aberdeen as we slowly buck and plunge towards the Bridge of Don. There it is! We can see the mouth of the river and the bridge itself. Aussie reports in and we are handed over to the Tower (118.10). The controller clears us for a right base approach to runway 34. I turn inland. Aussie tells me to steer north-west. There is a squat radio mast just south of the runway and we want to stay well clear of it. There is a tremendous downpour taking place in the vicinity of the mast and this blanks off the visibility. To the north-west we can see over the nose for at least

Above:
Being collected from a well tied-down Charlie Lima at Aberdeen.

seven or eight miles. The cloudbase has risen slightly and I climb up to 600 feet. There is still no sign of the airport. Surely it should be in sight now? A helicopter reports the cloud down to ground level up at Peterhead. We have been flying on the QFE for some time now and the airport is 215ft AMSL. Therefore the cloudbase here is above 700ft AMSL. Lower cloud forces us down again. Where on earth is the airport? The controller tells us she has us on radar four miles to the east and apparently still heading north. In fact we're heading north-west so Aussie tells her we are turning onto base-leg. This is very odd indeed. The Tower has confirmed our position to be just where we wanted to be. Whow! What a sight. A long low hill to

Below:
A British Airways 757 being quickly turned round at Aberdeen.

the east of the airport has blocked our view as we're so low down. The airport is ablaze in light, crystal clear and gleaming. We are spot on for right-base. I quickly tell Aussie I shall go for a fast approach, 75 knots, 10 degrees of flap and fly onto the runway until down to ten feet or so. If it looks good I'll pull the power. Any bad turbulence and I'll go around.

Aussie agrees with these precautions although even before we turn onto finals it is apparent that the ferocity experienced during the last fifteen minutes has died away. Aberdeen airport seems almost to be in the eye of the hurricane – surrounded by abysmal treacherous weather, this huge glittering expanse extends its welcome. The wind is strong and volatile as we fly towards the massive runway, all of 1829 metres long and 46 metres wide, but it is almost head-on presenting few problems. I am quite tense, expecting a strong gust to punch us any second. As we pass over the threshold at fifty feet it gets calmer. I fly down lower and lower. Still no gust. Sure, it is bumpy, but not unreasonably so. I juggle the controls but with quite small movements. This is it, decision time. I pull the throttle fully back, let Charlie Lima sink, pitch the nose up as the speed bleeds off and flare out, holding back, more, a little more, juggling around, keeping the wings level, pulling back firmly now, the nose rises and we're down. A little bump and skidding screech hardly worth noticing. We've done it!

The relief is overwhelming. I rely on Aussie to talk me through the ATC instructions towards our parking place in front of the highly stylish, ultra-modern, multi-layered control tower. Hours and hours of disciplined training take over. We complete all the shut-down checks one step at a time. At the end as the propeller thumps to a stop, radios OFF, Nav Aids OFF, thumbing the electrical switches OFF, Mags OFF, Master Switch OFF, Fuel Selector OFF, in the ensuing silence we turn to each other, size up the emotional response, and gasp a combined laugh and sigh of relief. We've done it! It is really very odd. At no time did I feel we were in any real danger. It was dammed hard work; sheer effort combined with resolute concentration. I know one thing for certain. I could never have done it on my own.

I realise this last bit may sound rather sycophantic so it needs to be qualified. Since he has over 7000 hours flying experience, I think it is a practical matter for me to trust Aussie to make the decisions. After all, he has been there many times before and I know very well that he is a cautious pilot. For me it was like climbing my own Everest. What I have just seen is the result of calm, reasoned, decision making. When training I often took the opportunity to fly in foul weather with seasoned instructors in order to gain some knowledge of what it can be like and what should be done about it. At any time we could have turned back and retreated to Edinburgh if necessary. Two points were of utmost importance. One; what are the actual conditions at the destination? Two; do we have a viable alternative or alternatives? If you are in trouble no aerodrome or airport can refuse to accept you, so RAF Leuchars becomes another alternative. In giving you this account it is impossible to relate everything raised or considered. Let me just say that at all points on the way an appraisal was made and a decision taken. A lot of discussion took place over our intercom. That is why we were firmly convinced we were not undertaking anything foolhardy or courting unduly dangerous circumstances. On a slightly frivolous note, would the Kittyhawk flight deliberately enter dangerous conditions? Of course not. For them it was part of the daily grind. For me, in a very small aeroplane it was very exciting, extremely demanding, and, having touched down safely, immensely rewarding.

Below:
Typical apron furniture at Aberdeen.

5.
Scotland to Yorkshire

We returned to the airport the next morning to find another mixed bag of violent weather confronting us. Once again I must emphasise that on our journey so far, every airport has provided a very cordial welcome and Aberdeen is no exception. Ranger 2, a Leyland DAF van of Sherpa origins has been placed at our disposal to take us around the airport. Our driver couldn't possibly be more helpful. Nothing is too much trouble. Photo opportunities abound. We have searing bright sunlight between colossal downpours. Aussie gets shots of airliners emerging from waterfalls. There is frenetic helicopter activity from three major operators supplying the North Sea rigs. The helicopters have to use approved runways and it seems incredibly weird to watch these large VTOL machines taxiing long distances to the departure points. Incoming flights follow a similar procedure. Aberdeen, with the helicopters, is the Heathrow of Scotland. Unlike Heathrow we watch with interest the passengers embarking clad in full survival gear. This shows us that the operations to keep the oil and gas flowing are a deadly serious business. At one point Ranger 2 is asked to undertake a runway inspection. Our ever tolerant chauffeur accepts the irreverent banter we produce as he lines up on 34. It'll never fly we advise him.

During a particularly bleak, wet and windy spell around half past two we paid a visit to the Met Office in the Tower. They painted a very grim picture for us. We certainly didn't lack for information. They regularly experience long spells of bad weather up here and understand what we require. However, when the Met officer says things like, "Don't even think of flying further north for the next four days unless you're prepared seriously to risk your life", even I know it's time to reconsider. Wick for example was reporting 55 knot surface winds plus the odd thunderstorm to enliven the proceedings. We had hoped to get up to the Shetlands and Orkneys via Inverness and Wick. Just as in Plymouth the weather has conspired to prevent us

Top:
Joining the runway inspection in Ranger 2. The aircraft ahead is off on a perilous over-water trip (bearing in mind the weather conditions) to Scandinavia.

Above:
Ranger 2 chasing a helicopter. The helicopter got away.

reaching the extremities of our green and very wet land. The 24, 48, 72, 96 and even the 120-hour forecast charts for the North Atlantic, covering a huge area stretching from eastern Canada to Russia and from the North Pole to North Africa complete the picture. It is no go.

It is now 15.20 on 15th October and winter has arrived early this year. There were heavy snowfalls in the Scottish Highlands last night. We now decide to see if it is possible to escape from Aberdeen. We request 'actuals' from Edinburgh, Dundee, Perth and Glasgow. In a couple of minutes we have them. What a strange contrast. They are all showing really quite favourable conditions. Basically, as the front batters its way southwards, struggling to get across and around the Highlands, the energy consumed in doing this is enormous. Having broken free there is nothing left and the front dissipates leaving brisk winds and small shreds of fluffy cumulo-stratus streaked across a largely clear sky. So, just as we saw yesterday, it still appears that if we can get to Stonehaven we will probably be in the clear. Either way, it is clear at Dundee and Perth. What we have to do is predict the arrival of a large gap, be ready for take-off just after it arrives, and fly in the gap to Stonehaven. Sounds feasible, doesn't it?

The time now is 15.50. Aussie is attempting to arrange clearance to orbit overhead if we get a decent sized gap. I have ordered fuel, written down our flight frequencies and plotted a course to Glasgow. The course is a very simple one – after Stonehaven we shall head south-west, following the A94 to Forfar. At Forfar is the start of a long wide valley, which takes us past Coupar Angus, to clip Perth on the north side, and continue through the valley to Dunblane. Here we turn south via Stirling to Cumbernauld whereupon we submit our fate to the whims of Glasgow Approach. While I'm waiting for Aussie and the fuel tanker to turn up let me tell you about a very novel feature on the chart for this area. It resembles a semi-circular fan spread around 100° of arc. The lines indicate HMRs (Helicopter Main Routes) and spread out from HMR Whisky which runs roughly north from Hackley Head, (on the edge of the CTR SFC-FL115), some ten miles up the coast from Bridge of Don. All the lines indicate radials from the VOR positioned 7 miles out on the extended centre lines from Runway 34. Out over the sea, parallel to HMR Whisky is HMR Echo, (Whisky = West, Echo = East), five miles distant. It sounds complicated but is pretty simple really and provides a no-nonsense answer to controlling dozens of helicopters spreading out all over the North Sea. Hold up . . . the tanker has arrived. "Fill her up please, both tanks".

16.20 hrs. We start up having copied Information Bravo, QNH 1001 etc, and taxi to Hold Charlie at the end of the helicopter Runway 33, (also the end of the short cross Runway 05/23). Whilst doing our power and take-off checks a S.61 lands and taxis close by. We hope the downdraught from the huge rotors won't tip us over. It is very close. We feel the buffets but they pass by safely. The rain is easing now and we can see the following brightness breaking through to the north. Fingers crossed. Let's hope it's a big one.

"Golf Charlie Lima is ready for departure".

"Golf Charlie Lima, Roger, you are cleared to line-up Runway 34. Right turn-out to Bridge of Don not above 1000ft. Squawk 7216". Aussie reads back the instructions.

"Read-back correct Golf Charlie Lima, you are now cleared take-off, surface wind 010°, 20 knots gusting 25".

In order to get off quickly we have taken a mid-point departure, The runway looks as long as it is wide. With the headwind we are off with plenty of room to spare. We are in luck. We are climbing out into a large sun-lit gap, encircled by monstrous cliffs of cumulo-nimbus cloud. We know that the tops are at 24,000ft. The altimeter needle winds round towards 1000ft.

Aberdeen airport is drenched and the reflected sun is dazzling. I reach back into my flight case for the sunglasses. Aussie flies while I do this. It is too good an opportunity to miss. Aussie calls the Tower requesting permission to turn back and climb to photograph overhead. We are told to "standby one". Our request is approved. I sling the right wing wind down, apply full power, and haul us round into a steep climbing turn. "Bleeding show-off", mutters Aussie. Then it's time to open the window. I reach across and pull the cabin heat knob fully out but it doesn't make much difference. It is freezing. I fly two orbits, Aussie closes the window and calls the Tower to tell them we're finished. I point the nose down for a fast descent to 1000ft heading for Bridge of Don.

"Hope you got some good ones, Charlie Lima, we're showing our best side, send us a print".

"Glad to oblige Aberdeen, lovely smiles, thanks for the help".

"Our pleasure, call Approach 120.4, bye bye".

I love it when the ATCOs have a lull in proceedings and get a chance to put their personalities on .

Aberdeen Approach instruct us to use the Stonehaven Lane not above 1000ft. This means we are back out over the sea for a while hoping that our Lycoming donkey is feeling fit and well. At this height there aren't many suitable spots on the shore for a forced landing and the sight of the waves crashing onto the rocks throwing up fiery cascades of spume and spray looks lovely until you contemplate having to swim ashore through it. However, another matter has caught our attention. We are catching up with the rear of the last squall line and we can't see a way

On the apron at Aberdeen with Charlie Lima prepared to sit it out.

Right:
Dramatic over the nose shot of the small gap in the clouds near Stonehaven which allowed us to escape to Glasgow. Cbs towered up to 25,000 feet above us.

through it. There is one gigantic mass just off the coast at Stonehaven apparently supported on a column of rain maybe five miles wide, five hundred feet high, and so dense with water it isn't possible to see inside. As we fly closer we spot what appears as a small arch beneath the front to our right at two o'clock. There is a brightness seeping through from beyond, a sign of clear sky. But how much clear sky? We decide that another decisive decision is called for. Oh heck!

"Do we got for it Aussie?"

"I don't think we have a choice do we?' He thumbs the transmit switch.

"Aberdeen, Golf Charlie Lima is four miles from Stonehaven, we require to head 240° in order to avoid a large Cb east of Stonehaven, is that approved?"

"That is approved, Golf Charlie Lima, no conflicting traffic in your area, call leaving frequency".

I fly towards the arch. As we get in line with it the brightness increases. Whump, we have just encountered the turbulence surrounding the Cb. This is very different from yesterday. These are short, sharp, powerful jabs, we literally leave our seats with the impacts. This is unnerving. We can see clear through now, there is some rain beneath, not much. Clear sky almost, so let's hope this doesn't last much longer because I really do not care for this one little bit. The turbulence stops as suddenly as it started.

We look around us. To our left vast banks of Cumulonimbus stretch to the horizon over the sea. Behind to our right, an equally vast line stretches across the snow capped mountains. In front there is the most beautiful vista as soft autumnal evening sun illuminates the land. The sky is ablaze with vivid colours created by the shreds and streaks of torn cloud, all that remains of the front. Shafts of golden light spread out from beneath the thicker patches and speckle the countryside.

"Aberdeen Approach, Golf Charlie Lima is clear of the front, changing to Scottish Information, 119.87".

The reply is just made out. Scottish Information are fresh out of product this evening and soon suggest we contact Leuchars on 126.5. They ask us to Squawk 2657 and also have little else to offer except the Tyne and Portree Regional QNH 993 and 1001 respectively. I have been noticing an odd phenomenon. The air is making Charlie Lima behave like a ship in a giant ocean swell as it flows from the mountains. We have climbed up to 2500ft so I throttle back a little but the VSI still shows us climbing so I give it more of the same. By the time I've got this trimmed out the reverse starts happening. We estimate that if I did nothing about it we would rise and fall by at least 500ft either way. We joke about calling Leuchars to say we're level at 2000 and 3000ft.

It is 18.10. Aussie is standing on the edge of the West apron at Glasgow International snapping airliners on the approach to Runway 05 as they sink down across the setting sun. What can I say about the rest of the flight. I don't know any superlatives that could adequately describe the sensation of beauty and isolation. We were quite alone in the sky as far as our eyes could see. And we could see for ever. That was just how it felt.

Leuchars suggested we gave Perth a call as we drew close. Perth had packed up their aeroplanes for the night. Leuchars had nothing more to offer so we went back to Scottish Information. We almost felt like apologising for keeping them awake. The airwaves were completely silent except for a diminutive Cessna, Golf Charlie Lima, putting along, vainly trying to catch the setting sun. We did an orbit over the Gleneagles Hotel. The golf courses with their bunkers looked like a surrealistic film set for an epic from World War One. As we turned south towards Stirling the wind died right down. Aussie made a call to Glasgow Approach (119.10) but it turned out they heard us although we couldn't hear them. This situation was rectified as we turned the corner at Cumbernauld. I pointed out the aerodrome there to Aussie. It was very hard to see but I knew where it lay. Glasgow Approach told us to route via the East Kilbride and Barrhead VRPs. My relatively good local knowledge made this task easy and I enjoyed pointing out items of interest. This amuses Aussie. I suspect he's hoping that we encounter an area in which I get lost. From Barrhead we were cleared for a right base approach to 05. Surface wind 330 at 10 knots. 100% crosswind component. At ten knots this was easy to deal with and I made a very nice soft touchdown. I was so pleased I forgot to keep the into wind aileron on and spoiled things by veering off to the right.

14.00hrs 16.10.92. I had a good time this morning. We were allowed out on the main apron to photograph the arrivals of two trans-

Above:
Approaching the Barrhead VRP and turning there for positioning into Glasgow.

Atlantic flights. A DC10 and a Boeing 767. Close up these machines are very, very big. I get some cracking shots that really emphasise this. An almost clear sky provided bright, bold colour combinations as swarms of service vehicles clamoured for attention, squeezing up close as if paying homage. We shall be off to Prestwick soon and I relish the prospect of getting into the air again.

And here we are at Prestwick, 15.35hrs. We have landed completing our 20th leg. Our logged flight time 'chock to chock' was 0.9 hrs. The distance as the proverbial crow flies from Glasgow to Prestwick is 23nm. As you will quickly realise we did a spot of dillying and dallying en route, taking the odd snap or two from above. This was not the only reason. As a VFR flight we are quite capable of proceeding from A to B under our own steam, but being in controlled airspace most of the time, we were directed to conform to certain patterns dictated by ATC. These don't usually equate to the proven direct passage followed by the proverbial crow. By adding insult to injury we will be charged for 'Navigation Services' which direct us over a more circuitous route. Bleeding marvellous, ain't it!

Prestwick is strange. Nicely strange. Peculiarly strange. The main Runway 13/31 is 2987 metres long, not far short of Gatwick or Manchester. It is 4 to 500 metres longer than Edinburgh or Glasgow. But only rarely do the big jets visit this airport now. We park Charlie Lima in a position which, thirty years earlier, would have been occupied by a Super Constellation or DC-7C which had just completed the hazardous voyage across the north Atlantic, or had flown up from Heathrow to refuel before departing to the west. In the 50s and 60s Prestwick hummed with activity. The arrival of the big jets plus

Top:
Aerial view of the substantial facilities at Prestwick, looking north.

Above:
Taxiing out to depart from Prestwick, Hold Lima, Runway 31.

other considerations signalled the end of that era. Prestwick lives in limbo, hoping for salvation in the form of an unexpected resurrection. All the equipment is in place. I walked through baggage reclaim facilities frozen as if in a time warp. There is a large well-equipped terminal building. The catering section is kept alive by two well-meaning and helpful ladies. Aussie has complex emotions about this place. As a kid of similar age, also ardent spotter and incipient 'anorak', I can readily empathise. His Prestwick in those days equated to my Gatwick. As a lad Aussie was brought up in the north-east between Sunderland and Teeside.

In the mid-fifties, to anyone interested in aviation, Prestwick was a Mecca. To us lads in the south, equipped with a bicycle, a telescope and a ten-bob note, if we were lucky, it was unattainable For Aussie it was a question of

making a special plea to mum and dad to divert when driving across Scotland on holiday. We are both pretty much the same age and just caught the tail-end of the big prop era. The new jet generation, the Boeing 707 and Douglas DC-8 finished the propliners off for good. Even so, after all these years I still see the Lockheed Constellation family and the Douglas variants, DC-4, DC-6 and DC-7C along with Boeing Stratocruisers as being *real* airliners. I sound like some old codger going on about stream trains. Even so, once heard, the sound of four turbo-compounds at full chat takes some beating. To a lad there was something exciting and romantic about them because of the danger. They couldn't really fly high enough to escape the worst weather. They were quite slow too. The crews really had to work hard at times. Aussie paints a word picture for me as we walk across the near deserted apron. To him it has the same effect as walking across the National Stadium in Cardiff would for a Welsh rugby fan. Apart from the Connies and 7Cs you could look across at the Scottish Aviation factory and see Twin Pioneers parked up next to Douglas Skyraiders waiting to be converted for target-towing duties with a 'scandiwegian' air force. There would be a long line of Royal Canadian Air Force CF-86 Sabres awaiting an uncertain fate. Looking up you might see a USAF Globemaster routing overhead, there might also be one on the apron possibly parked near a Lockheed WV-2 of the US Navy (a Constellation variant). Several USAF SC-54D Douglas Searchmasters (DC-4) could be spotted. In my mind's eye I can picture it. Definitely. Today we have a TNT BAe146, a RCAF Hercules and us. Scottish Aviation is part of British Aerospace now and they make the Jetstream here. Stopping and looking around I feel the familiar sensation when something is seen again for the first time since childhood. It ought to look bigger.

At 16.30 over a quick cup of coffee we decide to fly across to Newcastle via Carlisle. The weather is reported satisfactory for our purposes at both airports. We estimate a flight time of 1.3 to 1.5 hours depending on wind. We have refuelled at Glasgow so there is plenty of fuel in the tanks. I shall fly the leg and the pre-flight checks show Charlie Lima to be fully serviceable. At 16.55 we get engine start and taxi. We have copied Information Papa on the ATIS. Runway 21, QFE 1003, QNH 1005, wind as on landing, cleared VFR to Cumnock (VRP) not above 2000ft QNH and taxi to Hold Romeo. As we taxi out we request a mid-point departure as Romeo is at the far end of 31. This is approved and we are redirected to Hold Lima. This gives us in the region

of 1500 metres. Power and Pre-Take-Off checks complete, we are cleared to line-up, right-hand turn-out to proceed direct to Cumnock. This is our 21st leg. After 350 metres Charlie Lima is ready to fly and I pull back on the yoke. Ailsa Craig, gaunt and silhouetted like a giant Christmas pudding, appears out to sea. I climb out fast with a low angle of climb and pivot Charlie Lima on a wing-tip to turn cross-wind. Aussie has got used to my exuberance by now and doesn't say a word. He knows I'm enjoying myself this evening and lets me get on with it. Setting out for Cumnock I revel in finding the clues for our course, reading from map to ground, levelling off at 800ft. At Cumnock Aussie bids Prestwick Approach farewell and dials up Scottish Information on 119.87. Yet again, no conflicting traffic. Our route is along the valley via Sanquhar and Thornhill towards Dumfries. The evening light exudes ecstasy. It is absolutely beautiful. I decide to continue at low level dropping down to 500ft AGL to maximise our appreciation. At times the fields below appear as velvet laid upon the sea, the undulations look so much like waves. I'm flying IFR,R and R. 'I follow railway, road and river'. All

Charlie Lima having a good look round on the hallowed apron at Prestwick with the British Aerospace plant in the background but sadly, as the photos show, little other flying activity.

three are below and I bank Charlie Lima left and right to follow their course.

Cessna 172s have the best statistical safety record of all the popular light singles and Charlie Lima is proof positive as we thrum along, turning onto a heading of 150°, 6nm north of Dumfries. We've added fuel and a little oil from time to time and that has proved sufficient to carry us more than half way round Britain. Even so we still engage in a 'spot the field' exercise just in case of some unforeseen emergency. Aussie asks Scottish Information for the Newcastle weather. 330/10, Runway 07, 25kms, 1/15 Cb, 4/30, QNH 1001. So, probably a cross-wind landing, and scattered Cb's at 1500ft. I imagine these are the last remnants of the appalling conditions battering the eastern coast of Scotland. The low sun graphically illuminates concentric circles built up thousands of years ago to provide defensive protection for people long since forgotten in our dim and distant past. We see a few as we speed along and I throw Charlie Lima into a tight orbit over one as Aussie struggles to get a shot from the open window. To the camera the light is minimal. To our complex and incredibly adaptable 'Mark One' eyeballs it is still quite bright. I wonder at the fact that farmers have respected so many of these ancient monuments over the centuries. Aussie is shooting at a 60th of a second. Knowing his ability to judge the right milli-second to press the shutter release he'll probably get a result. Not crisp, but quite readable nevertheless. I wouldn't even attempt a shot below a 250th. That's the difference between a pro and an amateur.

Passing once again near Lockerbie, a small town whose name is indelibly etched into the memories of people not even remotely connected with aviation, Aussie transfers to Carlisle Approach/Tower. It seems to me that an age has gone by since we last landed there, so much has happened since. Edinburgh, Perth, Dundee, Aberdeen, Glasgow and Prestwick – I glossed over Glasgow to be honest. So much of interest happened there, I could almost devote a whole chapter. For a tiny example, we were lined up and held for almost two minutes for wake turbulence to subside following the departure of a medium sized jet airliner.

My biggest single problem is deciding what to include and what to leave out. Each individual leg involved enough to write a lengthy article on. It is an immense privilege to be involved in such a project and the experience enables me to dip into arcane areas which are usually the province of commercial pilots. All this occurs to me as we pass north of Carlisle. A band of low cloud apparently blocks our path eastwards to Newcastle. The base is quite low and beneath it looks so dark it might as well be night. It is very important that I recall precise memories of driving along the A69 because we need to follow that road. It is another IFR,R and R situation and the chart confirms this. From 15nm out there is a choice of valley. Getting closer I am positive about the A69 route. Aussie respects my memory and we plunge in below the cloud. We have everything relating to lights switched ON. Bands of rain pound across the airframe and windscreen as we push on deeper. It is so severe at times that Carb-heat is selected fully ON. Keeping the road, railway and river on the left I peer into the gloom in an attempt to isolate known way-points. It turns out not to be too difficult. The spur road into Hexham is easily identified and as we pass by the conditions improve.

Hexham is a VRP 4nm outside the western edge of the Newcastle CTA (1500'ALT to FL75) so Aussie calls up Newcastle Approach on 126.35. They have traffic approaching from the south to use the ILS and ask us to route to the radio mast situated 5nm north-northwest of Hexham. Upon reaching the mast we are cleared for a direct path onto Runway 07. As predicted there is a hefty crosswind but this time I manage to make a landing which satisfies me. There is a short back-track to Taxiway 2 and we park on the G.A. apron which is south of the of the runway at the western end opposite the terminal area.

Thankfully, the next morning is clear and bright since we plan a trip to part of Hadrian's Wall which Aussie definitely wants to photo-

Left:
On finals to Newcastle in the dusk. Notice the angle of the nose necessary to correct the drift in almost a crab-like approach.

graph. We take-off on 25 this time, back-tracking to the mid-point. Prior to departing west, Aussie asks if our request to orbit overhead is approved. It is, at 2000ft. We turn right to climb and make a wide sweep. As we circle up just east of the field I spot a 737 on short finals. Quickly I inform Aussie who snaps the window open and leans out. Got it! These will be spectacular shots. The timing is perfect. I fly directly over the 737 as if flares for touch-down.

The flight to Hadrian's Wall shows us the strange nature of the land here. It sweeps up in short escarpments and we see how the Romans exploited this feature to the full. I also exploit the opportunity to make swooping passes over points of interest. Lots of wing waggling, dives and climbs. Great stuff! Aussie shoots several films taking full advantage of the exemplary lighting conditions, the lowish sun throwing distinct shadows which gives the ruins crisp outlines. We return to Newcastle where there is more work to do.

Newcastle has interesting statistics. It is a very busy regional airport with a surprising number of diverse destinations. Charter flights depart for Austria, Bulgaria, Canada, Cyprus, France, Greece, Holland, Italy, Malta, Norway, Portugal, Spain, Turkey, Tunisia and the USA. Scheduled flights serve many UK destinations plus Holland, Norway, Belgium, Ireland and France. In 1990 they handled 1,626,306 passengers and recorded 61,472 movements, an unexpected hive of activity for a rank southerner.

Passing over the threshold to Runway 25 I can't resist the opportunity to show off a little. At ten feet I increase the power and slowly fly two-thirds of the way down the runway, putting Charlie Lima down very gently in plenty of time to taxi onto Taxiway 2. "Getting used to it now, aren't you". Aussie is right of course. With such intensive flying I am indeed managing to improve my capabilities. My enthusiasm is soon dampened, however, when the Magneto check on shut-down shows the right-hand side to be barely functioning. I tell Aussie I will sort it out while he photographs the terminal area. A prolonged burst at 2000 RPM didn't improve the situation at all.

It is Saturday afternoon and the resident engineering facilities are all but closed. No one can help. What to do? An enforced stay until Monday is not very acceptable. As a last resort I go to the Newcastle Aero Club to see if they have any suggestions. I have the good fortune to find Sue Boxall, an instructor there sipping coffee during a short break. She asks if I've tried the lean mixture technique. I confess I haven't and I'm not too confident about trying it. If overdone, it can inflict serious damage on the engine. Sue says she'll give Charlie Lima the 'once over', to see if it will cure the problem. The lean mixture routine involves running the engine at fairly high revs then pulling the mixture control out. Not too slowly and not too fast. As the mixture is leaned the cylinder head temperatures rises dramatically. The idea is to burn off excessive carbon deposits from the plugs. Hence the danger. Too much heat and whoops, there goes another engine. On the third attempt we have success. Both Mags are performing perfectly. As a very happily married man how can I show my appreciation? A handshake and sincere thanks will have to do. Sue leaves to do some line-training on a Short 330. Should she happen to read this book . . . Many thanks.

Arriving back Aussie metaphorically kicks himself. "That technique is exactly what we used on Daks (Douglas DC-3s) in the Caribbean". It obviously works just as well on lowly Lycomings.

Below:
Our angel of mercy, Sue Boxall, after fixing Charlie Lima.

Top:
Charlie Lima in front of the attractively serialled G-JANE at Newcastle. A Short 'Shed' in the background.

Above:
It may not be clear that this is in fact a restricted area but Danger Keep Out gets the message across. In fact the sign marks the edge of the ILS exclusion area.

The next stage is to depart for Teeside and photograph Newcastle, Sunderland, and other points of interest en route. Aussie has a site near Teeside to cover plus the village of Murton where he was born and raised.

We depart Newcastle on Runway 25, QFE 992, QNH 1001, and circle over the city centre before heading across to Sunderland making a quick orbit over the Nissan plant on our way. The sight of the sun reflecting off hundreds of windscreens gives a jewel-like quality to the huge parking lot where cars are stored after manufacture. The site is on an old aerodrome and the runway pattern is still clearly visible. A test track has been added and this is very evident as we pass overhead. Aussie has to suffer a fair amount of "one for me" on this particular leg.

Whilst overhead Newcastle city we were within the CTR and in contact with Newcastle

Above:
Yet another kind courtesy bus to save our feet, this one at Teesside

Approach They also provide the LARS service so we stay with them to Sunderland and beyond. High above is the NRASA (Northern Radar Advisory Service Area) which extends from FL100 to FL245. The weather conditions are still very good with a touch of haze into sun. We easily identify Murton and Aussie takes control for a bit and does a touch of sightseeing over his home town. After this we head off for Teesside and transfer onto Teesside Approach 118.85. Our departure pressures were QFE 992, QNH 1001. (Newcastle is 266ft AMSL), but we set the Regional QNH which is 1000. We locate the area which Aussie wants to photograph and do a couple of orbits. It is right on the coast near Redcar. The industry in the area west of us presents an abysmal picture of contamination. The land *looks* poisoned so I ask Aussie to take a couple of representative shots. Throughout our trip the contrast between country and industry is glaring from a couple of thousand feet. To our south-west the hills to the moors rise steeply, the tops being between 1400 and 1500ft AMSL.

Completing the task, Aussie asks Teesside for an approach and landing clearance. We get Runway 23, QFE 995. It is 15.20 and the light is still good. Aussie asks if we may continue in at 1800ft to orbit the airport. This is approved not below 2000ft on the QFE. The circuit pattern is right-hand and we slot in downwind from the overhead. Runway 23/05 is slightly shorter than Newcastle (2332 metres) at 2291 metres and as usual we take only a fraction for landing. I land long again to place us close to the Central Taxiway. We have a student on first solo behind and I don't want him to have to go around on our

account. The air is very calm now with little wind and we watch the student make a nice landing. The Tower offers congratulations and Aussie thumbs the transmit switch to give ours. I still vividly remember the same nice touch coming through my headphones. It tops off an experience that anyone can be proud of.

Although there are a lot fewer scheduled and charter operations from Teesside than Newcastle the 1990 figures show more movements (64,329). These I think are mainly training flights and not just the single-engined variety either. We've been watching a BAe 146 doing circuits and bumps for the last half hour. It is now 17.15 and we're strapping in for our departure for Leeds/Bradford where we aim to spend the night. Aussie decides it's high time he had a go. We take-off on 23 and notice clear signs that this was once a major military base. There are masses of dispersal areas. Our initial track is 185° and should take us over Harrogate. En route we shall spend most of our time inside the Vale of York AIAA (SFC to FL200). Aussie climbs to 2500ft on the QNH which has dropped to 999. Teesside then gives us the regional QNH which, as always, is lower (995). I have listed Linton and Leeming for a LARS service. After leaving Teesside Approach we try them both. It's the weekend and the evening so they've all gone home but this doesn't mean they aren't active with gliding, for example. We pass between Leeming on our right and Topcliffe and Dishforth on our left. Then we see a bright light heading straight for us on a constant relative bearing in our eleven o'clock. Just when we consider that evasive action may be a wise precaution a small bundle falls away from the light. Then another; they are parachuting. As the last jumper leaves, the aircraft makes a sharp right turn. We are still about three miles apart. This

Above:
Charlie Lima putting on the style in very exalted company.

Right:
CL getting ready for lunch - 90-plus litres of AVGAS 100.

Below right:
Aussie at the controls during our departure from Leeds-Bradford

hasn't taken us by surprise as Topcliffe is shown on the chart as a parachuting base.

Passing near Ripon I dial up the Leeds/Bradford ATIS and copy the details on Information Kilo. Wind 260/08, visibility 50kms, 1 OKTA at 5000ft. The runway is 32, QFE 976 QNH 999. Notice the big difference. Leeds/Bradford sits high on a hill 682 ft AMSL. Their call-sign is Leeds and I give them a call on the Approach frequency (123.75) as we fly over Harrogate. We are told Runway 32 but to expect 28. This is good news. Runway 32/14 is the main with 2250 metres. 28/10 is 1100 metres but is almost into wind. Lucky for Aussie.

Harrogate is a VRP and Aussie changes heading onto 210° which should set us up nicely for a right-base approach to 28 and will still suffice for 32. Closer in we are asked to contact Tower on 120.30. They clear us for a right base join for 28. We spot the airport lights quite easily and Aussie sets up the approach, placing Charlie Lima gently onto the asphalt in time to turn off via Hold Uniform. We are directed to park on the western end of the apron. While Aussie books in and telephones another friend who lives close by, I search around for tie-downs. There are several plastic 5 gallon containers nearby so I tie three to each wing and two to the tail. If the wind does get up they don't look as if the weight of the water inside will do a lot of good. Fortunately no high winds are forecast. We're in luck. Aussie's friend invites us to join them for dinner with another couple and insists we stay the night. We grab a taxi and set off, looking forward to a fine Italian meal.

Next morning I'm woken up by Aussie. A family illness means that we must break off our trip temporarily. We decide to fly down to Wycombe. Arriving at Leeds airport I'm surprised to find a Concorde sitting on the apron. It's doing one of those 'champagne lunch' flights. Aussie snatches a couple of shots while I pre-flight Charlie Lima. We need fuel and have to taxi across the airport via Hold Whiskey and X-Ray to get it. Aussie will fly the leg. Fully fuelled we are instructed to taxi to the Hold for One Zero. Shortly after a clearance to taxi to the 28 end is given. We shall take-off past Concorde which will be on my side. I get my camera ready and unlatch the window. We have bright sunlight coming through fairly large gaps in the clouds so I'm hoping we'll get a bright patch on Concorde when we take-off.

Just as our take-off clearance is given the sun comes out. Aussie immediately asks the Tower if we can do one low level circuit. We can and what height do we require? Aussie asks for 500ft and this is approved. Following that our departure route is south by the Dewsbury VRP. The QNH is 998. I take a couple of quick shots as we climb out. I don't have motor-wind on my camera and appreciate the extra circuit. Our route south is simplicity itself. Follow the M1. We fly over the eastern edge of Sheffield, past Mansfield, and call up East Midlands Approach on 119.65. A clearance to transit their CTA and CTR is received. We have to climb to 3000ft and reset the altimeter to their QNH of 1001. We're also asked to Squawk 7214.

Near Leicester we leave the CTA and drop back down below 2000ft and give Leicester Radio a quick call on 122.125 to let them know who we are and what we're doing. We see the massive runway at Bruntingthorpe, 3000 metres of runway that is barely ever used. It is 60 metres wide too, wider than most major airports like Birmingham, Gatwick, Manchester and Heathrow who all have 45 to 46 metres. At Northampton we turn south on a heading of 175°. This will take us straight to Wycombe. On reaching Princes Risborough I request joining and landing instructions on 126.55. Back into very familiar territory. Right base join, Runway 25, QFE 982. As we taxi in I feel disappointed that we couldn't finish the trip off. Such is life and it certainly can't be helped.

Below:
Checking the downwind circuit prior to joining right base for 25 at Wycombe Air Park

6.
The final legs

The time is 07.30 and the date is November 24th. Aussie is just steering his red Alfa Romeo into a parking bay outside Wycombe Air Centre. We returned from Leeds/Bradford on 18 October and over a month has gone by with no breaks in the weather at a time convenient for us both to get going again. We drove up to Wycombe yesterday to get checked out as neither of us had flown since the 18th. The conditions were very poor and few people were flying. Rather foolishly I decided to get checked out in a 182, a type I hadn't flown since August. What with the time lapse and the severe weather I had a hard time getting to grips with it. It looks like a slightly bigger 172 but handles very differently. At times I wondered if Nick my instructor, had any nerves at all. During the first and second landings which were pathetic, floundering, bouncing, botched-up affairs he never raised his voice once, nor, when he spoke did I detect the slightest quiver. When you're making a complete hash of things this is exactly the temperament that is required. I was glowing bright red with embarrassment but he made me persevere and eventually I started getting it right. Previously I have flown the 182 quite nicely and Nick has checked me out before. On that occasion I had inwardly glowed with pride when, having finished the check, he said I was one of a dozen or so pilots he'd encountered who could land a 182 properly. So. I'm sure you can now realise,I was keen to put in a polished, 'in control' performance. Instead, I got it all wrong, failing to flare sufficiently, and failing to compensate for the turbulent cross-wind. Frankly, getting over the severe dent in my self-esteem was the biggest problem. Under such circumstances it is easy to let the aircraft and the conditions get on top and find you can't catch up with events. Having an awful lot of hours under his belt, and somehow tacitly implying that he's been there before and it's not a problem, Nick slowly brought me round. I'm not saying my third, fourth and fifth landings were good but, they were workmanlike enough to pass the check. Like so much in avia-

tion, it taught me it can soon get very serious indeed.

Having got that out in the open, and, not feeling a great deal better for the confession, let's return to the present. The forecast was excellent for this morning so we made arrangements yesterday for an early departure before the aero-

Below:
Loading up CL for the final stages of our trip, on the apron at Wycombe with Aussie's car.

Bottom:
A final check to make sure that the approach is clear to Runway 25 at Wycombe, all the more necessary when the tower is closed.

drome opened. The forecast was correct. It is a very fine morning indeed. I have the keys to Charlie Lima plus the documentation folder which contains all the various items required when operating away from base. It is like a highly expanded edition of the MOT, Vehicle Registration Document, Insurance Certificate, routine you might go through when taking the car on holiday. We pack the rear seats and baggage compartment and set about the pre-flight checks. Charlie Lima was fully refuelled and topped-up with oil yesterday.

Having started up we make 'blind calls' on the radio because the Tower is not yet open. Our calls are on the Tower frequency 126.55. The QNH is set on the altimeter by calculating the QFE minus twenty feet for the apron level, (the QFE being the highest point on an aerodrome). One millibar of pressure equals thirty feet so we divide five hundred by thirty. By zeroing the altimeter at 999 we reset for 1016. Wycombe is listed as 520ft AMSL. Taxiing out to Hold Alpha Aussie makes another 'blind' call to say we're proceeding to Hold Bravo just in case someone is making a tight circuit to land on the gliding area. It might seem over-cautious but accidents often occur by ignoring these basic preliminaries. After all, we're operating before normal hours and who can say some other keen pilot hasn't got up early to take advantage of the excellent conditions?

Having completed the Power and Pre-Take-Off checks we 'blind call' our intentions to line-up on 25. Whilst Aussie does this I turn Charlie Lima vigorously around for a visual inspection of the circuit. No other traffic is seen. Taxiing out the short distance to the lining-up point I check the T's and P's and, with Charlie Lima pointing down the centre-line, check the alignment of the magnetic compass and DI. Both agree.

It is a nice familiar feeling sitting here, looking over the nose of Charlie Lima as we accelerate along the runway. The windsock is hanging limply straight down. This is our 24th leg and our destination is Coventry. Climbing away from runway 25 I steer a heading of 240° to avoid encroaching upon the noise abatement area and climb to 1000ft at which point we're just passing the south-west corner of the circuit. Banking the left wing down to afford a better view to the right and seeing the sky is clear I bank the right wing down and continue climbing to 1700ft on a heading of 345° which should bring us directly overhead the Silverstone Racing Circuit via Westcott, (a disused aerodrome that looks like a government research establishment), and has a NDB placed there and Buckingham which has

Top:
Climbing out and crossing the M40 near Wycombe, a lovely day but note the haze that becomes apparent when airborne.

Above:
Checking the course en route on the ICAO half-mil chart.

had its character assassinated by a bunch of morons who wouldn't recognise town planning if it fell on their heads. Enough of that. What a great morning! It makes one feel glad to be alive. Aussie is calling up Upper Heyford on 128.55. A laid back drawl accepts our details and tells us he will give us a Flight Information Service, no conflicting traffic, call turning over Silverstone. Regional QNH 1016 and Squawk 0260. It's a pity we can't see the owner of the drawl. I swear he's wearing a stetson.

Our intention now is to fill in the large gap in the Midlands and East Anglia. We have picked Coventry, Birmingham, Manchester, Humberside and Norwich as representative examples. Aussie drove up to East Midlands last week and got some cracking night shots. Gatwick, Heathrow, Luton and Stansted are all short drives too so he'll have to pick these off one by one on days when the weather is kind. I don't

Above:
Passing close to Silverstone race track with, in fact, a practice session in progress; but the runway and apron areas were deserted.

expect there will be many such days during this winter considering what we've seen so far this year. Silverstone is in view now but the track is deserted. Actually Aussie gave Silverstone a quick call because they do have ATC present from time to time. They retain one of the old runways, 06/24, 882 x 23 metres, and have a Tower/Radio frequency 121.075.

Directly overhead I bank left for a heading of 300° and Aussie informs Upper Heyford. I trust you'll remember the mention of the Upper Heyford Mandatory Radio Area. Silverstone lies just beyond the north-east corner and we've chosen this route to avoid it. A few minutes later Upper Heyford tells us that the Flight Information Service is terminated and resume own navigation. Aussie calls an acknowledgement and changes over to Coventry Approach on 119.25 after resetting the Transponder to 7000. From Coventry we learn that Runway 23 left-hand is in use. QFE 1006, QNH 1016 and we should call established down-wind. The join and approach is straight-forward and I land long on the runway (1615 metres) as the expected light aircraft parking area for visitors is at the far end beyond the Tower. Indeed, having made quite a nice landing, we are told to park on the Western area which is grass and soaking wet with a heavy dew. For those who want all the details, the Tower frequency is 124.80 and we were instructed to use this when closing in on the circuit. Today they don't appear to be using the Ground frequency on 121.70 for landing traffic.

While landing I caught a glimpse of some notable classic aircraft parked around the northern side. Coventry is home base for Air Atlantique which is a fascinating operation using Douglas DC-3 and DC-6 aircraft. This morning they have two '6s and five '3s in residence. The

'3s form the backbone of a fleet engaged on a pollution control contract. I take advantage of the permission granted to take photographs on the apron area and get right up close to one of the '6s which is being serviced. Up close it is 'eye-fuel' material. What a machine! These big piston engines never did think much of retaining their bodily fluids and oil drips off the nacelles and streaks across the wings. From a distance airliners like these appear sleek and smooth. From a few feet the panels look hand worked. Perhaps some are these days, as spares become rare. As a younger and incipient 'anorak' I had great regard for the Douglas family and their designs still please.

The light is excellent for taking photographs but I notice the first wispy traces high in the sky that indicate the warm front forecast to arrive this afternoon is on its way. A breeze has

Below:
One of the most enjoyable parts of the trip was the opportunity to view magnificent veteran aircraft at close quarters. Below is a handsome and venerable Air Atlantique Douglas DC-6 and at bottom an even more experienced group of DC-3s.

developed over the last half-hour and will steadily increase. However, we should still get a few more hours of bright sun with any luck. I go in search of Aussie. On the way I pause to snap a lovely little Cessna 152 tail-dragger resplendent in turquoise and white. 150/152 conversions are proving very popular and more appear at ever shorter intervals. I spot Aussie walking back from the second DC-6 parked at the end of Runway 17. As we meet he points out another rarity languishing in the bushes, in a sorry state and awaiting its end. It is a Percival Prince and once belonged to City Airways who (I think) now reside in the rich tapestry of aviation history. Further away, up in the north-east corner of the airport lives a very active museum which houses a variety of significant aircraft. It's a shame we can't spare the time for a proper visit. In the past I've only managed glancing glimpses. They have the mandatory Vulcan of course. Examples I would recommend, and not solely because of their rarity, include: let's see, the McDonnell F-101 Voodoo and Lockheed F-80 and Starfighter certainly, the Avro Anson (I luv 'em), Boulton Paul P.111A (unique?) and Fairey Ultra-Light Helicopter plus the Pou-du-Ciel. Many of the mainstay British military types are also represented.

Returning to the main apron we stop to inspect an Army Lynx helicopter en route to Booking Out. It looks to me like an exercise in induced drag, the fuselage resembling a threadbare camouflaged hedgehog with a bad attack of warts that's been hit by a high speed truck. It is ready to depart so we retire to the edge of the apron to spectate. The turbines whine and the main rotors slowly gather momentum. Bit by bit it beats itself into a manic, whirring, shrieking, screaming frenzy. At the point when it must surely self-destruct, the laws of gravity, mechanics and reason, beaten to pulp, give in and the machine leaves the ground. Passing by, the ugly angry beast whips us with wild winds as punishment for our doubts.

It is now exactly 10.30 and we are back in Charlie Lima with permission to photograph overhead. We shall turn right, climb above circuit height north of the airport then turn along the downwind in reverse direction. This is subject to the usual traffic and ATC considerations. Prior to start-up we double-check the procedure for Birmingham by reading though the notes in the Pooley's Flight Guide and dial up Birmingham ATIS on 120.725. The distance from Coventry airport to Birmingham International is 11nm so we need to familiarise ourselves as it will be a short fast flight when we depart overhead. The ATIS is broadcasting Information

Above:
Flying the flag above the brand new terminal at Birmingham.

India, and we copy the details. Runway 15, QNH 1013, QFE 1002, wind 180 at 8 knots, +6 +3, CAVOK, plus we are to report aircraft type and Information India copied on first radio contact.

Coventry clear us to Hold Alpha and we turn through the checks here before back-tracking to a position halfway along 23. I am flying the leg. There is a crosswind component from the south but nothing to cause any problems so take-off is straightforward as I'm used to having the window open by now. Even with headphones the noise level is high so I have to concentrate on hearing the ATCO on Tower 124.8. Having finished we are handed straight over to Birmingham Approach on 131.325. Aussie makes the call and we're cleared for a downwind join for 15, left-hand, squawking 7261. There is another light aircraft flying a right-hand circuit. The flight guide notes tell us that we must not join finals below 1500ft AAL and must not descend below the ILS glide-path. With a Cessna 172 and 2255 metres of runway, I'll want to land long anyway, and since the G.A. apron is on the south-west corner, these instructions are convenient to comply with. Our heading from Coventry is 290° and we're in Class D airspace. Although I've spent hundreds of hours in the National Exhibition Centre next door to the airport this will be my first flying visit.

The join and landing were uneventful. I touched down just beyond Taxiway 8, passed across the intersection with the much shorter 06/24 runway (1315 metres), departed right up Taxiway 7 and parked on the apron in front of the large hangars within the designated area. The Tower frequency was 118.3 and Ground 121.8. Aussie had rung an acquaintance before leaving Coventry and as I shut Charlie Lima down Ken, of the PR department, pulls up alongside in his car. We compliment him on his immaculate timing. He tells us that he'd monitored our calls on his radio. Ken has laid out the red carpet for us and will take us around the airport and aprons. The old terminal building reminds me of a large sea-side hotel as we drive past. It turns out that we were lucky because we've flown in just before the mid-day rush. This is good news for Aussie and we get cracking while the sun continues to shine although it is becoming intermittent as the front thickens. The new terminal complex is most impressive and as we make our way round the aprons, arrivals are coming in thick and fast. Jets and turbo-props from British Airways, Brymon European, Air UK and British Midland are liberally scattered around and the turn-round machine spools itself into action. It really is quite impressive to watch dozens of vehicles all slotting seemingly effortlessly into the complex but well rehearsed routine which will enable these aircraft to be back in the air earning their keep. I particularly like the very smart scheme worn by an Air 2000 Boeing 757. Before lunch, Ken, who is a keen photographer also shows us some fine prints he took of Concorde and a BA 747 using Birmingham.

The front is deepening quickly now and Aussie checks the actuals and forecast from Manchester. We want to take our night stop there and it's plain that we'd better get our skates on before conditions deteriorate too far. We start up at 14.25 with Information Tango. Runway 15, wind 160/150 at 14 knots. 6 OKTA at 1500ft, +10 +7, QFE 996, QNH 1007. Ground Control clears us to Hold Golf where we complete our checks.

Calling ready for departure, Ground tells us to call Tower on 118.3. After a short wait we are instructed to enter the runway turning left, then right up Runway 06 to Hold Charlie on Taxiway 10. We have to give way to a Citation before entering Taxiway 10. After a brief wait we follow the Citation who heads for Hold November at the end of Runway 15 but we are told to hold at Bravo on Taxiway 9 which is about three or four hundred metres before. We have to wait here for landing ILS traffic plus the take-off of a 737 already waiting at November. While we wait I'll give you a few statistics about Birmingham. In 1992 they logged 69,420 air transport movements and handled 18,556 metric tonnes of freight. On top of these were the executive and private flights. A lot of countries are served by scheduled and charter services. To give some idea here is a list of the principal destinations: Albania, Austria, Belgium, Bulgaria, Spain, especially the Costa Packets, Central and South America, Cyprus, Denmark, Eastern Europe, the Far East, France, the USA, Greece and its islands, the Netherlands, and Italy. Ireland isn't forgotten and more flights depart for Malta, Morocco, Sweden, Switzerland, Canada, Tunisia, Turkey and Germany plus several destinations in the UK. Quite a list! Okay we're off, We've been asked to expedite and turn right ASAP as the Citation is breathing down our necks. At 200 feet I bank Charlie Lima and fly across the apron we'd parked on. To stay well clear of incoming traffic I adopt an initial heading of 320°. Steadily climbing away we level out below the cloud base which is 1500ft exactly as given. The transponder is set for 7264 and Approach have cleared us VFR not above 1500ft (just as well!) to follow the M6 motorway out of the CTR (SFC to FL45) which stops just short of Walsall and below the CTA (1500ft ALT to FL45). After 5nm the base rises to 3500ft but we won't get that high. The cloudbase at Manchester was 4000ft so we should find the base rising further north. It should but it isn't showing any signs of doing so. In fact it starts raining as we pass Cannock and the traffic streaming south on the M6 is a blaze of headlights. Turbulence is fairly bad too.

It is getting pretty grim. Visibility has dropped to barely five miles and we are forced down to 1100ft. Aussie changes to 124.75, calls for a Flight Information Service and requests the 'actual' at Manchester. I fly around Stafford avoiding the built-up areas and, as we head north again for the Potteries, Aussie gets the details. They are quite good by comparison. Wind 130/17, 10 kms plus, NIL weather, 6 OKTAs at 3600ft, +9 +5 and QNH 1004. Runway is 24. Even more than at Birmingham there are masses of details listed in the Flight Guide.

Above:
Orbiting overhead Woodford aerodrome while holding for Manchester.

Above:
Manchester's Runway 24 just becoming visible through the rain.

As we forge ahead, Aussie runs through them again after changing the transponder to 7220 while I reset the Regional QNH to 996 on the altimeter. I would not like to attempt to handle all this on my own as the flying alone is demanding.

Clinging tenaciously to the M6 we skirt round the Potteries and I'm forced even lower dropping down to 600ft AGL at one point. It looks a bit better as the ground drops and levels out around Crewe and Kidsgrove. We predicted this should be the case but the rain has intensified making forward vision marginal. The strong tail-wind and our low altitude gives us a ground-speed of around 130 knots at times. I've climbed up a bit now and Aussie calls Manchester Approach on 119.4. They instruct us to turn right at Sandbach, routeing via Congleton and Macclesfield to the British Aerospace production facility at Woodford aerodrome. Aussie asks me if I'm confident about recognising Sandbach. I am. The motorway services will be our turning point and I know each one on the M6 better than the back of my hand. I don't know Congleton very well but it will be hard to miss. Good, it is coming up now. Let's double-check. The rain has eased off a bit but visibility is poor and it is quite dark. A railway runs through Congleton in a north-easterly direction and heads off to Macclesfield. Got it! Okay we're bang on track. The rain stops and we can see a lot better now. I get a good view of Macclesfield and identify an industrial estate familiar to me from years ago. Locating Woodford is easy and we're instructed to hold overhead.

Circling Woodford we see several examples of the BAe 146 scattered around in various states of undress. Indeed, one scantily clad example is only wearing its base primer. This aircraft

seems, as far as I can make out, to be very successful and I wonder why the British can make this size of aircraft which will sell well, (think of the Viscount and BAC 111), but fail miserably in the international market with larger types like the Britannia, Trident and VC.10. There is little time to ponder right now. We are more concerned with the wind direction and strength being given to airliners as they're cleared to land at Manchester. It is increasing rather quickly and gusting. We decide to give it one try and if it is too bad divert to Barton, a smaller grass aerodrome to the west of Manchester which has four runways, one of which (14-32) is almost into wind. An Aer Lingus 737 flies in and we're cleared to follow it, routeing initially towards Stockport before turning finals. After two orbits it has taken me a few seconds to get properly orientated. As I said, it is very gloomy beneath the cloud despite being just after three in the afternoon and specific features are difficult to make out beyond two or three miles. There is one advantage, the masses of lights on the airport provide a beacon of massive proportions. Once established on finals we are both convinced that the wind is much stronger than the Tower is giving. From past experience I know this can be the case in some unusual circumstances, and strong southerly winds are not common. Charlie Lima is bucking around like a buoy on a storm tossed sea and it doesn't get any better as we descend. I decide to approach right of centre and attempt to land at an angle to the centre-line in order to reduce the cross-wind. This is awful! I keep the airspeed up at 75 knots to improve controlability and select just 10 degrees of flap. I feel as if I'm fighting every inch of the way, so busy I haven't got time to scare myself. Lower and lower, bucking and twisting.

90

Just in control. Twenty feet, fifteen, ten, chop the power, heave back as the nose pitches down and try to flare.

In less time than it takes to blink a powerful gust tries to spin us round. Before I know what has happened Aussie grabs the yoke and heaves it fully over. Without thinking I shove left rudder on and we're down seemingly almost at a standstill. Whew! "Thanks Aus". Even at taxi speed we're being blown around. The actual touch-down was, to me, surprisingly smooth. Also, I should make a couple of qualifying remarks. First, with regard to wind speeds in gusty conditions, especially on large airports, the ATCO can only rely on the reading seen, and this reading is taken from a single point which may be a kilometer or two from the end of the runway. Large buildings like hangars can affect the airflows and produce variables depending on direction. Of much more relevance is the amount of experience the pilot has. As a PPL comparatively little of my flying is done in unfavourable conditions but I know full well that commercial pilots deal with these conditions frequently. Often they are much worse. For me it was a major problem encountering and dealing with this. For Aussie and so many of my erstwhile instructors it would be nothing worth writing home about. I realise this, but it was exciting I can tell you. Deep down the lesson proves yet again what it takes to fly for a living as opposed to flying as a hobby.

Having reached the apron on the north side which is reserved for G.A. visitors, and, having parked Charlie Lima into wind, we quickly make enquiries as to the short-term forecast. Winds of up to forty-five knots are anticipated so we set about getting Charlie Lima hangared for the night. Air Kilroe offer hangarage for £20 and we gratefully accept. We might get a much lower rate over on the south side but it would cost us much more just to taxi over there.

With Charlie Lima safely ensconed in the immaculate, almost surgically clean Air Kilroe hangar, it is becoming obvious that night photography here could be quite an ordeal. Weighing up the pros and cons we retreat in orderly fashion and re-assess our position. It should be much better in the morning although a few hours spent on site could add an extra day, possibly two. Aussie has some areas he wants to photograph to the east of the Pennines and with a quick start we could cover Humberside and Norwich and still be back in Wycombe before the aerodrome closes. Given the chance we'll try for a finish tomorrow as the longer term outlook is not too clever.

Above:
Charlie Lima on the apron outside the Air Kilroe hangar, Manchester.

It is just after 08.00 as our taxi drops us outside the offices of Air Kilroe. Straight away we set about ascertaining the Met situation. It is a bright sharp morning with a brisk wind. Bursts of blinding sun suddenly shoot through small gaps in the cloud. Leaving Manchester is not a problem. Getting across the Pennines is. The cloud base is fairly level at 2000 to 2200ft and the tops of the hills rise to 2077ft. I want to route up the valley beyond Hyde following the A628 to Barnsley. We are told this may not be possible and routing via the M62 is the most probably alternative. We have a classic cleft-stick conundrum. I do not favour the M62 route. It is higher and at the critical point allows much less room for manoeuvre. Whilst debating the final decision we get Charlie Lima towed out of the hangar and refuelled. Time passes very

Below:
Inside the Air Kilroe hangar, snug and cosy from the storm outside.

quickly in these circumstances. Having made a positive request for the southern route we strap in and contact Ground on 121.7. We get the start-up clearance at 09.25 and inform them we've copied Information Golf. the ATIS transmission tells us Runway 24, wind 170° at 14kts, +7 +4, QNH 998, QFE 989, and Link Foxtrot closed because of standing water 2cm deep. There is a lot of traffic arriving and our initial departure point is to be Thelwall Viaduct on the M6. I have listed Barton as a possible diversion where we just might have to land and re-evaluate our position. Ground clear us to Link Bravo and tell us to change to Tower on 118.625.

There is a Tri-Star on finals and the Tower instructs us to line up behind this, wait for wake turbulence to subside, route to the Thelwall VRP turning ASAP after take-off because of departing traffic and Squawk 7236. Our clearance to route via Hyde and Holmes Chapel is still denied. The heading for Thelwall is, we estimate, 290° allowing for the brisk cross-wind. Here we go, the Tower has just told us to line up. The Tri-Star is

Above:
A Tristar flares for touch-down as we squint into the sun at Manchester.

turning off a mile or so down the runway. There are a couple of jets behind us waiting for departure on Link Alpha. Mixing in with the big boys is quite exciting. To our right we see three more jet airliners moving away from their stands towards the Hold. A quick check round the panel and controls. All GOOD and CORRECT.

"Golf Charlie Lima is cleared take-off, surface wind 170° at 13 knots".

"Golf Charlie Lima, cleared take-off".

As Aussie thumbs the transmit button I push the throttle firmly fully open, shove the yoke fully forward, hold into wind aileron down and steer with the rudder. At sixty knots I pull back

sharply, unstick and crab down the runway centre-line. As the terminal slips by there is open ground beyond so I bank over and clear the runway passing just to the south of the Fairey apron.

"Thanks for the early turn Golf Charlie Lima, change to Approach 119.4." Aussie acknowledges and redials. "Approach, Golf Charlie Lima is with you".

"Roger, Golf Charlie Lima, I have your clearance to Holmes Chapel, steer radar vector 345° initially. What altitude do you want?"

We give each other a brief questioning look. "Thousand eight hundred?" asks Aussie. "Fine", I agree.

"Approach, we would like 1,800ft please, Golf Charlie Lima".

"That is approved Golf Charlie Lima, Squawk 7222 and call level 1,800".

A couple of minutes later Approach tells us to steer radar vector 055°. We are now heading back parallel with the runway. The wet concrete and asphalt areas gleam and dazzle, reflecting the sun.

It takes us four minutes to 1800ft without resorting to maximum rate of climb. Aussie calls in. There is a sliver of light between the hills and the cloud. Further on Approach ask us if we have the British Airways 757 in sight two miles in our two o'clock. Aussie confirms we do.

"Route direct to Holmes Chapel and report leaving frequency".

I head for the valley, which has a couple of long thin reservoirs. It is quite bumpy. We are just above the level of the ground to the north and below the ground to the south, the highest point of which is actually in cloud. The A628 weaves around below and steadily climbs up the valley. Ahead the cloud base rises considerably.

""Golf Charlie Lima, you are now clear of controlled airspace. Barnsley QNH 990".

"Golf Charlie Lima, Roger, clear of controlled airspace, 990, climbing to two thousand five hundred and QSY to Finningley 120.35, cheers and thanks".

Aussie contacts Finningley explaining that we're VFR from Manchester to Humberside and that we want to photograph south of Goole first then east-north-east of Sandtoft aerodrome. This means we want to operate in areas very close to the Finningley MATZ 'panhandle'. Fortunately the radar controller sees no problems at this time, gives us a new squawk of 0210, approves 2500ft ALT plus the Finningley QNH 999.

Flying just south of Barnsley, the nature of the country changes. It is quite different from anything we've seen so far. It's very flat and has a

Above:
The cloud sitting just above the hill tops as we make our way from Manchester to Humberside. Note the mast in the centre of the picture practically disappearing into the cloud.

lot of industry and power station cooling towers which dot the landscape. The site we are looking for south of Goole is easy to identify. Intensive peat removal has left a vast scar. Aussie asks for and gets 3000ft but we can't quite make it and clip the cloud-base at 2900ft. Following Aussie's instructions I circle round then descend bit by bit until we're at 500ft. Mission complete, Finningley clears us south, grants 1200ft, and asks us to call Sandtoft Radio on 130.425.

Sandtoft have nothing for us but we stay with them because our work takes place inside their ATZ to begin with. It is still turbulent and I have to do quite a bit of flying at 500ft here also. I'm very mindful of the need to keep the airspeed above 90 knots because as we turn *with* the wind, (given as 20 knots), we could lose airspeed in a tight turn and get dangerously close to stalling. The stall speed increases when turning and continues to rise as the bank angle steepens and the turn tightens. Consequently if Aussie wants a really tight turn at 60° of bank I only agree if we're turning into wind. I know he wants me to fly first and try to accommodate his requirements second. He has told me a couple of very hairy stories in which he has barely avoided disaster because the pilot has tried to fly too slowly in an attempt to please him.

Leaving the Sandtoft ATZ we go back to Finningley. It's very quiet round here on the radio this morning. Aussie wants to photograph the very long straight manmade rivers and drainage canals feeding into the Trent at Gunness just west of Scunthorpe. In between getting Charlie Lima and our flight details organised back in Manchester I'd spent some time closely examining an Ordnance Survey map making sure that Aussie's references were exactly pin-

pointed. Then I transferred to the ICAO chart and drew the areas in with a blue chinagraph. Having positioned ourselves in the area Aussie then double-checks the Ordnance Survey against his information to make sure I've got it right. So far so good. All in all the flight workload is quite high and this often increases dramatically at times, even with two sharing the duties.

Finishing off, Aussie calls Finningley with thanks and changes to Humberside Approach on 124.675. They clear us in via the disused aerodrome at Elsham Wolds. One thousand feet for Runway 21. Surface wind 210° at 20 knots and Squawk 4570. At last a wind straight down the runway, which is long too at 2230 metres. This time I want to land short because the terminal is on the right near the start of 21. With 20 knots on the nose we're definitely in STOL territory here. After a short run we're cleared to back-track and take the single taxiway to the apron, parking on Stand 13. A Queens Flight BAe146 is close by with a police vehicle in attendance. Although seemingly in the middle of nowhere, Humberside logged a creditable 47,045 movements in 1990, although Bond Helicopters have a base on the airport and I bet they accounted for a fair proportion. You'll know the routine as well as we do. Aussie gets snapping and I settle down to logging the route and flight frequencies for Norwich via another batch of interesting areas for photographing on the Trent south of Gainsborough. This time we'll be in close proximity to one of the most intensive military flying areas in England. A lot of training takes place and I think it will be interesting so say the least to discover how we'll get routed. We take a lunch break with the table awash with charts, maps, information sheets and last, but not least, our Flight Guides.

I fully fuelled Charlie Lima before lunch and paid the landing fee which I think is extortionate at £25.40 for a Cessna 172. To bring you up to date a little, here is a selection so far. Glasgow charges £12.50 and Manchester £15.00 while Aberdeen wanted £10, all plus VAT. If you don't want visitors this is one way of getting the message across. Unfortunately the CAA charges navigation fees at Glasgow and Edinburgh of £10 plus VAT which seems a bit of a cheek considering we were VFR.

We get an 'actual' from Norwich. The wind is 20 knots, gusting 30, but straight down the short Runway 04/22. The direction of the wind is unlikely to change much today so we give it a go. Our request for a low pass along the Humberside runway followed by a climbing orbit is approved and I thoroughly enjoy this. The

Tower on 118.55 has us squawking as before on 4570. As we pass the runway centre-line on the second orbit Tower hands us on to Approach. I set a heading of 235° and stay level at 1500ft. At ten miles out Aussie changes from Humberside Approach to Waddington who provide LARS for the Combined MATZ of Scampton. Waddington and Cranwell. He explains what we want to do, taking the three areas from 500 to 2200ft. This is approved with a new Squawk of 1751, Barnsley QNH 990. It is very turbulent and Aussie gets badly bruised trying to brace himself against the door and window frame. Aussie has also been handling the radio. Unlike this morning we're getting constant calls from Waddington. Then our intercom fails. Aussie explains this to Waddington and the radar controller tells us to call once we're finished. We continue monitoring the frequency of course and Aussie resorts to hand signals. It would be quite funny if it wasn't so serious and bloody uncomfortable.

I can't complain. I really wanted to be on this trip, and the main reason was the flying. Well I'm doing more stick and rudder flying in five minutes right here than most Jumbo pilots get in a round trip to Australia. I'm constantly correcting because of the buffeting. My left arm is aching with the effort of jiggling the yoke as we climb up turning, level out still turning, straighten out, dive, in fact we're performing like a demented seagull. My right hand controls the throttle and carburetter heat on descents. It's really great and we'll see some terrific shots, of that I'm certain. They will appear lit by dramatic effects. All the noise, cold and discomfort will have evaporated and be rarely recalled.

The radar controller at Waddington is concerned that we might encroach into the CMATZ. I assure him we will stay clear. Aussie wants to get very specific shots of the power stations plus individual features of the river both in close-up and with general views. In one or two places meanders have been straightened out and he wants to photograph these from several angles. What a perfectionist. He has been reading about the controversy surrounding the management of this area and intends to exploit this opportunity to the full. The camera bags in the back are awash with spent films. At last he is satisfied and he calls up Waddington for routeing to Norwich. The LARS controller brings us overhead at 2200ft on their QNH of 1001. Underneath we see two Short Tucanos and a Tornado apparently running the circuit. Hey! this is different. A trio of Boeing E-3D Sentry early warning jobs are spotted on the apron. The military in Britain need to be complimented here. In most countries we wouldn't get anywhere near these bases.

They realise that most private and commercial pilots are not in the employ of some Secret Service and anyway, we could find out ten times more about what goes on by using common reference books. Even so, we both appreciate the positive ATC work that allows us to witness these exciting goings-on. And positive it is too. After crossing the aerodrome we are told to head 090°. A Harrier comes hurtling by beneath and shortly after we are told to turn onto a heading of 180° which will take us between Cranwell and Coningsby. Waddington hands us over to Cranwell who ask us to Squawk 6570. I must stress that, although we see fast jet traffic above, below and around us and we are given very precise instructions, at no time are we given the impression that we are unwelcome in this area.

Cranwell pass us through to Coningsby on 120.8 and they give us another Squawk of 2677 among other things. As we approach the southern side of the 'panhandle' which forms a umbilical cord between Cranwell and Coningsby we get a direct route to Marham, tracking 123°. This keeps us within the Wash AIAA which adjoins the Lincolnshire AIAA south-west of Boston. I admit to struggling to maintain heading. Most of the time we have 30° of drift compensation. To our left over the Wash powerful jets are seen. We are puny in comparison. They are so fast and have so much sheer thrusting power I wonder if drift compensation forms much of a consideration in their calculations. It does of course. Those guys are honed to such fine degrees that my flying must seem like the bubblings of a blind incompetent idiot. Not so! I don't understand exactly why, but the controllers seem implicitly to understand the differences between flying heavy fast jets and small low-powered single-engined aeroplanes. I haven't put this very well. Of course they appreciate the difference. They are professionals but what I hadn't expected is the degree of tolerance.

Coiningsby pass us on to Marham and they route us in directly overhead squawking 6530. Handley Page (am I showing my age?) Victors of the K.2 variety are parked on the aprons below. Aussie wants to photograph some prehistoric ponds situated right on the edge of Danger Area D208 which turns out to be active. Marham direct us in via Watton and hand us over to Honington who give us another Squawk of 1414. Providing we stay clear of the Danger Area Honington raises no objections. Even Aussie, much better informed in matters of flying privileges, is impressed.

We have little difficultiy in identifying the ponds and start circling, careful not to stray into the Danger Area. Honington drops a gentle hint that live ammunition is being used. To add to the fun F-111s start appearing around us. Presumably they've been on exercise over the North Sea. The light is too poor for photographs and we don't want to linger amongst the fast jets. Calling up Honington Aussie says "We're heading direct track to Norwich." Shortly afterwards Honington suggests we 'free-call' Norwich on the Approach frequency 119.35.

Norwich clears us in for Runway 27, left-hand circuit, downwind join, QFE 1004. But, to expect a change to Runway 22. The strong wind is veering and backing between these two headings. Norwich city is easily spotted and pretty soon we identify the airport and set ourselves up for a down-wind join for 27. Approach hand us over to Tower on 124.25 as we fly into the ATZ. Still Runway 27. We turn base then finals. Now we approach 27 on finals. It's pretty blowy up here. I shunt the controls around as strong gusts shove us around. The stall warner blips as the turbulent air disturbs the flow over our wings. I try to keep the ASI reading a bit fast at 70 knots. Over the threshold. Arms and legs sawing away. Steady, steady, we drop, a burst of power, that's it, steady, a few feet above the runway, chop the power, flare, still sawing away and . . . we're down! Whew!

In fact we touched own at something like 35-40 knots ground-speed so the landing run was very short indeed. The Tower instructs us to taxi to the Terminal along Runway 22. We turn onto 22 and there is the new terminal. Right across the end of the runway! Now, that is novel. I am sure that 22 is only used by light aircraft in strong wind conditions so there is masses of room to spare. After parking and 'booking-in' we head straight for the cafeteria. We are in need of a good hot drink.

We sit down to a cup of coffee and discuss our situation. The Met reports show a large warm front approaching which would screw things up tomorrow. There are quite a lot of interesting things happening at Norwich especially with the Air UK base here. On the other hand we both have other commitments. A couple of quick calculations indicate that if we leave now we can beat the front into Wycombe. Sorry Norwich, we must go. Aussie rushes off to grab a few shots in the failing light. I quickly organise a re-fuel and plot a course back together with a list of all the probable frequencies. With start-up approved and details copied we make our way out to the Hold for Runway 22 this time. Our departure is brisk and unhindered. I head straight across the western edge of the city looking out for the A11. As before we get transferred

from Norwich Approach to Honington in the vicinity of Wymondham. As you know by now, it is customary to follow line features from the right. After Snetterton, however, the Danger Area D208 butts up to the A11, so we expect to have to adjust our course to Thetford by flying on the left. Although anticipated this doesn't happen. Honington direct us due south after passing Snetterton. As the aerodrome at Honington comes clearly into view we see the bright landing lights of a Tornado taking-off towards us (with a tail-wind), on a constant relative bearing which means collision! We are not in the slightest bit perturbed by this but view the speeding jet with considerable interest. About a mile away it banks in a spectacular turn which must have the occupants glued to their ejector seats. Show offs! We pass close by the aerodrome at Knettishall and identify the disused aerodrome called Shepherd Grove in our eleven o'clock. Honington then instruct us to head 230° which points toward Bury St Edmunds. As we turn we see a KC-135 heading towards Mildenhall banking steeply around in the distance at approximately 3000ft ALT. Honington tell us that an emergency has been declared and traffic is descending through Flight Level 110 to 65 to land at Honington. We should maintain altitude and heading.

Aussie, who to my untutored mind appears to possess clairvoyant abilities, leans forward and points forward and up. Two F-16s in incredibly tight formation are hurtling down and pass directly above. What a sight! The wing man was so close it thrills my imagination that people posses such abilities to fly so accurately. Shortly after Honington very kindly inform us that the problem aircraft has landed safely. Aussie quickly passes a brief message to the effect that we are pleased to hear this. The KC-135 then

Below:
Is it possible to encounter more rain? Poor Charlie Lima nearly swimming at Norwich as we prepare for our final flight.

resumes its extended left-base approach to Mildenhall and Honington warn us of possible wake turbulence as it passes very close above. If it was light enough Aussie would have the chance to get a superb air-to-air shot of this. The radar controller is very correct to issue the warning but fortunately we cross the path of the KC-135 without experiencing any difficulty. Just as well! These large aircraft certainly stir the air. The KC-135 passed across our path about one mile ahead and one thousand feet above. Seems like a lot doesn't it? Not so, it was very close and reinforces our opinion that these controllers work to very precise limits.

We have our start-up time logged at 15.15 at Norwich and it is now approaching 16.30, close to official night. As we head towards Newmarket we leave the Honington Military Control Zone (SFC to 4000'ALT) and change frequency to Stansted on 125.55. I now see a new dimension to Aussie. I don't have a Night Rating let alone an Instrument Rating. Aussie informs Stansted that the status of our flight is being amended. It is now IFR and the captain's name is Brown. In effect I can sit back and enjoy. Aussie spools up and gets the ADF and VOR instruments earning their keep for real. Despite this he still respects my opinion as to our course. It is very interesting. The primary conurbations can be more easily identified at night, if you know what to look for, than by day. I have had some experience at night plus taking a keen interest on commercial flights into London when visibility allows.

Although more than capable on his own, Aussie actively involves me in the navigation and decision making process. This is great and I put all my enthusiasm and land-based experience into effect. Stevenage appear with the A1M sandwiched between Letchworth and Hitchin. No doubts here. Stansted pass us across to Luton Approach on 129.55. They are so quiet at this time, that we feel like apologising for disturbing them. They pass us through as Aussie follows the VOR towards Bovingdon. Luton airport shows up on our right bright and clear as we fly steadily on. Hemel Hempstead is easily identified. From such a low altitude, (just over two thousand feet), the bright intensely lit areas sparkle and gleam with complex interwoven patterns. It really is magical and throws whole new perceptions on familiar places. Aussie gets on with the flying and brings in a stark realistic reminder. "Where would we put down if the engine fails now?" I don't have an answer. The inky black areas between the lights offer no indications as to what lies within.

Passing over Bovingdon, black and invisible, only the instruments tell Aussie precisely what has occurred as we head toward Wycombe. It is very real, ominous, yet enchanting. I struggle to achieve correct orientation now. Aussie dials up the VOR at Compton which will place us directly towards the runway at Wycombe if he follows the 250° radial, I now realise how serious this is getting. It is one thing to read about it. It is quite different to see it in action. Calling up Wycombe on 126.55, we are cleared in for a long finals direct approach. We spot the bright green aerodrome identity beacon flashing its cryptic message. No approach aids here. Just green lights across the front of the runway, white lights on either side and a line of red lights at the far end.

Our world is so completely, totally, transformed, I feel as if we are floating in a void. The actions are familiar but seem to have little effect. A red light in the roof of our cabin illuminates the instruments each one of which has a single bulb casting a glow. Aussie reaches out for the dimmer control and the cabin grows darker. The instruments glow softly now. Sensations of speed and distance, minimised in daytime flight, are almost frozen. The ASI tells me that airspeed is reducing as Aussie pulls the throttle back, carb-heat ON, and applies back-pressure to the yoke. Aussie drops the flaps as the ASI needle falls below 80. Now the reduction in noise really emphasises the floating sensation. The runway surface is pitch black, darker than any night, a featureless black hole. The runway lights start rushing towards us. Aussie cuts the throttle back to idle and pulls the yoke back in small decisive increments, judging the flare. This is weird, landing on a surface we still can't see. In the darkness the unseen under-carriage emits a quiet screech as the wheels struggle to speed up. We're down. The end of the 29th leg.

"Golf Charlie Lima, backtrack to Hold Bravo".

"Backtrack to Hold Bravo, Golf Charlie Lima", Aussie calls back and swings Charlie Lima around. We taxi between the lights broadly spaced now but which had appeared compressed together on the approach. Turning off the runway now we hear, "Golf Charlie Lima, cleared to the apron". Aussie taxis in and we spot an empty slot just outside the entrance to Wycombe Air Centre.

While Aussie shuts down I note the time: 16.55 and the DATCOM; 98.5. The total trip from Top Farm 36.2 logged flying hours. Aussie leaves to get his car and I start packing up our things and securing the aircraft for the night. Aussie pulls up alongside on the left. I prise the door lever vertical and push the door open. In response the heavens open. The front has arrived.